Tupolev Tu-4
Soviet Superfortress

Yefim Gordon and Vladimir Rigmant

Original translation by Sergey and Dmitriy Komissarov

Midland Publishing

Tupolev Tu-4: Soviet Superfortress
© 2002 Yefim Gordon and Vladimir Rigmant
ISBN 1 85780 142 3

Published by Midland Publishing
4 Watling Drive, Hinckley, LE10 3EY, England
Tel: 01455 254 490 Fax: 01455 254 495
E-mail: midlandbooks@compuserve.com

Midland Publishing is an imprint of
Ian Allan Publishing Ltd

Worldwide distribution (except North America):
Midland Counties Publications
4 Watling Drive, Hinckley, LE10 3EY, England
Telephone: 01455 254 450   Fax: 01455 233 737
E-mail: midlandbooks@compuserve.com
www.midlandcountiessuperstore.com

North American trade distribution:
Specialty Press Publishers & Wholesalers Inc.
39966 Grand Avenue, North Branch, MN 55056, USA
Tel: 651 277 1400 Fax: 651 277 1203
Toll free telephone: 800 895 4585
www.specialtypress.com

© 2002 Midland Publishing
Design concept and layout
by Polygon Press Ltd (Moscow, Russia)
Line drawings © Vladimir Klimov

This book is illustrated with photos from the
archives of Yefim Gordon, Vladimir Rigmant,
Sergey and Dmitriy Komissarov, the Tupolev
OKB, the Yakovlev OKB, Avico Press Ltd
and the Russian Aviation Research Trust
and photographs by Helmut Walther and
Keith Dexter.

Printed in England by
Ian Allan Printing Ltd
Riverdene Business Park, Molesey Road,
Hersham, Surrey, KT12 4RG

Contents

**Title page: A still from a cine film showing a
production Tu-4 as it 'cleans up' after take-off.**

**Below: A Long-Range Aviation crew receives final
instructions beside a late-production Kuibyshev-
built Tu-4 coded '28 Red' (c/n 2806303).**

Introduction

The epic story of how the Tu-4 aircraft came into existence is one of the thrilling pages in the history of aircraft technology development in the USSR. Events relating to this project and fitting into the 1943-1949 time frame were instrumental to a great extent in shaping the Soviet aircraft industry in the period following the end of the Second World War and in promoting its subsequent leap to the forefront of the world's jet-powered aviation; they also laid the foundation of the strategic parity between the USA and the Soviet Union which secured the survival of mankind in the era of global nuclear confrontation.

It can arguably be stated that before 1943 neither the military nor the political leaders of the USSR had any information on the work being conducted in the USA at that time with a view to creating the newest 'superbomber' – the Boeing B-29 Superfortress, which became the mainstay of the American strategic air power a few years later. Soviet intelligence agencies were engrossed in penetrating the secrets of the American nuclear programme and in studying the work that went ahead in the USA in the fields of electronics, jet aviation and other breakthrough technologies in the field of military hardware; thus, the development of the B-29 escaped their attention and, most importantly, the attention of the leaders in Moscow. The situation changed in 1943 after Eddie Rickenbacker's visit to the USSR. This visit can be regarded as the starting point for the story of 'how the B-29 became the Tu-4'.

Captain Edward V. Rickenbacker, a former fighter pilot and a hero of the First World War, became President Franklin D. Roosevelt's advisor on aviation matters during the Second World War; he was sent on a mission to the USSR for the purpose of getting acquainted with the situation in Soviet aviation and with the utilisation in the USSR of the American aviation materiel supplied under the Lend-Lease arrangement. This visit confronted the foreign relations department of the Soviet Air Force (VVS – *Voyenno-vozdooshnyye seely*) with a fairly delicate problem. On the one hand, being a presidential advisor, Rickenbacker was entitled to an appropriate retinue, at the level of generals at least. On the other hand, after the end of the First World War he retained the rank of Captain of the US

Army; hence, according to diplomatic canons he could not receive as escort an officer of a rank superior to his own. As a result, the person selected to accompany him was Captain A. I. Smoliarov, a young officer who had recently graduated from the Air Force Academy. He had a decent command of English, was well versed in aviation technology and had a reasonably good knowledge of electronics into the bargain. As witnessed by subsequent events, the foreign relations department of the Air Force could not have made a better choice: no general, even the highest-ranking one, could have procured for the Soviets such initial information on the B-29 as this modest young Captain of the Soviet Air Force. In this particular case the famous maxim coined by Stalin: 'Personnel is the decisive factor' – proved correct by a full 200%, thanks to Smoliarov's excellent work and Rickenbacker's talkativeness.

In the USSR Rickenbacker was shown a number of Soviet aircraft factories and military units, including those operating American-supplied aircraft. A specially equipped Douglas C-47 was used for travelling from one airfield to another. The conditions on board were fairly austere for that kind of travel, but the lack of 'creature comforts' was more than recompensed by the hosts' cordiality and an unlimited supply of liquor. During the flights Smoliarov and Rickenbacker whiled away the time by discussing all sorts of subjects; quite naturally, aviation matters were predominant among them. During one such conversation with Smoliarov the American guest mentioned a new American 'superbomber', the B-29, and informed Smoliarov about its high performance. After Rickenbacker had departed to the USA, Smoliarov submitted, as was required of him, a detailed report on this visit to his direct chief. In this report he cited the information on the new American machine, committing to paper in the minutest detail everything that Rickenbacker had said about the B-29 during his visit.

This part of the report attracted interest on the part of Smoliarov's direct superiors. The name of a general who was Smoliarov's chief was substituted for the original signature on the report (curiously, the text of the report remained unchanged and the pronoun 'I' came to refer to the general) and the report

was sent to the higher echelon. Its contents, now suitably classified, began to make the rounds of important persons' studies in the People's Commissariat of Aircraft Industry (NKAP – *Narodnyy komissariaht aviatsionnoy promyshlennosti*), in the various organisations and institutes under NKAP and in the command of the Air Force, the Red Army and the intelligence services. The initial source of the information was soon forgotten and the American B-29 bomber became the object of a systematic search for information through all available official and unofficial channels. For the Soviet military and political leaders the B-29 became a reality and an eventual threat at a later stage, as well as a standard to the attainment of which the Soviet aircraft industry was to be geared.

To begin with, unsuccessful attempts were undertaken to obtain the B-29 legally from the USA within the framework of deliveries of war materiel under the Lend-Lease arrangement. On 19th July 1943 General Beliayev, the chief of the Soviet military mission in the USA, sent to the appropriate US authorities an enquiry concerning the possibility of deliveries of the Lockheed P-38 Lightning, Republic P-47 Thunderbolt, Consolidated B-24 Liberator and Boeing B-29 to the USSR. Out of this list, the Soviets received only the P-47 fighter. The Americans continued to turn down Soviet requests for four-engined heavy bombers, being of the opinion that these were not really needed by the Red Army's Air Force for its mainly tactical operations at the Soviet-German front. The USSR made another request for deliveries of B-29 bombers from the USA during its preparations for entering the war against Japan. Availing themselves of the fact that the Allies were interested in the USSR entering the war in the Far East at the earliest possible date, Soviet representatives made one more attempt to obtain the B-29. On 28th May a request was sent for the delivery of as many as 120 B-29s for the purpose of using them in the forthcoming war against Japan; yet again not a single B-29 was supplied by the Americans. Right from the start of the war the Soviet Union repeatedly asked the USA for the delivery of the four-engined Boeing B-17 Flying Fortress and B-24 bombers, and each time the USA turned down such requests – primarily because the Anglo-American allies had placed their bets on a strategic air offensive in Europe in their war against Germany and needed such aircraft themselves in ever-increasing numbers. Besides, the Allies did not want to create future problems for themselves, always bearing in mind that the Second World War was bound to be followed by a Third World War – and it was uncertain on which side of the front the traditionally anti-Western Russia would be in a new confrontation. Everybody in the West had the brief flirtation of the Soviet National Communists with the German National Socialists in 1939-1941 fresh in their memory.

It should be noted that it is the USSR that must be credited with being the first to create a strategic bomber force. By the early 1930s the Soviet military leadership had worked out a sufficiently clear concept concerning strategic use of the Long-Range Aviation (ie, strategic bomber force). The main emphasis in these plans was put on the use and expeditious development of multi-engined heavy bombers. The young Soviet aircraft industry, thanks to the incredible straining of the entire country's economy and mobilisation of the industry's main resources, succeeded in launching into series production the TB-3 (ANT-6) four-engined bomber developed by Andrey Nikolayevich Tupolev's design bureau. More than 800 machines of this type were built in the 1930s; they equipped the world's first air force units capable of accomplishing major strategic tasks on their own. However, the TB-3's design dated back to the mid-1920s and was already obsolescent by the time the bomber reached production status and began to be delivered to service units. It was no longer on a par with state of the art in aviation technology and, most importantly, with the rapidly developing means of anti-aircraft defence available to the leading aviation powers. In the light of the new realities, from the beginning of the 1930s onwards, work was initiated in the USSR with a view to creating a modern high-speed high-altitude long-range bomber similar in its concept to the Boeing B-17. The prototype of its counterpart, the TB-7 (ANT-42), took to the air at the end of 1936. However, a spate of technical and organisational problems, coupled with the general disarray in Soviet society and industry in the wake of mass purges of the late 1930s and further compounded by complete uncertainty and incessant 'ideological vacillations' in the approach of the Stalinist leadership to the role of strategic aircraft in the future war, delayed the launching of series production of the TB-7; limited production did not start until the eve of the Second World War. When Germany invaded the USSR, massed strategic operations were no longer on the agenda – the front required thousands of relatively simple and cheap machines; hence the

TB-7 (renamed Petlyakov Pe-8 in 1942) was built on a very limited scale.

In all, only 93 TB-7 aircraft were produced in the USSR between 1936 and 1945; for various reasons only 60 to 70% of these saw active service. This bears no comparison with the thousands of American B-17s and B-24s, British Avro Lancasters and even the hundreds of German Focke-Wulf Fw 200 Condors and Heinkel He 177 Greifs. Yet, in overall performance Tupolev's TB-7 was no worse than the B-17 (at the time when the two prototypes made their appearance in the mid-1930s) and, given better circumstances, could have gone on to become the mainstay of the Long-Range Aviation of the Red Army.

At the beginning of the Great Patriotic War the long-range bomber units lost a good deal of their hardware, in part during the first days marked by disarray and panic, and in part when wastefully used for tactical strikes against the German armour and motorised infantry units rapidly advancing into Soviet territory. The few strategic air operations undertaken by the long-range bomber units during the initial period of the war pursued primarily limited political objectives and were not always efficiently planned and executed, resulting in considerable losses both of materiel and personnel. As a consequence of all this, by the beginning of 1942 the strength of Soviet long-range bomber units was cut by two-thirds. In the spring of 1942 Stalin, taking into account the experience of the war and influenced by Aleksandr Ye. Golovanov (the future Commander-in-Chief of the Long-Range Aviation) and many officers of this branch, grouped all long-range bomber units into a separate structure and subordinated it directly to himself. From the spring of 1942 onwards the Soviet Supreme Command was in possession of a powerful instrument for the conduct of strategic operations – the Long-Range Aviation headed by a dynamic C-in-C, General Golovanov. (In December 1944 it was transformed into the 18th Air Army subordinated to the Air Force command but reinstated as an independent structure, the Long-Range Aviation of the Soviet Armed Forces, in April 1946.) By the end of hostilities the units of the Long-Range Aviation, as a tool of the Supreme Command, represented a sufficiently effective and mobile force. However, in its composition and equipment this force primarily corresponded to the peculiarities of the fighting at the Soviet-German front, where the outcome of a battle, the question of victory or defeat, was determined mainly in the tactical or minor strategic depth of the enemy's defence. Accordingly, the aircraft equipping the Long-Range Aviation units reflected to a certain extent the tasks posed for it. By the time the war ended, the lion's share of the Long-Range Aviation's 2,000 air-

craft was made up of twin-engined bombers such as the Il'yushin DB-3 and IL-4 (DB-3F), the North American B-25 Mitchell, a small number of Yermolayev Yer-2s and a vast number of Lisunov Li-2s (a version of the Douglas DC-3 built in the Soviet Union under licence; in this context, the bomber-configured Li-2VP). They were supplemented by Pe-8s, plus a few dozen damaged B-17s and B-24s that were appropriated by the Red Army in Eastern Europe and subsequently restored to flying condition. This air armada could tackle its tasks with a fair degree of success in the course of the Great Patriotic War, but it was obviously les than suitable for the new post-war reality involving an eventual confrontation with the extremely powerful American war machine.

It should be noted that already in the course of the Second World War the Soviet leaders had turned their attention to the problem of creating a prospective multi-engined bomber for their Long-Range Aviation. There were several important reasons for this. Massed employment of strategic aircraft by the Allies against Germany showed the Soviet government what a potent force emerged when hundreds and thousands of heavy combat aircraft were brought together within strong units. Secondly, as a reaction to information from Soviet secret agents from the USA on the first successes of the American nuclear programme, work was speeded up on the creation of the 'Red superbomb'. The future 'wonder weapon' required an adequate carrier aircraft, the Pe-8 being obviously unsuitable for this role. Design work on a new heavy bomber had to be initiated. What should it be like? Very aptly, more or less credible information on the B-29 became available at that moment. It was deemed that this four-engined bomber should become a beacon to which Soviet designers should turn their attention when creating a new bomber for the Long-Range Aviation.

From the autumn of 1943 onwards three Soviet design bureaux were tasked with creating new four-engined high-speed high-altitude long-range bombers by the NKAP. A design bureau (OKB – *opytno-konstrooktorskoye byuro*) headed by I. F. Nezval' was tasked with a thorough modernisation of the series-built Pe-8. In the course of 1944 the OKB prepared a project for the thorough modernisation of the aircraft, envisaging a considerable improvement of its performance. Additionally, in 1944 work was initiated under Nezval's direction on a long-range high-speed high-altitude bomber similar in its design features and performance to the American B-29. During the same period Vladimir M. Myasischchev's OKB worked on two projects – the DVB-202 and DVB-302 (DVB = *dahl'niy vysotnyy bombardi-*

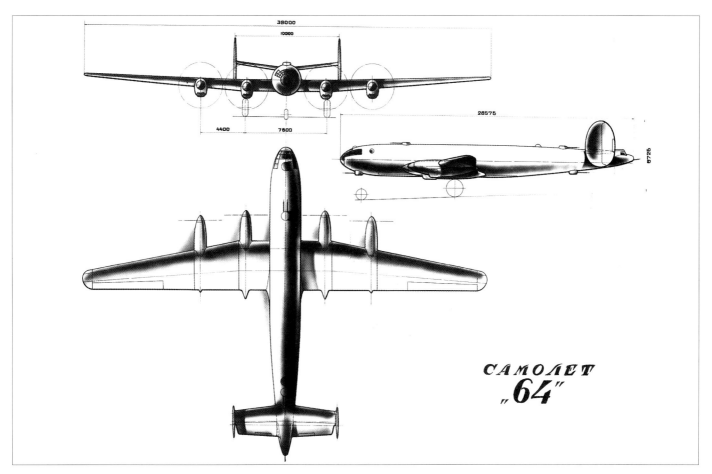

Above and below: Two advanced development project configurations of Tupolev's 'aircraft 64' long-range heavy bomber which never reached the hardware stage. Note the individual 'bug-eye' canopies for the pilots on the lower three-view which was the ultimate configuration.

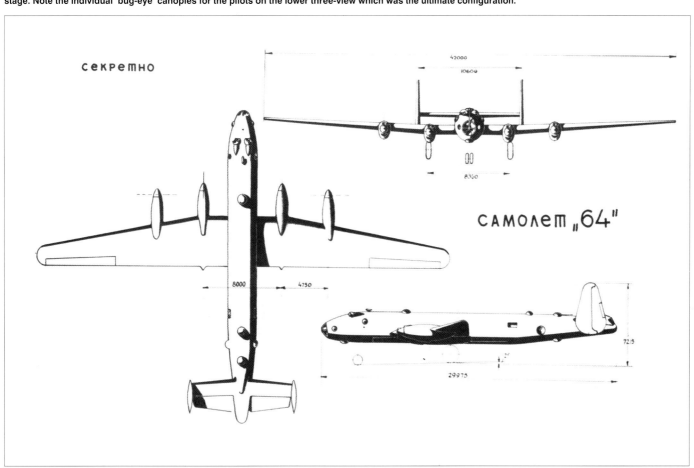

A desktop model of the 'aircraft 64' in its ultimate guise, showing the sharply raked nose gear strut and extensively glazed navigator/bomb-aimer's station.

rovschchik – long-range high-altitude bomber) which, in their approach to technical problems, were very close to the American machine. At that time Sergey V. Il'yushin's OKB-240 was working on a project of a similar four-engined bomber designated Il-14 (the first aircraft to have this designation which was eventually reused for a twin-engined airliner). All these projects did not progress further than the preliminary design stage and were shelved when work on the Tu-4 started. It was A. N. Tupolev's design bureau (OKB-156) that had progressed furthest in creating a Soviet 'competitor' to the B-29.

In September 1943 the Design Bureau was instructed to evolve an advanced development project and to build a mock-up of a heavy high-altitude bomber powered by 2,200-hp Shvetsov M-71TK-M radial engines and provided with pressurised cabins and cannon armament for defence. The aircraft was to possess the following basic characteristics:

Top speed at 10,000 m (32,810 ft)	500 km/h (311 mph)
Range at 400 km/h (249 mph):	
with a full bomb load	5,000 km (3,107 miles)
with a bomb load of 7,000-	
8,000 kg (15,432-17,637 lb)	6,000 km (3,728 miles)
Bomb bay capacity	10,000 kg (22,046 lb)

The OKB was to design a heavy bomber emulating the class and performance of the B-29, while making use of well-established indigenous production techniques, materials and equipment that were available at that time. The new machine, which received the in-house designation '**aircraft 64**' and the official designation Tu-10 (later re-used for a Tu-2 derivative), was being projected simultaneously in two versions: a bomber and a transport/passenger aircraft. Assessment of the requirement issued to the OKB, which was undertaken within the framework of the design studies, showed that the 'aircraft 64', while possessing (as stipulated) dimensions similar to those of the ANT-42, would have to be twice as heavy. This posed a number of difficult problems for the designers and structural strength specialists, since the loads in structural members of the 'aircraft 64' would be twice as high as those in the corresponding structural elements of the ANT-42. The country was at war and it was unrealistic to

Another view of the same model. The 'aircraft 64' was to bristle with defensive armament.

expect the acquisition of new materials and intermediate products, modern equipment and hardware. At best, the designers could only see in aeronautical magazines all those things that were available to American engineers when they were designing the B-29.

Notwithstanding all the difficulties, the advanced development project of the new bomber was ready in August 1944. According to this project, the 'aircraft 64' was a heavy four-engined bomber intended for performing daytime missions deep in the enemy's rear areas. High cruising speeds and flight altitudes coupled with potent defensive armament enabled the aircraft to perform missions in areas where the enemy's anti-aircraft defence was at its strongest. The aircraft could carry a bomb load of up to 18,000 kg (39,683 lb) while using bombs weighing up to 5,000 kg (11,023 lb) apiece. The bombs were housed in two capacious bomb bays fore and aft of the wing centre section. The provision of pressurised cabins for the crew enabled the aircraft to perform flights at altitudes of up to 8,000 to 10,000 m (26,247 to 32,808 ft). Structurally, the aircraft was an all-metal monoplane with mid-set wings. The fuselage had a monocoque construction with a thick stressed skin. The wings featured a two-spar construction and were fitted with efficient lift-augmentation devices for take-off and landing. The tail unit featured twin fins and rudders. The aircraft had a tricycle undercarriage. As for the powerplant, the 'aircraft 64' was to use one of the following engine types: the 2,000-hp Mikulin AM-42TK, the 2,300-hp AM-43TK-300B, the 1,900-hp Charomskiy ACh-30BF diesel (all liquid-cooled 12-cylinder Vee engines), the 1,900-hp Shvetsov

ASh-83FN 14-cylinder two-row radial, or the monstrous 2,500-hp Dobrynin/Skoobachevskiy M-250 24-cylinder liquid-cooled engine featuring power recovery turbines. Design studies and performance calculations were made for versions with all these engines. The defensive cannon armament of 20 to 23-mm (.78 to .90-in) calibre was to be installed in two twin-cannon fuselage turrets featuring electrically actuated remote control and in a tail turret with one or two cannon. Navigation, radio communications and radio engineering equipment was to comprise the most up-to-date items that could be produced by indigenous industry. The 'aircraft 64' was to feature a large number of electrically actuated systems – all the main systems of the aircraft were electrically actuated, with the exception of units designed to sustain especially heavy loads which were hydraulically actuated.

In the course of design work several variants of the '64' were considered. They featured differences in basic dimensions and also differences in the fuselage layout, equipment complement, weapons fit and crew accommodation.

In August 1944, proceeding from the preliminary work on the '64' aircraft, the Air Force issued a specification for a high-altitude long-range bomber powered by four AM-42TK engines which eventually could be replaced by AM-46TKs or M-84s. In the long-range bomber version the aircraft was expected to operate at altitudes of 9,000 to 10,000 m (29,528 to 32,808 ft), to possess a combat radius not less than 2,000 km (1,243 miles), a bomb load of at least 18,000 kg (39,683 lb) and be fitted with potent defensive armament comprising 12 cannon of 20 to 23-mm (.78 to

.90-in) calibre; the tail turret was later to receive 45 to 57-mm (1.77 to 2.2-in) cannon.

By September 1944 the full-scale mock-up of the 'aircraft 64' had been completed and was presented to representatives of the VVS for inspection. This inspection resulted in a large number of critical remarks, including, in particular, a demand that a 360° bomb-aiming radar be installed, as was the case with the B-29. On 7th April 1945 the specification for the aircraft was endorsed. The Air Force wished the industry to produce a bomber possessing the following performance characteristics:

Max. speed at nominal power	610 km/h (379 mph)
Max. speed at combat power	630 km/h (391 mph)
Service ceiling	11,000 m (36,089 ft)
Range with a 5,000-kg (11,023-lb) bomb load	5,000 km (3,107 miles)
Tactical range with a 14,000-kg (30,865-lb) bomb load	2,000 km (1,243 miles)
Take-off run	800 m (2,625 ft)

The aircraft's powerplant was expected to comprise supercharged Mikulin AM-43TK-300B or AM-46TK-300 engines.

The mock-up was approved on 27th April 1945. After the end of the war with Germany OKB-156 started issuing detail drawings of the machine; the OKB's experimental production facility initiated preparations for the construction of the first prototype. The airframe and the powerplant (with the exception of the turbosuperchargers) presented virtually no problems, but fitting the aircraft with modern equipment meeting the requirements of the Air Force within the specified time limits became a real stumbling block. Subcontrac-

A cutaway drawing of the 'aircraft 64'. Note that the rear bomb bay is much more capacious than the forward one which is encroached upon by the forward dorsal gun barbette.

7

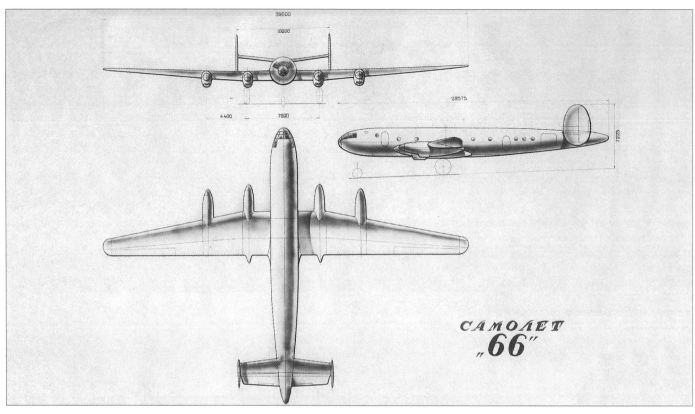

This three-view drawing illustrates the projected 'aircraft 66' airliner derivative of the 'aircraft 64' bomber.

tor enterprises were unable at that stage to provide for the 'aircraft 64' the necessary navigation and radio equipment and the automated remote control system for the cannon armament.

It became obvious that the work on the creation of the first Soviet aircraft intended for the strategic weapon carrier role was reaching a state of deadlock. Worried by the state of affairs in the work on the 'aircraft 64', the nation's leaders took the decision to organise series production of a copy of the B-29 Superfortress bomber in the USSR; this was now possible, since four examples of the B-29 had been impounded in the Soviet Far East. A. N. Tupolev's OKB was entrusted with the task of copying the B-29 and all the resources of the design bureau were concentrated on this task

which enjoyed the highest priority. Gradually all the work on the 'aircraft 64' wound down, although it still figured in the OKB's plans in the course of the following two years. One more project based on the aircraft was prepared; it was reworked completely to incorporate the knowledge gained as a result of closely studying the B-29. The revised aircraft received a low-set wing which simplified its adaptation for a passenger aircraft role; it was to be powered by AM-46TK-3PB engines delivering a maximum of 2,300 hp apiece, the equipment complement was to include a Kobal't (Cobalt) bomb-aiming radar etc. Apart from the bomber version of the 'aircraft 64', the OKB prepared two further projects based on it – an airliner (project '66') and a military transport.

Basic design specifications of the 'aircraft 64' with four AM-46TK-3PB engines

Length	30 m (98 ft 5 in)
Wing span	42 m (137 ft 10 in)
Height	7.2 m (23 ft 7 in)
Wing area	150.3 m² (1,618 sq ft)
Normal take-off weight	38,000 kg (83,776 lb)
Maximum speed at normal take-off weight	650 km/h (404 mph)
Service ceiling	11,000 m (36,089 ft)
Maximum range with a 4,000-kg bomb load	6,500 km (4039 miles)
Cannon armament	10 x 20-mm (.78 calibre) Berezin B-20 cannon
Crew	10

A diagram illustrating the VIP interior layout of the 'aircraft 66' airliner powered by Mikulin AM-43TK-300B engines.

Chapter 1

Presents from America

As noted in the introduction, the USA persistently turned down Soviet requests for the delivery of B-29 bombers. Yet, despite this discrimination on the part of its ally, by the beginning of 1945 the USSR had obtained three flyable Superfortresses. Where had they come from? The origin of this miracle, very timely for the USSR, is as follows.

From 1944 onwards the USAAF units equipped with the latest B-29 bombers began to systematically raid territories occupied by Japan, followed by bombing raids against the Japanese Islands themselves. In the course of these raids several damaged aircraft made forced landings in the Soviet Far East. It should be noted that during the first raids the B-29 crews ran a fairly high risk of not returning to base. Apart from the danger posed by the Japanese anti-aircraft defences, the fate of the crews depended on the reliability of the aircraft's systems – which left a lot to be desired in the aircraft of the first production batches. Engine troubles were especially numerous. The Wright R-3350 Twin Cyclones of early B-29As were extremely unreliable and the service life was only 15 hours; there were frequent failures of the defensive armament etc. This was the usual complement of 'teething troubles' of a new and highly complicated machine which was hastily pressed into combat service with all its vicissitudes. Besides, the first crews could not use the aircraft to its full potential. This was especially

true for long-range flights. Not until 1945 did the Americans master the technique of cruising at the aircraft's service ceiling while heading for the target; this technique substantially reduced fuel consumption, enabling the pilots to reach the bomber's design range.

The first Superfortress made a forced landing at the Soviet Navy airbase Tsentral'-naya-Ooglovaya, 30 km (18.6 miles) east of Vladivostok, on 20th July 1944. The machine, a Wichita-built B-29-5-BW (USAAF serial 42-6256) christened *Ramp Tramp* because of its lengthy stays on the ground for maintenance and piloted by Captain Howard R. Jarnell, belonged to the 770th Bomb Squadron/462nd Bomb Group (Heavy). The aircraft was damaged while bombing the Showa Steel Works at Anshan, Manchuria. Two of the bomber's engines were knocked out by anti-aircraft fire and the pilot decided to play safe and land on Soviet territory. Yakovlev Yak-9 fighters of the Pacific Fleet Air Arm intercepted the aircraft and conducted it to the airfield in the vicinity of Vladivostok where the crew and the aircraft were interned.

A month later, on 20th August 1944, another crippled 'Superfort', a Renton-built B-29A-1-BN of the 395th BS/40th BG(H) (42-93829 *Cait Paomat II*), crossed the Soviet border over the Amur River. The aircraft had been damaged during a raid against steel foundries in Yawata, Japan. With the radar inoperative, the B-29 lost its way in the clouds

where it had taken cover from Japanese fighters, straying into Soviet territory as a result. The pilot, Major R. McGlinn, ordered the crew to bale out. The entire crew parachuted to safety and the uncontrolled B-29 crashed into the foothills of the Sikhoté-Alin' mountain range in the vicinity of Khabarovsk. Although the bomber was a complete write-off, the wreckage was salvaged and delivered to Moscow for close examination.

On 11th November 1944 B-29-15-BW 42-6365 piloted by Captain Weston H. Price was hit by flak over the town of Omura, Japan. (Some sources, though, claim it flew into a typhoon during a raid against the Japanese islands and was severely damaged by a lightning strike.) The crew managed to limp to the Soviet coast, landing at Tsentral'naya-Ooglovaya AB. This B-29 belonging to the 794th BS/468th BG(H) was christened *General H. H. Arnold Special* to commemorate a visit paid to this particular aircraft by General Henry 'Hap' Arnold; the same was witnessed by a memorial plate affixed in the aircraft's cockpit. It was this aircraft that was dismantled in Moscow and used for making outlines of all parts and copying the dimensions for the purpose of issuing working drawings for Tu-4 production. The memorial plate was removed and kept as a souvenir by Leonid L. Kerber, a leading equipment specialist of the Tupolev OKB; later he gave it to Maximilian B. Saukke who also took part in the work on the Tu-4.

Still in USAAF markings, Boeing B-29-5-BW 42-6256 *Ramp Tramp* sits at Tsentrahl'naya-Ooglovaya airbase in the Soviet Far East after force-landing there on 20th July 1944, with Soviet Naval Aviation/Pacific Fleet pilots in the foreground.

The three pictures show B-29-15-BW '358 Black' (ex USAAF 42-6358) at Izmaïlovo airfield, Moscow.

The fourth aircraft, B-29-15-BW 42-6358 *Ding Hao!* (794th BS/468th BG(H)) piloted by Lieutenant William Micklish, fell into Soviet hands ten days later. On 21st November 1944 it was hit by AA fire during a raid against a target in Japan (some sources claim it was attacked by Japanese fighters when bombing Omura). One of the engines was damaged and went dead. On three engines the aircraft reached the Soviet coastline where it was met by Soviet fighters; they escorted it to an airfield where the bomber made a safe landing.

So far, Western publications say four Superfortresses were lost in this fashion. Some sources, however, claim that much later, on 29th August 1945, a fifth and final B-29 found its way into the USSR. Japan had already ceased resistance but the Act of Capitulation was not yet signed, and pilots of the Pacific Fleet's fighter element were on combat alert, ready to engage the enemy at a moment's notice. The B-29 made its appearance over Kanko airfield where the 11th IAP (*istrebitel'nyy aviapolk* – fighter regiment) of the Pacific Fleet Air Arm was based. Two pairs of Yak-9s scrambled to intercept the B-29. Hot-tempered naval pilots made a firing pass at the 'American', putting one of its engines out of action. The machine made a forced landing at Kanko.

Now the first three B-29s that had made forced landings were interned by the USSR on a perfectly legal basis, whatever Western authors may say about it being 'contrary to agreements with the United States'. In April 1941 a Pact of Neutrality was concluded between the USSR and Japan with a five-year term of validity; in April 1945 the USSR denounced this Pact. While this Pact was still valid, the Soviet Union abided strictly by its stipulations and fulfilled its obligations over Japan, including the clauses providing for the internment of Allied combat materiel and personnel in the Far Eastern theatre of operations. In the course of virtually all four years of the Great Patriotic War the Japanese threat hanging over the Soviet Union was something to be reckoned with. Should Japan undertake an offensive in the East, this, coupled with powerful German blows, at least in

The same aircraft at Tsentrahl'naya-Ooglovaya airbase near Vladivostok prior to the ferry flight to Moscow, with typical rugged local scenery in the background.

1942-43, could place the USSR on the brink of total disaster. Therefore the Soviets diligently complied with all the clauses of the 1941 Pact, interning any and all American aircraft and crews that landed in the Soviet Far East. The first to land in the Soviet Union in 1942 was a B-25B from the famous group led by Lieutenant-Colonel James H. Doolittle which attacked the Japanese islands on 18th April after taking-off from the aircraft carrier USS *Hornet* with a 'one-way ticket'. Then a considerable number of B-25s, B-24s, Lockheed PV-1 Venturas and PV-2 Harpoons made landings on Soviet territory. Some of them were in airworthy condition; later they were taken on strength by the VVS and even took part in combat against Japan in 1945.

The three slightly damaged B-29s that had landed in the USSR in 1944 were interned on the same legal basis. The fifth Superfortress, however, which landed at Kanko in August 1945 was handed over to the Americans together with its crew, since the stipulations of the Soviet-Japanese Pact were no longer enforced. All the interned crews of Allied aircraft were sent to a special NKVD (Soviet secret police) camp near Tashkent. Before being sent there they were allowed a meeting with the US consul who promised to send a message to the USA informing their relatives that they were alive. When the airmen asked when they would be set free, the consul could only answer that they were interned in conformity with the Geneva convention and that they would have to wait. The camp was subjected to observation by Japanese officials and the Soviet administration had to be extra careful.

It should be noted that conditions in the camp were comfortable by Soviet standards of the day; they could be compared neither with the Soviet camps for war prisoners from the Axis powers, nor with camps for former Soviet prisoners of war, nor even with the conditions for soldiers of the regular Red Army units while in reserve regiments before being sent to the front. The rooms accommodated 15 to 20 persons; the Americans got decent food; they could practice sports, play games etc. The fairly liberal regime in this camp is testified to in the memoirs of one of the B-29 crew members who related how a Russian general came to the camp on Christmas Day in 1944 and began to deliver a speech; at that moment one of the internees flung a salted cucumber at him which hit him squarely in the eye. Naturally, everybody believed they all would soon be shot, but the matter was sorted out without any dire consequences.

The camp was populated by some 200 internees at any one time; people came and went. The Allies were perfectly well informed about all these incidents involving their personnel and materiel but did not interfere

Above and below: B-29-5-BW 42-6256 with Soviet insignia but still carrying the original *Ramp Tramp* nose art. The USAAF serial has been removed but the Soviet serial '256 Black' not yet applied.

because they were well aware that they ought to avoid provoking Japan and that the appearance of one more front in the Far East could not only lead to a debacle for the Soviet Union but also compromise the success of their struggle against Japan. From time to time Soviet authorities allowed the interned airmen to 'vanish'. They were transported in closely shut Studebaker trucks to Iran, part of which was occupied by the US Army. There they took a bath, changed into fresh clean uniforms and were shipped off to the United States. Before boarding the ships they were warned that they had better keep their mouths shut, or else Stalin would not let the remaining Americans go. The American airmen from the B-29 crews travelled along that route, too.

The return scheme was operated on condition that the American side would observe the strictest secrecy. The USAAF Command made the returning airmen sign a document stipulating that they would not breathe a word about their stay in the Soviet Union for several years to come; no entries were made in their personal files about their stay in the USSR. After return to the US they were no longer posted abroad. Personnel officers of the units where they continued to serve were informed that these people had served in a top secret unit 'D' and that it was strictly forbidden to ask them any questions about their previous service. Yet, a leak did occur; some information found its way into the press – apparently someone from these crews had blabbed. News of this was brought to Stalin's notice. 'Uncle Joe' was enraged and immediately put a stop to the process of 'vanishing'; rumours were current among Americans that

Another view of one of the captured B-29s at Izmaïlovo airfield.

Top and above: In the closing stages of its flying career B-29-5-BN 42-6256 (by then repainted in Soviet markings and serialled '256 Black') was used as a 'mother ship' for the DFS 346 rocket-powered experimental aircraft designed by captive German engineers. These views show the special rack for the DFS 346 fitted between the bomber's Nos. 3 and 4 engines.

Below: Apart from showing some design features of the DFS 346 (the T-tail, the two-chamber rocket engine and wing boundary layer fences), this view illustrates how the suspended experimental aircraft severely restricted the bomber's flap deflection angle.

Stalin had ordered all the internees liquidated. These rumours were readily given credence by those who knew the true nature of the Soviet regime. Only a personal intervention on the part of the US Ambassador in the USSR helped hush up the affair.

As for the interned aircraft, they should have been returned to the USA once the Soviet-Japanese Pact was denounced, but the Americans did not bother much about this problem. Their reasoning was quite logical: three flyable B-29 would not be a decisive factor; they would not dramatically raise the power of the Soviet Air Force. As for the Russian aircraft industry copying the latest American technology and, in consequence, putting these machines into series production, they simply did not believe in such a possibility. Even when the first three production examples of the Tu-4 – a copy and analogue of the American B-29 – flew over Moscow's Tushino airfield, for a long time people in the USA remained under the impression that the machines seen at Tushino were the very B-29s interned by the Russians in 1944. Thus, by the beginning of 1945 the USSR had at its disposal three virtually operational B-29s.

The machines were in the charge of the Pacific Fleet Air Arm. People's Commissar of the Navy Admiral Nikolai G. Kuznetsov issued an order calling for a careful examination of the American machines. Vice-Chief of Flight Inspection of the Naval Air Arm Colonel S. B. Reidel was sent on a mission to the Far East. Reidel had prior experience of testing and developing aviation materiel of the Naval Aviation, he spoke English and, by virtue of his professional skills, was exactly the right person to tackle the task of breathing new life into the American machines. To assist him, Major Vyacheslav P. Maroonov and one more pilot were sent from the Black Sea Fleet, as both of them had some experience with American aircraft. Engineers A. F. Chernov and M. M. Krooglov were seconded by the Pacific Fleet Air Arm. (Subsequently both Maroonov and Chernov were employed by the Tupolev OKB, flight-testing a number of aircraft, including the Tu-4. Both of them were involved in the crash of the first prototype of the Tu-95 turboprop-powered strategic bomber (Tu-95/1) on 11th May 1953; co-pilot Maroonov parachuted to safety while flight engineer Chernov was killed in the crash.)

Reidel mastered the B-29 on his own, making use of his knowledge of English and the flight and maintenance manuals discovered in one of the aircraft (subsequently these documents were transferred to the Tupolev OKB and were used by the OKB personnel when working on the Tu-4; several books from this set of documents are now preserved in the archives of the museum of the present-day Tupolev Joint-Stock Company. Reidel

Above: A head-on view of '256 Black' with the DFS 346 suspended under the starboard wing. Note the cine camera under the wingtip filming the drop sequence.

Centre and above: Two more views of B-29-5-BN '256 Black' with the DFS 346 aircraft. Note that the armament has been removed and the locations of the gun barbettes faired over.

performed several taxying runs on the airfield, followed by brief hops and, finally, by the first real flight. From January 1945 onwards the B-29 became the object of systematic study. As of 1st January, two B-29s were in the charge of the Pacific Fleet Air Arm command and one more was operated by the 35th Independent Long-Range Bomber Squadron. This air unit was formed specially for testing the B-29; eventually it came to comprise two B-29s and one B-25. Flights were performed from Romanovka airbase which was best suited for flights of heavy aircraft in the class of the B-29. One of the machines was flown by Reidel, while Maroonov and Chernov mastered the other one. They were given two days to get acquainted with the machine. Their English being far from perfect, they spent these two days mainly crawling all over the bomber, armed with a thick English-Russian dictionary. On the third day Reidel made them sit and pass an exam. On 9th January Maroonov flew as co-pilot in the right-hand seat, the left-hand seat being occupied by Reidel. Two days later Maroonov performed a flight on his own, piloting 'the American' from the captain's seat.

Flight-testing of the B-29s in the Far East went on until 21st July. In the course of these tests the bomber's basic performance characteristics were recorded, proving to be somewhat inferior to figures obtained from the USA. This is natural: the machines were not new, having seen a good deal of wear and tear. Several high-altitude flights were undertaken to check the maximum range in a circuit and to perform bombing. The basic performance characteristics determined by the naval pilots are given in the table on this page.

In June and July two B-29s were ferried to Moscow. The first machine was piloted by Reidel, with Major Morzhakov as co-pilot and Krooglov as flight engineer. The names of the airmen piloting the second machine are unknown; however, it is certain that Maroonov was not one of them. By then he had already been transferred to one of the regiments converted to the Tu-2; shortly thereafter he took part in the fighting against Japan. Some time later the third B-29 was also ferried to Moscow. The B-29s arrived at Izmaïlovo airfield on the outskirts of Moscow where they joined the 65th Special Mission Air Regiment. (Now this place is within the city limits, the airfield is long since closed and the land redeveloped; one of the authors lives not far from the former airstrip where the B-29s landed.) At the request of Air Marshal Aleksandr Ye. Golovanov, Commander of the 18th Air Army, one of the B-29s (42-6256) was transferred to the 890th Air Regiment based at Balbasovo airfield near the town of Orsha. Apart from nine Soviet-built Pe-8s, the regiment operated twelve restored ex-USAAF B-17s and nineteen B-25s (the latter were supplied under the Lend-Lease agreement); this was a result of the scarcity of flyable bombers forcing the Soviet Air Force to repair every available aircraft. The Superfortress remained with the 890th Air Regiment until May 1945. As soon as discussions concerning the possibility of copying the B-29 began at the highest level, the machine was ferried to Moscow by the famous test pilot Mark L. Gallai who took the first Tu-4s into the air two years later.

Thus, as the new year of 1945 set in, the most horrendous war in the history of humanity was drawing to an end. The victors and the vanquished alike had in store for them peacetime years during which the former allies would soon be divided by a new front – the front of the Cold War. In the East this was clearly understood, and preparations for this situation were made in advance. The setbacks suffered by Tupolev's '64' project made it imperative that alternative ways be sought. In a gesture of despair, someone in the Air Force command suggested reinstating production of the Pe-8 in 'as-was' condition, without even modernisation. The idea was rejected outright. Stalin was furious; as was his wont, he tried to seek out those who were to blame for the Soviet Union's lagging behind the West in the field of heavy bomber technology (which was actually due to perfectly objective circumstances). Thunderous accusations were hurled at those responsible for the current condition and technical level of Soviet aviation. While the war was in progress, he did not touch anyone, but a year later his heavy-handed chastisement was inflicted on the People's Commissar of Aircraft Industry Aleksey I. Shakhoorin, VVS Commander-in-Chief Novikov and some other high-ranking aircraft industry officials and officers of the Air Force command.

This 'emotional' situation, characteristic of the final months of the war, induced many top-ranking Air Force officers and aircraft industry officials to ponder over the solution of the 'long-range high-speed high-altitude bomber' problem. It is hard to say now who was the first to suggest solving the problem by copying the B-29 – the aircraft industry or the Air Force. According to V. V. Reshetnikov, the former Commander-in-Chief of the Long-Range Aviation, it was Golovanov who dared to approach Stalin with this proposal. According to Golovanov, Stalin's reaction was more than positive, it was coined in his succinct remark: 'All our aircraft that have fought the war must be scrapped, and the B-29 must go into production!' The first mention of the idea of copying the B-29 in the NKAP documents can be found in a letter written by V. M. Myasishchev to People's Commissar A. I. Shakhoorin and dated 25th May 1945. The letter stated, among other things: '…*all the work on issuing production drawings can be effected by the OKB led by Comrade Nezval', by the production engineering section and by some designers of our OKB residing at Plant No.22 which has been relieved of the work on production Pe-2 bombers…*' Myasishchev proposed that the Soviet copy of the B-29 be powered by indigenous Shvetsov ASh-72 engines and Berezin B-20 cannon be installed instead of the American machine-guns. Gradually all this mosaic of opinions on the problem transformed itself, in the minds of the Soviet leaders, into a firm conviction that it was necessary to initiate work on creating a Soviet copy and analogue of the B-29. This was a case of 'quantity transitioning into quality', as a philosophic maxim has it. Unperturbed by this unanimous opinion, Andrey N. Tupolev continued his work on his project '64', without giving any thought to the possibility of copying the American machine. But Stalin, being well aware and appreciative of Tupolev's energy and thrust, selected precisely him for the implementation of this work. In the early summer of 1945 A. N. Tupolev and Aleksandr A. Arkhangel'skiy (one of his aides) were summoned to Stalin. They surmised that the conversation would be concerned with the work on the '64' aircraft, so they brought along an album with a graphic presentation of this machine in colour (the artwork of B. M. Kondorskiy). However, almost right from the start Stalin began discussing the B-29, and the conversation ended with Stalin's instructions to Tupolev requiring him to copy the B-29 within the shortest possible time frame. Shortly thereafter an appropriate directive of the State Defence Committee and a suitable order of the NKAP were issued. The ball was set in motion.

Normal all-up weight	47.6 tonnes (104,939 lb)
Maximum all-up weight	54.5 tonnes (120,151 lb)
Empty weight	32.2 tonnes (70,988 lb)
Normal payload	15.4 tonnes (33,951 lb)
Maximum payload	21.7 tonnes (47,840 lb)
Maximum range without bombs	6,760 km (4,200 miles)
Range with a 4-tonne (8,818-lb) bomb load	5,310 km (3,299 miles)
Maximum speed at normal all-up weight	580 km/h (360 mph)
Time to 5,000 m (16,404 ft)	16.5 minutes
Take-off run	960 m (3,150 ft)

Chapter 2

A Monstrous Task

As noted earlier, by the beginning of 1945 the leaders of the aircraft industry, as well as the leaders of the country, including Stalin, fully realised that development of any indigenous equipment for the 'aircraft 64' by dozens of design bureaux and scientific institutes subordinated to various People's Commissariats (ministries) would take a lot of time; and that in the near future the USSR would not obtain an aircraft capable of carrying a nuclear bomb which was so necessary for ensuring national security. Stalin took the decision that was the only right one under the circumstances – to organise series production of a copy of the American Boeing B-29 Superfortress bomber with all its systems within the shortest time possible, using the four aircraft which had fallen into Soviet hands as recounted in the introductory section.

It was Andrey N. Tupolev's OKB-156 that was tasked with copying the B-29 and putting it into series production; the bomber's initial Soviet designation was B-4 (for *bombardirovschchik*), aka *izdeliye* R. (*Izdeliye*

(product) such-and-such is a commonly used code for Soviet/Russian military hardware items.) On 6th June 1945 the State Defence Committee issued directive No. 8934; it was followed by Order No. 263 issued by the People's Commissariat of Aircraft Industry (NKAP) dated 22nd June 1945. In accordance with this order A. I. Kuznetsov (chief of the 10th Main Directorate of NKAP and Vice People's Commissar responsible for series production of heavy aircraft), V. A. Okulov (Director of aircraft factory No.22 in Kazan') and A. N. Tupolev (Chief Designer) were required to organise production of the four-engined B-4 bomber at Plant No.22. The NKAP order stated: *'Chief Designer Comrade Tupolev is to start immediately the work on preparing technical drawings, mould lofts and technical documentation for the B-4 aircraft; this work is to be considered a primary task for the design staff and production personnel of Plant No. 156 [...] For the purpose of speeding up the work on the B-4 aircraft as much as possible, an experimental design bureau*

(OKB) for the B-4 bomber is to be set up to aid the main OKB led by Comrade Tupolev; this new OKB is to comprise the whole personnel of the OKB led by Comrade Nezval', Comrade Myasishchev's OKB at Plant No. 22 and the experimental workshop of Plant No. 22.'

The text of the NKAP order set out more precisely the whole range of tasks assigned to different organisations and enterprises of the aircraft industry. Tupolev's OKB was entrusted with breaking down the B-29 into separate units and assemblies, reverse-engineering the theoretical outlines of all parts, dismantling different items of equipment and transferring them to appropriate enterprises. The All-Union Institute of Aviation Materials (VIAM – *Vsesoyooznyy instituot aviatsionnykh materiahlov*) was assigned the task of organising the examination of all structural materials used in the B-29's airframe; it was also to issue orders to factories for the production of materials which had not been previously produced by Soviet industry. The Central Aero Engine Institute (TsIAM – *Tsentrahl'nyy insti-*

The team which was responsible for copying the B-29. Left to right: B-4 chief project engineer Dmitriy S. Markov, OKB-156 chief structural strength engineer A. M. Cheryomukhin, Chief Designer Andrey N. Tupolev, his deputy Aleksandr A. Arkhangel'skiy and general arrangement group chief Sergey M. Yeger.

Above and below: The exhibition in the mock-up hall of the Tupolev OKB showing all units and equipment items of the Tu-4 and naming the organisations and officials directly responsible for each item.

toot *aviatsionnovo motorostroyeniya*) was to study the engine/propeller assemblies and conduct the necessary test and development work that would make it possible to equip the new aircraft with Soviet-designed ASh-73 engines (a further development of the ASh-72) and with special turbosuperchargers. The Central Aero- and Hydrodynamics Institute named after Nikolai Ye. Zhukovskiy (TsAGI – *Tsentrahl'nyy aero- i ghidrodinamicheskiy institoot*) was entrusted with studying the aircraft's aerodynamics and structural strength. The Special Equipment Research Institute (NISO – *Naoochnyy institoot spetsiahl'novo oboroodovaniya*) was to study the B-29's equipment and prepare technical requirements that would be issued to Soviet enterprises for the purpose of putting all the various equipment items into production.

Meanwhile, preparations for ferrying the three flyable B-29s to Moscow were getting underway in the Far East. The runways at the two airfields where the bombers had landed had to be extended to cater for the B-29's long take-off run and the Pacific Fleet Air Arm crews who were to fly the Superfortress started mastering it. As already mentioned, in June and July 1945 all three bombers arrived at Izmaïlovo airfield on the outskirts of Moscow.

Work on copying the B-29 started with determining the fate of the three machines. It was decided to transfer B-29-5-BW 42-6256 to the Flight Research Institute (LII – *Lyotno-issledovatel'skiy institoot*) in the town of Ramenskoye south of Moscow for the training of personnel and for preparing flight and servicing manuals. B-29-15-BW 42-6365 was to be disassembled for the purpose of studying the airframe and preparing working drawings. Finally, 42-6358 was to be left as a reference specimen. On 5th July 1945 NKAP issued Order No. 278 placing in the charge of the Tupolev OKB a hangar at the territory of the Central airfield; it was this hangar that came to house the B-29 No.42-6365 which was placed there on the night of 11th June after being ferried from Izmaïlovo.

The stipulated time limits were extremely stringent. Having examined the machine, Tupolev assessed the scope of the forthcoming work as equivalent to three years. To substantiate this term, he pointed out that American technology and production methods differed from those of the Soviet industry not only in aircraft construction but in other branches as well. In response to Tupolev's arguments Stalin granted him the widest possible powers and support from Lavrentiy P. Beria, the influential and feared People's Commissar of the Interior, into the bargain, but the time frame for launching series production of the B-4 was limited to two years. The first Soviet-built bombers were to take part in the traditional air display at Tushino in the summer of 1947. (Actually, original plans required the first Soviet B-29 to be submitted for testing in a year – in June 1946, in the hope that the most complicated units and sub-assemblies for the first B-4s – the AN/APQ-13 radar, the BC-733 blind landing system, the Hamilton Standard propellers, the engine starters, the landing gear wheels etc. – would be purchased in the USA; however, it soon became apparent that in the atmosphere of the 'Cold War' the Americans would sell nothing to the Soviets, and the time limits had to be extended.)

The work on the new aircraft encompassed some 900 enterprises and organisations subordinated to different People's Commissariats of the country; some enterprises were created specially for the purpose. In particular, several new design bureaux were set up within the system of the aircraft industry; they were tasked with copying various items of equipment, including radio, electronics, electrical equipment and instruments, and mastering production of same.

Tupolev started his preparations for the work by establishing a 'think tank' comprising the leaders of the OKB teams, each of which was responsible for this or that part of the work. Dmitriy S. Markov was appointed chief project engineer. In the autumn of 1945 Tupolev and his associates undertook another inspection of the B-29. After the inspection Tupolev said, *'This is a normal aircraft, I see nothing unusual in it. But, frankly, I cannot imagine how you will sort out all this tangle of wiring covering all of the machine, how you will ensure the linkage between the numerous sights and the weapons' remote control system, how you will tackle the control and navigation system – it beats me. A number of other questions are unclear, too. The defensive weapons and bombs will be of our own design, no doubt. The instrument dials will be converted to the metric system, but what about the IFF system, crew gear, parachutes and so on? All these issues must be thoroughly worked out and the results incorporated into one more directive – lest we should debate these questions endlessly.'*

As early as the summer of 1945, immediately after the arrival of the first B-29 at Moscow's Central airfield named after Mikhail V. Frunze (better known as Khodynka), a special task force was set up at Tupolev's order for preparing outline drawings of the aircraft's main assemblies. An album with these outline drawings was ready at the beginning of August; it became a graphic visual basis for discussing the problems associated with copying the B-29. Preparation of these sketches revealed that it would be impossible to reproduce this aircraft in the USSR without radical technological changes in the aviation

More views of the 'exhibition'. Above: The highly polished wind tunnel model manufactured by TsAGI is in the foreground, with the full-scale B-29 visible beyond. The lower photo shows landing gear components.

ПРИБОРЫ СЛЕПОЙ ПОСАДКИ

МАРКЕРНЫЙ ПРИЕМНИК
типа ВС-357

ПРИЕМНИК СЛЕПОЙ ПОСАДКИ
типа ВС-733

Сигнализирует прохождение са-
молетом маркерного передатчика.
Рабочая частота — 75 мгц.
В полете н е управляется.
Антенна-горизонтальный диполь.

Диапазон – 108,3 ÷ 110,3 мгц.
Число фиксированных волн – 6.
Управление для смены волн в
полете - дистанционное.
Антенна – шлейф-диполь, уста-
новлена на фюзеляже.

ПЕРЕДАЮЩЕЕ УСТРОЙСТВО СВЯЗНОЙ РАДИОСТАНЦИИ
типа AN/ART-13
„БЕРКУТ"

ПЕРЕДАТЧИК

БЛОК УДЛИНИТЕЛЬНОЙ
КАТУШКИ

ЩИТОК УПРАВЛЕНИЯ

ЩИТОК ВЫПУСКА
АНТЕННЫ

Излучаемая мощность - 90÷6 вт.
Диапазон –   200÷1500 кгц.
                2,0÷18,1 мгц.
Число фиксированных волн - 11.
Род работы-телеграф и телефон.
Управление для смены волн в
полете - дистанционное.

АВТОМАТИЧЕСКИЙ РАДИОКОМПАС типа SCR 269 G
„Аист"

Диапазон – 200 ÷ 1750 крц.
Дальность действия-1000 км,при
мощности радиомаяка 1000 квт.
Точность ориентирования – 2÷3°.
Отсчет пеленга – непрерывный и
автоматический.

Opposite page:

Above: This page from a Soviet engineering album shows some of the B-29's equipment items copied and produced by Plant No. 327: the BC-357 marker beacon receiver and the BC-733 blind landing system receiver.

Below: More copied B-29 components from the same album (this time manufactured by Plant No. 197), namely the AN/ART-13 communications radio (called Berkoot (Golden Eagle) in the USSR). Left to right: the extension coil, the trailing wire aerial control panel, the transmitter and another control panel.

This page:

Above: Still more copies. The SCR-269G automatic direction finder was copied by Plant No. 528 as the Aist (Stork). As on the other sheets, product specifications are given in a box.

Right: These three artist's impressions show how the B-4 bomber should look.

Above: The Shvetsov ASh-73TK 18-cylinder radial engine.

nents of the B-29 were expressed in inches; when converted to the metric system, they were approximated to the standards adopted within this system. Later, venomous tongues cracked a joke that Tupolev had been awarded the title of Hero of Socialist Labour and the Stalin Prize for converting the screw threads from inches to the metric system. In reality, however, Tupolev and his team had to shoulder the extremely heavy burden of co-ordinating the activity of different industry branches involved in the programme and bringing them up to the state-of-the-art level of technology and production processes. After carefully analysing the B-29's structure A. M. Cheryomukhin, the OKB's chief specialist in structural strength issues, came to the conclusion that the Superfortress had been designed with substantially lower ultimate loads in mind than those prescribed by the Soviet Strength Standards then in force. As a result, the Strength Standards were reworked and approximated to those adopted in the USA; subsequently this facilitated the design work on Soviet heavy aircraft.

One item in the American manuals puzzled the Soviet engineers mightily. It was a phrase reading 'Start the putt-putt'. None of the engineers could recall coming across this term before; the team researched much aviation literature but to no avail. The mystery was solved by pure chance when someone started the emergency generator/auxiliary power unit which was driven by a two-stroke engine and this started emitting an unmistakable *putt-putt-putt-putt-putt…* The Soviet engi-

metal industry. The vast majority of technical features and materials used by the B-29 were new for the Soviet aircraft industry. Many intermediate products (metal sheets and plates, stamped and shaped structural sections, special nuts, bolts and fasteners), as well as up to 90% of the materials, had never been produced until then by the Soviet aircraft and metal industry. Also new were the production techniques involved in the manufacture of the aircraft's airframe.

In accordance with Stalin's directions no deviations from the American patterns were tolerated in any of the parts reproduced. For this reason the OKB's structural strength specialists had to tackle a 'reverse engineering' task: they were expected to issue specifications to the metal industry regarding the new alloys to be created, proceeding from the actual dimensions of the parts and strength characteristics of their materials, not vice versa. Besides, the dimensions of all compo-

B-29-15-BW '365 Black' in the mortician's... sorry, the hangar at Sokol'niki where it was dismantled completely for the purpose of studying the design and taking the dimensions of all parts and components.

neers may have been well versed in English aviation terminology, but nobody had counted on SLANG!

Issuing the technical drawings for the production Plant No. 22 was preceded by a systematic breakdown of B-29 42-6365 into separate assemblies. Major assemblies were detached from each other, every single unit was studied by a specially assigned team of designers and production engineers. The unit or part was weighed, measured, photographed and described. Then all detachable elements of the subassembly were removed, revealing the basic framework. All parts were subjected to spectral analysis in order to determine the material. A total of 40,000 A4-size sheets of manufacturing drawings were issued on the basis of that research. Preparation of the drawings was completed in March 1946.

Almost all items of equipment that had been removed from the airframe when disassembling the aircraft, totalling 350 units, were sent to specialised design bureaux for studying and copying.

The question of engines for the B-4 found a relatively simple solution, as since the 1930s the Perm'-based OKB-19 led by Arkadiy D. Shvetsov had been engaged in putting engines designed in the USA by the Wright Aeronautical Corporation into production under licence. In the late 1930s and the early 1940s OKB-19 evolved two 18-cylinder two-row radials – the 2,000-hp M-71 and the 2,250-hp M-72 – which were similar in their design features and production techniques to

A ground test rig for the ASh-73TK duplicating the complete engine nacelle with a section of the wing.

the Wright Twin Cyclone engines powering the B-29. Therefore there was no need to copy the Wright R-3350-23A; the engine that was put into production was the indigenous ASh-73TK – a further development of the M-71 and M-72, which differed in being fitted with twin TK-19 turbosuperchargers (TK = *toorbokompressor*). The supercharger with its control system, the magneto generator and the heat-resistant bearings were copied from the American engine.

This kind of Russian-American symbiosis resulted in the creation, within the shortest possible time frame, of the ASh-73TK engine which fully met the requirements of the aircraft designers.

The ASh-73TK was likewise an 18-cylinder air-cooled two-row radial fitted with a single-speed engine-driven supercharger and two exhaust-driven superchargers. The engine's displacement was 58.1 litres (3,543 cu in), the reduction gear ratio was 0.375. The

A scale model of the B-4 in one of TsAGI's wind tunnels.

Above: The first Soviet-built Tu-4 (c/n 220001), originally known as the B-4, was completed by the Kazan' aircraft factory No. 22 in February 1947. It is seen here at the factory airfield.

The first B-4 carried no markings other than Soviet national insignia on the wings, fuselage and tail.

A three-quarters rear view of B-4 c/n 220001, showing the radome of the Kobal't navigation/attack radar.

Секретно

Front view of B-4 c/n 220001. The inscription in the upper right-hand corner reads *Sekretno* (Classified).

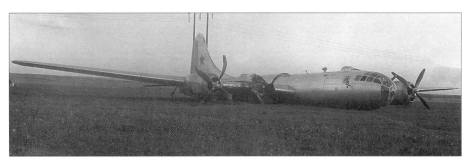

Above and below: Tu-4 c/n 220101 after crash-landing in a field near Kolomna on 18th September 1947 due to a fire in the No. 3 engine. The aircraft broke its back on impact and was declared a write-off.

Above: This photo shows how the fuselage broke in two aft of the wings.
Below: The twisted remains of the No. 3 engine nacelle; the engine is gone, having broken away in flight.

engine delivered 2,400 hp at 2,600 rpm for take-off, with a combat rating of 2,200 hp at 2,400 rpm up to an altitude of 8,000-8,700 m (26,247-28,543 ft) and a nominal rating of 2,000 hp at 2,400 rpm up to 8,600-9,300 m (28,215-30,512 ft). Specific fuel consumption (SFC) at nominal power was 310 to 330 g/hp·hr, the engine's dry weight was 1,275 kg (2,811 lb).

In contrast, copying the equipment proved to be a far greater challenge. The leaders of some design bureaux responsible for various units and systems persistently sought to be exempted from copying the American prototypes, claiming that the equipment developed in their OKBs was in no way inferior and was already series-produced into the bargain. However, it was perfectly clear to Tupolev that, should one relinquish the principle of strict copying, this would entail a host of co-ordination problems and completing the work on the B-4 within the specified time frame would be jeopardised. Both Stalin and the Government shared Tupolev's opinion. Tupolev resorted to an unusual step: at his initiative an exhibition was arranged in the mock-up hall on the fifth floor of his design bureau, presenting virtually all the units and equipment items of the aircraft. They were accompanied by notice boards specifying the ministries, enterprises, stipulated delivery dates and names of the officials directly responsible for the item. Members of the Politbureau, ministers, chief designers and factory directors were invited to the exhibition. It became a peculiar kind of tool for putting pressure on the enterprises responsible for the equipment, making it possible to take expeditious administrative measures against those chief designers or factory directors who displayed negligence or reluctance. Thus, the mentioned visit to the exhibition resulted in a decision to remove from his post chief designer M. Oikher who had persistently criticised the American prototype of an instrument and refused to copy it, proposing that an instrument developed by himself be used instead. Subsequent events proved this policy to be the right one. The pressure brought to bear on the subcontractors yielded the desired result; deliveries of equipment for the production B-4 bombers were made on schedule and, most importantly, the home-produced subassemblies and equipment items were not overweight compared to their American prototypes. When the first Soviet B-4 was completed, the empty weight of the aircraft was 35,270 kg (77,757 lb), the corresponding figure for the B-29 being 34,930 kg (77,007 lb); the difference did not exceed 1%, which was a remarkable result.

There were only two instances where Stalin's order to copy everything strictly was not observed. Firstly, it was the case with the identifcation friend-or-foe (IFF) system – which was perfectly natural, since it was the American air defence system that the B-4 was to penetrate; secondly, a more up-to-date American short-wave command radio was copied and fitted.

The B-4's defensive armament differed from that of the B-29. The 12.7-mm (.50 calibre) machine-guns were replaced initially by 20-mm (.78 calibre) Berezin B-20 cannon and then by 23-mm (.90 calibre) Nudel'man/ Rikhter NR-23 cannon; on the other hand, the defensive armament control system of the B-29 was retained. This decision was justified: a more potent cannon armament considerably enhanced the B-4's defensive capabilities compared to those of the B-29. An indirect corroboration of the advantages of the defensive cannon armament was provided by combat episodes in the Korean War where Soviet-produced MiG-15 fighters could often make a firing pass at a B-29 while remaining outside the effective range of its heavy machine-guns. Had the MiGs' adversaries been Tu-4s armed with cannon, not B-29s, the fighters would have had a much more difficult task to tackle.

It proved to be an arduous task for the Soviet industry to master production of American materials, especially the non-metallic ones: plastics, high-quality rubber, synthetic fabrics. This was due to the general backwardness of the Soviet chemical industry. As a rule, factories and research institutes persistently proposed that the American materials be replaced by traditional materials that were already well-established in production, such as Bakelite, fibre, Plexiglas etc. Yet Tupolev and his deputies were adamant; they understood full well that failure to use new materials would result in a substandard aircraft, and insisted that the subcontractors strictly abide by the specification.

By mastering the whole range of the B-29's design features, materials and technologies the Soviet aircraft industry and associated industry branches created a potent material basis which enabled Soviet aviation to attain world standards by the early 1950s, and then to surpass them on some counts. The work effected then was so wide-ranging and anticipatory in its scope that to this day instruments or equipment items that were put into production in 1946-47 and were either modelled directly on those of the B-29 or represented their further modernisation can be found in Soviet/Russian-built aircraft.

Construction of a full-scale mock-up of the B-4 began in mid-1946. All design faults and discrepancies that came to light were rectified and appropriate corrections were immediately made to the working drawings in the presence of a supervisor; the corrections were checked out on the mock-up and cor-

rected drawings were sent to the production Plant No. 22. In this way it proved possible to reveal most of the mistakes which were caused by the slam-bang tempo of the work and by fatigue suffered by the personnel who had only one day off in a month. When the mock-up was completed, all of its hatches were provided with locks and no one could get access to the inside of the mock-up without permission from Tupolev or D. S. Markov, the chief project engineer. This was done to rule out any attempts to undertake modifications without putting them on record in the production drawings.

In accordance with the order issued by the Ministry of Aircraft Industry (MAP – Ministerstvo aviatsionnoy promyshlennosti) on 23rd March 1946, all items of equipment manufactured by the industry and intended for the B-4 were entered in a special list and checked out against B-29 '358 Black' (ex 42-6358; after being repainted in Soviet markings the three B-29s received abbreviated versions of their USAAF serials) that had been retained as a specimen, to make sure that they were suitable for installation in the B-4. This saved a lot of time and spared the design personnel a lot of nervous stress, ruling out unpleasant surprises in the process of fitting the equipment to the real aircraft.

At the same time a large-scale wind tunnel model was produced for TsAGI; it was used for studying the peculiarities of the aircraft's aerodynamics.

B-29 '256 Black' (formerly 42-6256), which was in airworthy condition, was test-flown to check the aircraft's controllability, powerplant operation and obtain more precise performance data. In the autumn of 1945 it made a flight to Kazan' providing an opportunity for the employees of Plant No. 22 to examine the aircraft first-hand. At the same time training was started of the flight crews that were expected to test the first B-4s; this work was effected by test pilot Major Vyacheslav P. Maroonov, a former Naval Aviation pilot who had mastered the handling of the B-29 during his service in the Far East.

Tupolev's OKB was expanded to suit the needs of the B-4 programme. Not only did it obtain authority over the hangar at the Central airfield where the dismantling, examination and copying of the B-29 'No. 365' (ie, 42-6365) took place; it came to include the personnel of the OKB-22 – the design bureau of the production Plant No.22 led by I. F. Nezval' which became the Kazan' branch of A. N. Tupolev's OKB. The OKB also came into possession of a supplementary production facility in Moscow near the Paveletsky railway station.

The Kazan' branch of the Tupolev OKB undertook a considerable portion of the work. Making use of the ready parts of B-29 42-6365

which were received from Moscow, Kazan' branch personnel prepared technical drawings of landing gear doors, bomb bays, crew seats, outer wing panels, the aft portion of the wing centre section, the stabilisers, elevators, fin, rudder and the centre pressurised cabin. The drawings were completed by 1st January 1946; in all, the branch issued 1,383 drawings and 657 specifications. It also prepared theoretical outline mould lofts for the B-4, which the plant was gearing up to build. In December 1945 the Kazan' branch began restoring some subassemblies of B-29 42-6365; subsequently these were used to build the prototype of an airliner derivative of the B-4 – the 'aircraft 70', also designated Tu-12 (the latter designation was later reused for the 'aircraft 77', a jet-powered derivative of the Tu-2, while the 'aircraft 70' came to be referred to as the Tu-70).

Mastering the B-4 was a new and fairly complicated task for the Kazan' aircraft factory No.22. A number of workshops had to be rebuilt, completely new production processes had to be mastered, a considerable proportion of equipment and machine tools that was obsolete and worn out during the war years had to be replaced. Tooling up for production in Kazan' involved developing no fewer than 30,000 new manufacturing techniques, producing 27,000 pieces of rigging and 40,700 templates. The new equipment obtained by dismantling some factories in the vanquished Germany started arriving at the end of 1945. Some of the new machine-tools came from the final deliveries under the Lend-Lease agreement.

The B-4's airframe manufacturing technology, based on the use of mould lofts, was completely new for the plant. Quite different production methods had been used earlier during series production of the Pe-2 and Pe-8 bombers. A mould loft department was set up at the factory; at the initial stage it received a lot of support from the OKB's head office and the Kazan' branch.

Many problems were posed when mastering the manufacture of nut-and-bolt pairs for screw jacks, sighting blisters, astrodomes and other aircraft parts that were new for the plant. The B-4 introduced new complex navigation, electronic support measures and radio communications equipment systems, as well as the remote-control system for the defensive armament; this necessitated the setting up of a whole network of laboratories for studying these systems at the factory. In these laboratories various items of equipment were subjected to bench testing and adjusted with the participation of specialists from subcontractor enterprises, prior to being installed in the aircraft. Specialists from the OKB and its Kazan' branch also took part in the process of joining together major subassemblies and

The pilots who test-flew the first Tu-4s. Top row, left to right: Nikolay S. Rybko (crew captain of Tu-4 c/n 220001), A. G. Vasil'chenko (crew captain of Tu-4 c/n 220101) and Mark L. Gallai (crew captain of Tu-4s c/ns 220002 and 220405). Bottom row, left to right: Kazan' aircraft factory test pilot N. I. Arzhanov (crew captain of Tu-4 c/n 220402), Vyacheslav P. Maroonov (crew captain of Tu-4 c/n 220102) and A. P. Yakimov (crew captain of Tu-4 c/n 220103).

installing the equipment in the final assembly shop, which helped avoid errors in the installation and adjustment of the bomber's systems.

This immense, thorough and carefully planned work resulted in the completion of the first production B-4 (construction number 220001 – ie, Plant No. 22, Batch 00, first aircraft in the batch); the unserialled aircraft was rolled out on 28th February 1947 – ten months after the factory had received the manufacturing drawings in April 1946. Adjustment and development work went on until mid-May, whereupon the aircraft was ready for the first flight. This took place on 19th May; the bomber was captained by test pilot Nikolay S. Rybko, with A. G. Vasil'chenko as co-pilot and V. N. Saginov as leading engineer. Two

weeks later, after a few development flights, the aircraft was ferried to the LII airfield in the town of Zhukovskiy for further testing. (This town, formerly Stakhanovo, was renamed in early 1947 to celebrate the 100th anniversary of N. Ye. Zhukovskiy, the founder of Russian aviation science.)

At the end of June the second production B-4, serialled '202 Black' (c/n 220002), was handed over to a crew captained by test pilot Mark L. Gallai. The first flights of the first two aircraft took place in the presence of senior OKB staff headed by Andrey N. Tupolev.

In August the third production B-4 (c/n 220101) was handed over to a crew captained by test pilot A. G. Vasil'chenko; that same month a crew captained by V. P. Maroonov took charge of the fourth production aircraft

(c/n 220102). In the course of the summer and autumn of 1947 a further ten or so machines were manufactured, test-flown and ferried to Zhukovskiy.

The Government ruled that the B-4 bombers were to be immediately submitted for State acceptance trials involving a total of 20 aircraft. Holding the trials on this scale was expected to speed up obtaining the necessary data on B-4 operation, yielding more comprehensive information which would then be summed up; thus, the test results would be obtained within the shortest possible time, including information on the operational reliability of the aircraft and its entire equipment complement. However, certain difficulties arose in ensuring such a large-scale trials programme, unprecedented in the USSR. First of all, it was necessary to select the required number of pilots and engineers and form flight and ground crews. A stock of spare parts had to be provided for the aircraft; repair teams had to be formed; it was necessary to ensure efficient co-ordination with production plants delivering equipment and engines.

A special headquarters headed by Chief Air Marshal Aleksandr Ye. Golovanov representing the Air Force and Deputy Minister Pyotr V. Dement'yev representing the Ministry of Aircraft Industry was formed to supervise the trials. Permanently present in the headquarters were representatives of the organisations and plants responsible for the equipment and of the ministries directly involved in the B-4 programme; Dmitriy S. Markov was the permanent representative of the Tupolev OKB.

The trials were expected to be completed in 1948, whereupon the aircraft would achieve initial operational capability (IOC) with the Soviet Air Force.

The best test pilots of MAP and the VVS were entrusted with the testing of the B-4. In addition to the crews captained by Rybko, Gallai, Vasil'chenko and Maroonov, further aircraft were handed over to crews captained by B. V. Govorov, A. P. Yakimov, S. F. Mashkovskiy, F. F. Opadchiy, V. V. Ponomarenko, A. D. Perelyot, I. Sh. Vaganov, K. K. Rykov, M. V. Rodnykh and others. The LII airfield was chosen as the place for the test programme.

Before the work on determining the performance characteristics of the aircraft and its equipment could be started, much time had to be spent on adjustment and development work. Gradually the aircraft forming the initial production lot of 20 machines were brought up to the full complement of equipment and started flights in accordance with the test programme. At the initial stage the testing of the first B-4s looked more like development work on certain systems and, as often as not, individual units and equipment items such as variable-pitch propeller governors, undercarriage and flap actuators (faulty functioning of screwjacks was common in the early days and was cured by selecting the right type of lubricating oil), electric motors, generators, the powerplant (primarily the ASh-73TK engine itself). There were many complaints concerning the functioning of radar equipment and the synchros in the cannon armament control system. Despite these faults, the crews that test-flew the B-4 had a fairly high opinion of the aircraft – they recognised its good performance and handling, modern equipment, comfortable and well-designed crew workstations, and the provision of all sorts of service devices which facilitated the piloting and eased the crew workload. The pilots also voiced some complaints, however: they were not quite happy with the glazing of the front cabin (flight deck) which distorted the view, the rather heavy controls of the first machines and the lack of a de-icing system on these aircraft. The main drawbacks were eliminated during the course of flight-testing of the first batch of B-4s.

The first three machines took part in the traditional Air Display in August 1947. Rybko and Gallai flew their aircraft, while the lead aircraft was piloted by Chief Air Marshal A. Ye. Golovanov. The three B-4s made a dramatic pass at low altitude over the Tushino airfield, producing the desired impression on the Government and the attending foreign military attachés. Curiously, as already mentioned, for a long time the West was under the impression that it was the refurbished B-29s that had been shown at the Air Display, being of the opinion that the USSR was unable to copy and put into series production an aircraft as complicated as the B-29. Yet, the fact had to be faced: at the price of unbelievable exertion, Russia succeeded in mastering technologies of utmost complexity within a year and a half, furnishing a first-rate machine for its aviation. Later, when the West learned the truth, NATO's Air Standards Co-ordinating Committee (ASCC) allocated the reporting name *Bull* to the Tu-4.

After the Air Display the testing resumed. On 18th September 1947 a fire broke out in the No. 3 engine of B-4 c/n 220101 when the engine seized during a regular test flight. Crew captain A. G. Vasil'chenko ordered the crew to bale out; only Vasil'chenko himself and flight engineer N. I. Filizon remained on board. Filizon did his best, trying to extinguish the fire, but to no avail. The burning engine broke away and the fire spread to the front part of the wing centre section. In this critical situation Vasil'chenko managed to make a belly landing in a field 7 km (4.3 miles) southwest of the town of Kolomna. Having extricated themselves from the burning machine, Vasil'chenko and Filizon attacked the fire with hand-held fire extinguishers with which the bomber was provided; the fire was eventually put out completely by local peasants and a fire engine that appeared on the scene. Yet, the aircraft was damaged beyond repair, breaking its back aft of the wings, and could only be used for spares.

A second and far more serious accident took place in October 1947 when the 13th production B-4 (c/n 220303) was ferried from Kazan' to Moscow to take part in the fly-past over the Red Square on 7th November to mark the 30th anniversary of the October Revolution. (In connection with this parade Plant No. 22 urgently stepped up its work on the initial batch of 20 aircraft, responding to a Government decision that a large formation of B-4 bombers – by then redesignated Tu-4 – should be displayed at the parade.) During the flight to Moscow three (!) engines caught fire one after another, and the crew chose to make a forced landing rather than bale out. The aircraft landed in a field, which turned out to be too short, and crashed into trees at the end of the landing run. The fire went out on impact, but the front cabin was crushed and two crew members were killed. Would you doubt the magic power of the number 13 after that?

It must be noted that powerplant problems figured most prominently at the initial stage of the Tu-4's flight-test programme. For a long time the crews of the first Tu-4s were plagued by engine failures, malfunctioning of engine accessories and failures of the propeller feathering system. Much trouble was caused by two cases of propeller overspeeding which occurred on the aircraft piloted by Gallai and Maroonov. In Gallai's case the crew eventually managed to feather the propeller and the consequences were limited to a wrecked engine; in Maroonov's case the propeller broke off at great speed, striking the fuselage and the neighbouring engine, and it was a miracle that the crew survived. Subsequently, when the aircraft was already in widescale operational service, there were several cases of the engine mounts failing due to metal fatigue. Step by step these faults were eliminated by the aircraft and engine designers; the engine mounts were reinforced and alterations were introduced into the engines' shock-absorption system.

In the autumn of 1947 the testing of the first Tu-4s for maximum range commenced, two machines (c/ns 220002 and 220102) being used. The two bombers took off simultaneously from the LII airfield and each one followed its own route (Zhukovskiy – Sevastopol' – Zhukovskiy for Gallai's aircraft and Zhukovskiy – Sverdlovsk – Chelyabinsk – Zhukovskiy for Maroonov's machine). The first aircraft, flying under adverse conditions (heavy icing and extra drag created by bomb bay doors opened inadvertently due to a crew member's negligence), covered a distance of 2,560 km (1,591 miles). The aircraft's all-up weight was 49,100 kg (108,247 lb), including a bomb load of 1,500 kg (3,307 lb). The second machine covered a distance of 3,123 km (1,940 miles), staying airborne for 7 hours 39 minutes; the average speed was 400 km/h (248 mph). The flight was performed at an all-up weight of 50,000 kg (110,231 lb), including a 1,500-kg (3,307-lb) bomb load.

Another long-distance flight was performed by a pair of Tu-4s, c/ns 220102 and 220201, the fourth and sixth production aircraft. (**Note:** With the exception of the first two batches containing two and three aircraft respectively, there were typically five aircraft to a batch in the case of Kazan'-built examples, though the last batches were of ten air-

Above: '202 Black' (c/n 220002), the second Kazan'-built production Tu-4.

A side view of Tu-4 '202 Black' in the course of the flight-test programme.

Above: A three-quarters rear view of the second production Tu-4.

A full frontal of the same aircraft.

craft.) Their route took them from Zhukovskiy to Turkestan (Yany-Kurgan railway station) and back again. The first machine covered a distance of 5,380 km (3,343 miles) at an average speed of 384 km/h (239 mph), the all-up weight being 58,200 kg (128,309 lb) with a bomb load of 2,000 kg (4,409 lb). The remaining fuel upon landing was 2,294 kg (5,057 lb). The second machine covered 5,090 km (3,162 miles) at an average speed of 390 km/h (242 mph), the all-up weight being 57,900 kg (127,648 lb) with a bomb load of 2,000 kg (4,409 lb). The remaining fuel upon landing was 2,428 kg (5,353 lb). Design range, with full use of fuel, was calculated to be 5,800-6,100 km (3,604-3,790 miles).

The maximum range testing of the first production Tu-4s marked the completion of the initial stage of the State acceptance trials. MAP test pilots turned two machines, followed by another three, over to the Red Banner State Research Institute of the Air Force (GK NII VVS – *Gosoodarstvennyy krasno-znamyonnyy naoochno-issledovatel'skiy institoot Voyenno-vozdooshnykh sil*) for further work within the test programme. Gallai's original aircraft (c/n 220002) was the first to be transferred; instead, Gallai received the twentieth machine (c/n 220405), the last in the initial batch, for development and testing.

At the end of 1947, summing up the test results of the first Tu-4s, LII issued report No. 47-178 which cited the performance characteristics of the type as shown in the table on page 32.

This performance basically met the requirements set forth in directive No.1282-524 issued by the Council of Ministers on 29th June 1946, according to which the final performance characteristics of the Tu-4 (speed, range and payload) were to be endorsed after the completion of State acceptance trials of the first aircraft. At the same time it was stipulated that maximum speed at sea level should not be lower than 470 km/h (292 mph), maximum speed at altitude should be at least 560 km/h (348 mph), maximum range with a 1,500-kg (3,307-lb) bomb load should be at least 5,000 km (3,107 miles), maximum range with a 7,128-kg (15,714-lb) bomb load should be at least 3,000 km (1,864 miles).

Tests of the initial batch of 20 Tu-4s at GK NII VVS went on for another 18 months; they comprised the performance testing, tests of the aircraft's offensive and defensive armament and verification of the bomb-aiming radar. Additionally, various bomb load options were carefully tested because the Tu-4 was intended to be used as a strategic bomber armed with nuclear weapons (the weight of the first Soviet atomic bomb was expected to be within 6 tonnes (13,228 lb).

In the bomber's normal and overload configurations the 6,000-kg (13,228-lb) bomb was suspended in the rear bomb bay. If M-43 and M-44 conventional high-explosive bombs were used, the bomb load was 7,120 kg (15,697 lb), or 12,000 kg (26,455 lb) in the case of M-46 bombs. In overload configurations, when the all-up weight exceeded 60,000 kg (132,277 lb), an extra amount of fuel weighing 5,300 kg (11,684 lb) was placed in additional fuel tanks in the forward bomb bay; in such cases the aircraft's empty weight rose by more than 1,000 kg (2,204 lb) due to the additional weight of the fuel system.

Flight testing and special tests of such magnitude and involving such a large number of aircraft required considerable time; in consequence, they lasted throughout the year of 1948 and well into 1949.

While the State acceptance trials were in progress, the Kazan' aircraft plant was launching full-scale production of the Tu-4. In 1947 a Government directive was issued requiring Plant No.18 in Kuibyshev (now renamed Samara) to join in the series production of the Tu-4, but the Kazan' plant retained its status as the chief production plant responsible for the type. In 1948 Plant No. 22 together with the OKB branch residing there started tooling up for the construction of the first machines in Kuibyshev. A year later, in February 1949, the first production machine manufactured by the Kuibyshev plant took to the air. In 1948 the Government took the decision to task one more aircraft factory, namely Plant No. 23 in Fili, an area in the western part of Moscow, with manufacturing the Tu-4. Series production of the type was launched there by the beginning of 1950.

By mid-1949 a large number of Tu-4 aircraft had been produced by Plant No. 22 in Kazan'; all of them had been flight-tested in accordance with the State acceptance trials programme, but the VVS refused to accept them. The stumbling block lay in the fact that the Final report on the completion of State acceptance trials had not yet been signed. A paradoxical situation had arisen: the aircraft industry turned out by the dozen a bomber that was badly needed by the country, yet the re-equipment of the Air Force *en masse* with these aircraft could not take place. An urgent resolution of the matter was required, and the Tu-4 became the only aircraft in the history of Soviet aviation to have a final report on its State acceptance trials personally endorsed by Stalin. The way it happened is related by Pyotr V. Dement'yev, who at the time was first deputy of Mikhail V. Khroonichev, the Minister of the Aircraft Industry:

'In the evening Khroonichev received a telephone call from Poskryobyshev, Stalin's secretary, who gave the message: "The Master (ie, Stalin) asks for the final report on the testing of the Tu-4 to be brought to him at his suburban country house" (that was the term used for Stalin's residence in Koontsevo, now within the boundaries of Moscow – translator's note). The Minister invited me to accompany him, since I had been in charge of the testing of the aircraft at LII and knew all the details. Stalin was obviously in a sullen mood. Having leafed through several pages of the report, he shoved it aside and said in a dull voice: "Exactly one year behind schedule". The beginning of the conversation was obviously strained. Stalin asked a couple of questions concerning the Ministry's current affairs and invited us to have supper with him. The meal passed in painful silence. Having finished eating, Stalin rose from the table and, taking the report with him, left us without saying goodbye. There was nothing we could do but sit and wait. At least an hour had elapsed when Vlasik (a general, the chief of Stalin's personal bodyguards) entered the terrace and told us that we could go to Moscow. I made a step towards the telephone to summon a car, but he stopped me, saying, "no need to". We went out into the garden and saw a ZiS-110 (a limousine of the kind then used by the Kremlin garage – translator's note) parked near the entrance; an officer carrying a pistol and holding a big Manila envelope in his hands was standing near the driver. We climbed into the car and started off. The car passed Arbat Street and Manezhnaya Square (places in the centre of Moscow – translator's note) and was now heading for Lubianka Street (notorious for the secret police headquarters – translator's note). We had no idea as to where we were being taken and what was in store for us. Frankly, we were nervous, but we kept silent. However, the car went past the building of the Ministry of State Security, drove up to our Ministry and stopped. The officer gave us the envelope, saying, "Open it when you get to the office", and we went to our offices. We rose to the third floor, entered Khrunichev's study and plumped into the armchairs in silence...' The envelope, of course, contained the Final report on the State acceptance trials of the Tu-4 with Stalin's personal signature.

As a reward for the creation of the Tu-4 bomber and the organisation of its large-scale production, the leaders and many employees of the Tupolev OKB and production plants were awarded Government decorations and the title of a Stalin Prize laureate.

Three plants being engaged in Tu-4 production, this inevitably entailed the need for all components of the aircraft built in Kazan', Kuibyshev and Moscow to be interchangeable, which meant that the jigs and tooling at all three plants had to be standardised. To check the interchangeability, the Customer (as the Air Force was euphemistically referred to) arranged at one of the plants a check-up joining of airframe subassemblies manufactured at different plants. This procedure went

The photos on this page show the first production Tu-4 (c/n 220001) at the LII airfield in Zhukovskiy during trials.

Chairman of the USSR Supreme Soviet Mikhail Shvernik hands the Order of Lenin to Andrey N. Tupolev. Tupolev received this award for the copying of the B-29 and the creation of the Tu-4.

smoothly, no adjustments being needed to any of the parts. The units thus checked comprised the basic airframe subassemblies and the engine/propeller packages together with cowlings and engine mounts, as well as the engine exhaust manifolds. The results corroborated the high technical level attained by production factories manufacturing the Tu-4 and eliminated a great number of questions concerning the repair of operational aircraft.

Available information concerning series production of the Tu-4 (which ended in 1952) is extremely contradictory. According to the late Dmitriy S. Markov, nearly 1,000 machines were built (he quoted this figure to the authors in 1987). Referring to MAP sources, Ivnamin S. Sultanov, a well-known aviation historian, asserted in the early 1990s that 847 Tu-4s had been built. Two years ago the *Kazan'* magazine cited the production run in Kazan' as 655

machines; however, in 2002 the Kazan' Aviation Production Association, named after Sergey P. Gorboonov (KAPO, as Plant No. 22 is now called) provided the following information concerning Tu-4 output: one aircraft in 1947, 12 in 1948, 120 in 1949, 170 in 1950, 191 in 1951 and 150 in 1952, which amounts to 644 aircraft, not 655!

According to information received from Samara the local production run at Plant No. 18 was 480 aircraft. An article by the Russian aviation writer Nikolay V. Yakubovich based on archive material cites the following Tu-4 production figures: 655 in Kazan' (1948-1952), 481 in Kuibyshev (1949-1953) and 160 in Moscow (1950-1952), which totals 1,296!

The *Dvigatel'* (Engine) magazine No. 6-2001 has published the following figures for the year-by-year breakdown of aggregate production: 17 Tu-4s in 1948, 161 in 1949, 312 in 1950, 321 in 1951, 368 in 1952 and 16 machines in 1953 (?!), which totals 1,195!

The Tu-4 remained in service until the early 1960s. From 1953 onwards all three plants began mastering production of turbine-powered aircraft: Plant No. 22 switched to manufacturing the Tu-16 *Badger* twinjet medium bomber in 1953, Plant No. 18 started producing the Tu-95 *Bear* four-turboprop bomber in 1955, while Plant No. 23 started turning out production Myasishchev M-4 *Bison-A* four-jet strategic bombers in 1954. Successes scored in mastering quantity production of new jet aircraft were based in many respects on the experience of modern aircraft technology gained during the years of Tu-4 production.

The work on the Tu-4 marked a new, fundamentally important stage in the activities of the OKB led by A. N. Tupolev; it formed the basis for all subsequent piston-engined and jet-powered aircraft of OKB-156.

The Tu-4 was mostly produced in the standard bomber version suitable for conversion into a long-range reconnaissance aircraft. A few aircraft were modified into nuclear-bomb carriers. Several dozen aircraft were converted into missile carriers armed with anti-shipping cruise missiles. The Tu-4 served as a basis for various special mission aircraft: airborne command posts, different flying testbeds, aircraft for aerial film shooting, transport and paratroop-carrier machines, tankers for transporting fuel, ice reconnaissance aircraft for Aeroflot's Polar aviation directorate, navigator trainers etc.

The work on the Tu-4 formed the basis for producing the Tu-70 passenger aircraft prototype, the Tu-75 military transport prototype and the 'aircraft 80' bomber prototype; all of these are dealt with in separate chapters of this book.

Tu-4 performance obtained during tests at LII

Maximum speed at an all-up weight of 47,700 kg (105,160 lb):	
at sea level	427 km/h (265 mph)
at 1,000 m (3,281 ft)	442 km/h (275 mph)
at 3,000 m (9,842 ft)	471 km/h (293 mph)
at 5,000 m (16,404 ft)	500 km/h (311 mph)
at 8,000 m (26,247 ft)	543 km/h (337 mph)
at 9,600 m (31,496 ft)	557 km/h (346 mph)
at 11,000 m (36,089 ft)	543 km/h (337 mph)
Rate of climb and time to height at an AUW of 47,700 kg (105,160 lb):	
at sea level	4.6 m/sec (905 ft/min); 0 min
at 1,000 m (3,281 ft)	4.6 m/sec (905 ft/min); 3.7 min
at 3,000 m (9,842 ft)	4.5 m/sec (886 ft/min); 11.0 min
at 5,000 m (16,404 ft)	4.2 m/sec (827 ft/min); 18.7 min
at 8,000 m (26,247 ft)	3.3 m/sec (596 ft/min); 31.8 min
at 9,000 m (29,528 ft)	2.9 m/sec (571 ft/min); 37.1 min
at 11,000 m (36,089 ft)	1.5 m/sec (295 ft/min); 51.9 min
Service ceiling	11,500-11,600m (37,730-38,058 ft)
Range:	
with a 54,800-kg (120,813-lb) AUW and 1,500 kg (3,307 lb) of bombs	5,150 km (3,200 miles)
with a 58,000-kg (127,868-lb) AUW and 2,000 kg (4,409 lb) of bombs	6,000 km (3,728 miles)
with a 57,500-kg (120,834-lb) AUW and 9,000 kg (19,842 lb) of bombs	3,320 km (2,063 miles)
Take-off run/take-off distance at an AUW of 47,850 kg (105,491 lb)	980/2,200 m (3,215/7,218 ft)
Landing run/landing distance at a landing weight of 44,000 kg (97,003 lb)	870/1,970 m (2,854/6,463 ft)
Landing speed at a landing weight of 44,000 kg (97,003 lb)	170 km/h (106 mph)

Chapter 3

Tu-4 Versions

Independent Development

Boeing B-29 pattern aircraft

As already mentioned, the first thing the Soviet Air Force did with the three captured B-29s after repairing them for ferrying to Moscow and future use as pattern aircraft for the Tu-4 was to apply Soviet red stars and new serials matching the last three digits of the original USAAF serials – '256 Black', '358 Black' and '365 Black' respectively.

B-29-5-BW '256 Black' was initially earmarked for use as a testbed for the ASh-73TK engine. Accordingly the aircraft was handed over to LII, participating in the Tu-4's flight-test programme and then in test and development programmes associated with other types. Later '256 Black' was ferried to the Kazan' aircraft factory No. 22 in accordance with MAP order No. 210 of 16th April 1948 and converted into a 'mother ship' for rocket-powered experimental aircraft. A special pylon was installed under the starboard inner wing panel between the Nos. 3 and 4 engines for carrying the B-5 aircraft designed by Matus R. Bisnovat or the German '346' (DFS 346, aka Siebel Si 346); the latter was designed by Hans Rössing who completed development of this aircraft while working in captivity in the USSR as head of OKB-2.

The converted bomber was flown to the airfield in Tyoplyy Stan on the south-western

The seventh production B-4 (c/n 220202) during trials. Unlike most Kazan'-built examples, it carried an abbreviated c/n (the last three digits) on the nose; these have been retouched away by military censors.

outskirts of Moscow (no longer in existence) where trials of the '346' had been going on since 1948. In 1949-50 it made a number of test flights with three prototypes of the '346'; the experimental aircraft was dropped at altitudes up to 9,700 m (31,824 ft), making both gliding and powered flights. After the end of the '346' programme '256 Black' remained in use at LII as a testbed for some time yet until finally struck off charge and scrapped.

B-29-15-BW '358 Black' did not fly again after arriving at Izmaïlovo airfield; it was permanently hangared there, serving as the pattern aircraft for checking the dimensions and functions of Soviet-made B-4 airframe components and equipment items against 'the real thing'. Eventually it, too, was broken up.

Finally, as noted earlier, B-29-15-BW '365 Black' was disassembled completely for the purpose of studying and copying the design.

B-29-5-BW '256 Black' sits on a snow-covered airfield amid a line of unserialled Tu-4s, with c/n 220102 (marked '102') nearest to the camera and c/n 220103 next in the line-up. Note the hatch for the oblique camera aft of the star insignia on the fuselage.

Some of its components were reassembled in 1946 and used to build the prototype of the 'aircraft 70' (Tu-70) airliner.

Tu-4 (B-4, *izdeliye* R) long-range bomber

As already mentioned, the Soviet-built Tu-4 (formerly B-4) long-range bomber, aka *samolyot* R (aircraft R) or *izdeliye* R, was not a 100% carbon copy of the B-29, having a different powerplant (indigenous ASh-73TK engines) and heavier defensive armament. The aircraft was intended for delivering massive bomb strikes with conventional bombs against strategic targets located deep in the enemy's rear area, both singly and in groups, day and night, in any weather. The first production Tu-4 took to the air on 19th May 1947 and large-scale production continued at three factories until 1952.

In the course of production the bomber was progressively upgraded by installing more capable equipment and more potent armament. The first three Kazan'-built examples featured two 12.7-mm (.30 calibre) Berezin UBK machine-guns in the dorsal and ventral barbettes and three in the tail barbette. From the fourth aircraft (c/n 220102) onwards the machine-guns were replaced with 20-mm (.78 calibre) Berezin B-20E cannon; later these gave way to more powerful 23-mm (.90 calibre) NR-23 cannon developed by A. E. Nudel'man and A. A. Rikhter (two in each barbette).

The Tu-4 remained on strength with the Soviet Air Force until the early 1960s. Twenty-five of these bombers (Kazan'- and Kuibyshev-built aircraft) were delivered to the People's Republic of China free of charge in the 1950s, some examples of which soldiered on in service with the People's Liberation Army Air Force until the 1980s; the Chinese even developed a couple of special mission versions powered by turboprop engines, of which more will be said later.

The basic performance of a typical late-production Tu-4 is illustrated by the table on this page.

Tu-4 specifications

Length overall	30.179 m (99 ft 0 in)
Height on ground	8.460 m (27 ft 9 in)
Wing span	43.047 m (141 ft 3 in)
Wing area	161.7 m² (1,740 sq ft)
Empty weight	36,850 kg (81,240 lb)
All-up weight:	
normal	47,850 kg (105,491 lb)
maximum	55,600-63,600 kg (122,577-140,214 lb)
Top speed (with normal AUW):	
at sea level	435 km/h (270 mph)
at 10,250 m (33,629 ft)	558 km/h (346 mph)
Service ceiling	11,200 m (36,745 ft)
Climb time to 5,000 m (16,404 ft)	18.2 minutes
Range at 3,000 m (9,842 ft) with 10% fuel reserves:	
with a 55,600-kg (122,577-lb) AUW and 1,500 kg (3,307 lb) of bombs	4,200 km (2,610 miles)
with 63,600-kg (140,214-lb) AUW and 3,000 kg (6,614 lb) of bombs	5,400 km (3,355 miles)
with 63,600-kg (140,214-lb) AUW and 9,000 kg (19,842 lb) of bombs	3,580 km (2,224 miles)
Range at 3,000 m (9,842 ft) until fuel exhaustion:	
with a 55,600-kg (122,577-lb) AUW and 1,500 kg (3,307 lb) of bombs	4,850 km (3,014 miles)
with 63,600-kg (140,214-lb) AUW and 3,000 kg (6,614 lb) of bombs	6,200 km (3,852 miles)
with 63,600-kg (140,214-lb) AUW and 9,000 kg (19,842 lb) of bombs	4,100 km (2,548 miles)
Take-off run:	
with a normal AUW	960 m (3,150 ft)
with a 55,600-kg (122,577-lb) AUW	1,255 m (4,117 ft)
with a 63,600-kg (140,214-lb) AUW	2,000 m (6,562 ft)
Take-off distance:	
with a normal AUW	2,210 m (7,251 ft)
with a 55,600-kg (122,577-lb) AUW	2,585 m (8,481 ft)
with a 63,600-kg (140,214-lb) AUW	3,830 m (12,566 ft)
Landing run:	
with a 47,850-kg (105,491-lb) landing weight	1,070 m (3,510 ft)
with a 41,000-kg (90,389-lb) landing weight	920 m (3,018 m)
Landing speed:	
with a 47,850-kg (105,491-lb) landing weight	172 km/h (107 mph)
with a 41,000-kg (90,389-lb) landing weight	160 km/h (99 mph)

Tu-4A nuclear-capable bomber

A version of the Tu-4 designated Tu-4A (**ahtomnyy** – in this context, nuclear-capable) was developed as a delivery vehicle for the first Soviet free-fall nuclear bombs. It differed from the basic Tu-4 bomber in having an electrically heated, thermostabilised bomb bay equipped with an electronic control system. The suspension system for the bulky nuclear munition had to be designed anew and special shielding installed in the pressure cabins to protect the crew from radiation in flight.

Ballistic tests of the first Soviet nuke developed by KB-11, the RDS-1 (also known as *izdeliye* 501), began in the first half of 1948. Initially dummy bombs were dropped by a Tu-4 at the proving ground in Noginsk east of Moscow which was run by the 4th Directorate of GK NII VVS; the bomber was flown by LII test pilots A. P. Yakimov and S. F. Mashkovskiy. These test drops and other research conducted by KB-11 jointly with TsAGI showed that the bomb was not stable enough as it travelled on its ballistic trajectory. The manufacturer had to optimise the design by streamlining the bomb and shifting its cg.

Further ballistic tests were then performed at the 71st Test Range at Totskoye in the Orenburg Region No fewer than 30 test drops from a Tu-4 were required before KB-11 had achieved the required degree of accuracy and made the necessary trajectory measurements to be used in developing the *izdeliye* 501's automatic control system.

Tests of the Tu-4A nuclear-capable bomber and its specialised equipment were duly completed in 1951. On 17th May 1951 the Air Force Commander-in-Chief signed an order appointing a State commission for holding ground and flight tests of two *Bulls* which had been converted by OKB-156 to Tu-4A standard. The commission was chaired by Major-General G. O. Komarov, Director of the 71st Test Range; it included representatives from the Tupolev OKB and KB-11.

Upon completion of the tests the commission ruled that the Tu-4As were suitable for carrying and accurately delivering RDS-3 (*izdeliye* 501-M) nuclear bombs and that a series of measurements could be undertaken in the interests of both design bureaux. The commission did not focus on the carrier aircraft's flight safety when subjected to the factors of a nuclear explosion; this aspect would have to be dealt with separately.

Live tests of the RDS-3 nuclear bomb were scheduled for 18th October 1951. A highly experienced Tu-4 crew was entrusted with performing the first-ever live drop. It comprised crew captain Lieutenant-Colonel Konstantin I. Oorzhuntsev (Hero of the Soviet Union), co-pilot Lieutenant (senior grade) Ivan M. Koshkarov, navigator Captain Vladimir S. Suvorov, bomb-aimer Captain

Boris D. Davydov, radar operator Lieutenant (Senior Grade) Nikolay D. Kiriushkin, radio operator Lieutenant (Junior Grade) Vladimir V. Yakovlev, flight engineer Major Vasiliy N. Trofimov, gunner Private Arkadiy F. Yevgodashin, technician Lieutenant Arkadiy F. Kuznetsov and test engineer for the nuclear bomb Lieutenant Al'vian N. Stebel'kov.

For the sake of reliability a second Tu-4 was to accompany Oorzhuntsev's aircraft. The crew of this aircraft comprised crew captain Captain Konstantin I. Oosachov, co-pilot Lieutenant (Senior Grade) Vasiliy I. Kooreyev, navigator Captain Aleksey A. Pastoonin, bomb-aimer Lieutenant (Senior Grade) Gheorgiy A. Sablin, radar operator Lieutenant (Senior Grade) Nikita I. Svechnikov, radio operator Sergeant (Senior Grade) Vladimir B. Zolotaryov, flight engineer Lieutenant Pyotr P. Cherepanov, gunner Sergeant (Senior Grade) Nikolay D. Borzdov, technician Lieutenant Filaret I. Zolotookhin and test engineer Lieutenant Leonid A. Blagov.

Extremely stringent security measures were taken during the final preparations. The armed, checked and double-checked RDS-3 bomb was placed on a ground handling dolly, carefully draped in tarpaulins to disguise its outline and slowly towed to the parking ramp where the Tu-4A was waiting. The ramp itself was surrounded by a tall fence and had a separate checkpoint at the only entrance which was the taxiway. The refuelled aircraft was parked over a special trench lined with concrete; this was necessary because the bomber's ground clearance was insufficient to accommodate the bomb on its ground handling dolly. By then the bomb bay doors had been opened and fitted with four mechanical hoists for the bomb. To further enhance security the bomb bay area was curtained off by a canvas tent preventing unauthorised personnel from seeing the bomb. After the RDS-3 had been uncovered and slowly hoisted into position, an electrical connector was locked into place on the bomb's rear section and the approved time delay and critical barometric altitude settings were downloaded to the detonation mechanism, using the aircraft's control panel.

Next the crew commenced their pre-flight checks. The crew captain and the navigator inspected the bomb bay, satisfying themselves that the bomb was properly secured and all electrical connectors were in place. Together with a representative of KB-11 they activated the bomb's electric locks, checking that the appropriate signal lights were on; the keys were then handed over to the crew captain in case the aircraft had to make an emergency landing away from its home base. After checking the bomb control panel readings to see that they matched the entries in the log the bomb bay doors were closed and sealed

The globular RDS-1 bomb of 1949 was the first Soviet nuclear munition. The two huge 'eyes' gave the bomb an eerie look. Note that the attachment lugs are mounted transversely.

by a KGB officer. Finally the crew captain and the navigator signed their acceptance of the aircraft in the log book.

With the entire crew lined up in front of the bomber, Oorzhuntsev reported his readiness to Major-General Komarov and the KB-11 representative. Receiving the go-ahead, the crew took their seats and the aircraft taxied out for take-off. At 7.00 AM Moscow time on 18th October 1951 the Tu-4A lifted off the runway at Zhana-Semey airfield in Kazakhstan; the first-ever take-off with a nuclear bomb in the Soviet Union went without a hitch.

Minutes later the back-up aircraft captained by Oosachov took off. This *Bull* carried a dummy FAB-1500 HE bomb. In the event the nuke-armed aircraft's targeting systems failed the back-up would change formation and become the flight leader, proceeding to the target range as planned while transmitting a series of tone-modulated radio signals to the Tu-4A until the predesignated bomb release time. The signals and the moment when the back-up aircraft dropped the dummy bomb would tell the crew of the Tu-4A when it was time to drop the real thing.

En route to the target the bombers were escorted and protected by constantly shifting pairs of Lavochkin La-11 fighters. The flight was controlled from the Main Command Centre where all the people in charge of the tests were assembled; these were Igor' V. Kurchatov (head of the Nuclear Physics Institute), Yu. B. Khariton, Ya. B. Zel'dovich, B. L. Vannikov, P. M. Zernov, M. I. Nedelin, V. A. Boliatko and, representing the Air Force, General G. O. Komarov and engineer Major S. M. Kulikov.

The Tu-4A climbed to 10,000 m (32,810 ft) and proceeded to the target in strict accordance with the schedule; its progress was

monitored on a map display at the Main Command Centre. The Centre maintained HF and VHF radio communication with the bomber, using special code tables; for good measure the most important commands to the crew were backed up by the target range's support service.

The weather was favourable, all systems functioned perfectly, and right on schedule the Tu-4A crew was authorised to make a practice pass over the target while transmitting special radio signals so that the final adjustments could be made to the test range instrumentation. Finally it was time for the live bombing run. The range command post reported 'all systems are go' and the permission to drop the bomb was given. The bomber began sending special signals over the HF and VHF channels: T minus 60 seconds… T minus 15 seconds… The last signal came at 9.52:08 when radar operator Kiriushkin pushed the bomb release button. Lights started illuminating on the display showing the bomb's trajectory as the automatic control system was powered up, the multi-stage safety system was deactivated, the detonator was armed and the barometric altitude sensors switched on. This was the first evidence that the bomb was functioning normally. The next and final evidence was earth-shattering; the ground shook violently and a tremendous boom came from outside, confirming that the Soviet Union's first mid-air nuclear test had been performed successfully. The 42-kiloton RDS-3 had detonated at 380 m (1,247 ft) above ground level.

The Tu-4A landed safely at its home base. In his post-flight report Konstantin I. Oorzhuntsev described how the effects of the explosion were felt inside the aircraft. He also reported that no problems were experienced with flying the aircraft manually (as recommended by TsAGI and Andrey N. Tupolev) when the blast wave hit. No equipment failures occurred as a result of the explosion. We'll let bomb-aimer Boris D. Davydov, 'the man who pushed the button', tell the story:

'The weather that day was good enough for me to see the target in time, take aim and drop the bomb accurately. All systems, including the transmitters sending radio signals which activated the ground equipment, functioned without a hitch. When the bomb was gone and the doors closed the crew prepared for the flash and the blast wave: we switched off the autopilot, drew the protective curtains and donned protective dark goggles, decompressed the cabins and put on our oxygen masks. We used a stopwatch to check the anticipated moment of detonation.

'The first thing we knew was a tremendous flash. Then the first and quite powerful blast wave caught up with the aircraft, followed by a weaker second wave and a still weaker third wave. The flight instruments went crazy, the needles spinning round and around. Dust filled the cabin, even though the aircraft had been vacuumed clean before the flight. Then we watched as the dust and debris cloud grew; it quickly mounted right up to our own flight level and billowed out into a mushroom. There was every thinkable colour and shade to that cloud. I am lost for words to describe what I felt after I had dropped the bomb; I was perceiving the whole world, everything I could see, in a different way. I guess that was because I had my mind focused on this important mission which I could not fail for many days before the drop and it just shut out everything else.

'After landing we taxied in to our special parking area and climbed out, still wearing our parachutes and oxygen masks – we were still breathing pure oxygen from the bottles that came with the parachutes. The ground crew checked us and the aircraft for radioactive contamination; a washing-down station had been set up at the aircraft parking area, and after showering and changing into fresh clothes we were taken by car to the headquarters to file our reports.'

The State commission declared that the Tu-4A carrier aircraft equipped with a bomb bay heating system, modified bombing equipment and other associated mission systems permitted safe and reliable carriage of the RDS-3 nuclear bomb and accurate delivery of same. By decree of the Presidium of the USSR Supreme Soviet of 8th December 1951 Lieutenant-Colonel Konstantin I. Oorzhuntsev was awarded the Order of Lenin; Captain Boris D. Davydov (promoted to Major after the test), Captain Konstantin I. Oosachov, Lieutenant Al'vian N. Stebel'kov and Lieutenant Leonid A. Blagov were awarded the Order of

the Red Banner of Combat. All the other crew members of both aircraft involved in the first test were also the recipients of Government decorations.

The successful first test prompted the decision to add nuclear weapons to the inventory of the VVS. The Tu-4A and the RDS-3 nuclear bomb were put into production. As early as 1952 a production Tu-4A and an RDS-3 of the first production batches passed checkout tests at the Totskoye range.

In mid-1953 four Tu-4As were deployed to Kazakhstan along with several other aircraft to undertake live nuclear bomb drops at the nuclear test range near Semipalatinsk. In addition to the actual drops, two such aircraft fitted with dose meters were used to measure radiation levels near the mushroom clouds and at long distances from the epicentre – right up to the Sino-Soviet border. On these missions the crews wore isolating gas masks to protect their lungs; tragically, on one occasion a defective gas mask cost one of the crewmen his life.

In September 1953 the Tu-4A took part in the tests of the new RDS-5 nuclear bomb; these served to check some of the bomb's design features, including the neutron initialisation system. As had been the case with the very first test, a pair of Tu-4As ('live' and backup) was involved, with V. Ya. Kutyrchev and F. P. Golovashko as crew captains; the drops were performed at 9,000 m (29,530 ft).

Tu-4K (Tu-4KS) missile strike aircraft

Development of the *Kometa* (Comet) weapons system comprising the Tu-4K carrier aircraft (the K denoting Kometa), the KS-1 air-launched anti-shipping cruise missile and the Kometa-1 and Kometa-2 guidance systems began pursuant to a Council of Ministers directive dated 2nd August 1948. The KS-1 (*izdeliye* KS; NATO code name AS-1 *Kennel*) looked like a scaled-down MiG-15*bis*P (*izdeliye* SP-1) interceptor minus cockpit canopy, featuring mid-set swept wings, a swept cruciform tail unit, a pitot air intake with a guidance antenna radome on top and a 1,590-kgp (3,505-lb st) RD-500 centifugal-flow turbojet, the Soviet licence-built version of the Rolls-Royce Derwent V. It was developed by OKB-155 under Artyom I. Mikoyan and Mikhail I. Gurevich – or, to be precise, a

Basic performance of the Tu-4K (Tu-4KS)

Normal AUW with two	
KS-1 missiles	52,000 kg (114,640 lb)
Maximum AUW	62,000 kg (136,686 lb)
Top speed at high altitude	485 km/h (301 mph)
Service ceiling	8,600 m (28,215 ft)
Normal range with two	
KS-1 missiles	4,000 km (2,485 miles)

section of it led by Aleksandr Ya. Bereznyak and tasked with designing air-to-surface missiles (which later became a separate design bureau). The guidance systems were products of OKB-1 then headed by Sergey L. Beria – the son of the infamous Lavrentiy P. Beria. (After Stalin's death in 1953 L. P. Beria was found guilty of high treason and executed, sharing the fate of many he had sent to death. Hence Sergey Beria was removed from office and replaced by Konstantin Patrookhin.)

Overall co-ordination of the Kometa project was the responsibility of the Third Main Directorate of the Soviet Council of Ministers. The whole programme was shrouded in utmost secrecy and only a few people had access to it (on a 'need to know' basis).

The task of A. N. Tupolev's OKB-156 was to equip a Tu-4 bomber with the Kometa-2 guidance system, including the Kometa-M search/target illumination radar (a version of the Kobal't-N modified for working with the missiles), and a pair of BD-KS pylons under the wings for the KS-1 missiles (BD = *bahlochnyy der**zhah**tel'*, beam-type [weapons] rack). The advanced development project of the Tu-4K (also called Tu-4KS) was ready in 1949; the missile pylons were to be mounted between the inner and outer engines.

By 1951 the Mikoyan OKB had verified the guidance system on MiG-9 *Fargo* and MiG-17 *Fresco-A* fighters converted into avionics testbeds (the MiG-9L and MiG-17SDK respectively). The next step was to build a simulator aircraft – a piloted version of the actual KS-1 with a bicycle landing gear and a cockpit instead of the explosive charge (called *izdeliye* K or *izdeliye* KSK, ie, *izdeliye* KS *s kabinoy*, with a cockpit). Concurrently, the Tupolev OKB completed the first prototype of the Tu-4K (no serial, c/n 224203). In 1951-52 the prototype passed manufacturer's flight tests at Chkalovskaya airbase and the Bagerovo test range near Kerch on the Crimea Peninsula, in the course of which the system was brought up to scratch.

LII test pilots Amet-Khan Sultan and Sergey N. Anokhin (some sources state Fyodor I. Boortsev) made numerous flights in the *izdeliye* K aircraft which was carried aloft and launched by the Tu-4K; the first such flight was performed by Amet-Khan in May 1951. Two 'manned *Kennels*' were always carried but only one was launched at any one time. The bomber's propeller discs were uncomfortably close to the cockpit and the pilots were reluctant to gun the engines immediately after separation, fearing a collision; as a result, the *izdeliye* K would drop 600-800 m (1,968-2,625 ft) below the bomber's flight path, which made it hard to engage the midcourse guidance beam. Test pilots Fyodor I. Boortsev, Pyotr I. Kaz'min and V. P. Pavlov also participated in the Tu-4KS programme.

Above: The Tu-4K prototype (c/n 224203) toting two *izdeliye* **K missile simulator aircraft. Note the bulges on the underside over the** *izdeliye* **K's wheel wells and the cutout in the bomber's missile pylon to accommodate the cockpit canopy.**

Right: A real KS-1 missile under the wing of a production Tu-4K.

The State acceptance trials of the Kometa weapons system began in July 1952, continuing until January 1953. During one of the live launches a single hit by a KS-1 missile with its 500-kg (1,102-lb) warhead proved enough to sink the target, the decommissioned light cruiser SNS **Krahs***nyy Kavkahz* (Red Caucasus; SNS = Soviet Navy ship) sailing in the Black Sea about 100 km (54 nm) from Feodosia. The trials were deemed successful and the Kometa system was added to the Soviet Naval Aviation (AVMF – *Aviahtsiya voyenno-mor***skovo flot**a) inventory for use against large surface ships.

The basic performance of the Tu-4K (Tu-4KS) is indicated in the table on page 36.

The KS-1 cruise missile entered production at the Doobna Machinery Plant, Moscow Region. The carrier aircraft, on the other hand, was not built as such; about 50 bombers were converted to Tu-4K (Tu-4KS) standard by

Plant No. 22 in Kazan' and Plant No. 23 in Moscow. The type saw service with two regiments (one in the North Fleet Air Arm, the other in the Black Sea Fleet Air Arm) until the mid-1950s when it was replaced by the jet-powered Tu-16KS *Badger-B* equipped with the same weapons system. Afterwards most Tu-4Ks were stripped of their mission equipment and converted to Tu-4D transport/troopship aircraft.

Tu-4D military transport/
troopship aircraft (*izdeliye* **76)**
As early as 1947 the Tupolev OKB considered using the Tu-4 as a military transport carrying various combat vehicles on underwing racks (with or without streamlined containers or fairings). The following payload options were proposed:

a) two self-propelled howitzers weighing 3,800 kg (8,377 lb) each under the wings. At

Tu-4K c/n 224203 on the ramp at Bagerovo airfield with two 'manned *iKennels***'.**

Above and below: A production Tu-4K (c/n 226305) with two live KS-1 missiles, probably at Zhukovskiy.

Above and below: Two more views of the same aircraft. The radome of the Kometa-M radar is fully extended.

This unserialled Moscow-built Tu-4 (c/n 230320) was one of 300 converted to Tu-4D transports/troopships. Note that the cargo pods have stabilising fins.

an all-up weight of 60,000 kg (132,277 lb), including 14,100 kg (31,085 lb) of fuel, the Tu-4's estimated performance is shown in the table below.

b) two experimental 76-mm (2.99-in) OSU-76 wheeled self-propelled howitzers.

This time, carrying the howitzers without fairings was out of the question; calculations showed that the aircraft would be unable to take off even with a reduced TOW of 54,500 kg (120,152lb) because of the extremely high drag. The Tu-4's estimated performance in

	without fairings	with fairings
Top speed at sea level	340 km/h (211 mph)	405 km/h (251.5 mph)
Rate of climb at sea level	1.7 m/sec (335 ft/min)	2.9 m/sec (570 ft/min)
Climb time to 1,000 m (3,281 ft)	11 minutes	7 minutes
Range at 1,000 m (3,281 ft)	3,400 km (2,113 miles)	4,400 km (2,734 miles)
Service ceiling	2,500-3,000 m (8,202-9,842 ft)	5,000 m (16,404 ft)
Take-off run	2,500 m (8,202 ft)	2,200 m (7,218 ft)

The Tu-4 as a cannon-armed assault aircraft? No, this is just a self-propelled gun in a cargo pod under the wing of a Tu-4D; the barrel was too long to fit inside the pod!

this configuration is shown in the table at the foot of the page.

c) one OSU-76 SP howitzer with a fairing installed under the centre fuselage. With a 54,000-kg (119,049-lb) take-off weight the estimated range in this configuration was 3,350 km (2,082 miles).

In the early 1950s the Air Force proposed converting existing Tu-4 bombers into transport/troopship aircraft designated Tu-4D (*desahntnyy* – for paradropping). This involved outfitting the bomb bays to accommodate 28 paratroopers in extremely spartan conditions. Additionally, combat vehicles such as BTR-40 armoured personnel carriers could be carried under the wings in P-90 cargo pods or P-85 containers; these were suspended in a similar way to the KS-1 missiles on the Tu-4K. The Tu-4D could be reconverted to bomber configuration should the need arise.

One of the Tu-4s thus modified was tested at GK NII VVS in various configurations (with P-90 and P-98 pods, paratroopers and P-85 containers). These trials confirmed the

Top speed:	
at sea level	389 km/h (242 mph)
at 4,000 m (13,123 ft)	418 km/h (260 mph)
Rate of climb:	
at sea level	2.4 m/sec (472 ft/min)
at 4,000 m (13,123 ft)	1.1 m/sec (216 ft/min)
Climb time:	
to 1,000 m (3,281 ft)	7 minutes
to 4,000 m (13,123 ft)	37 minutes
Range at 1,000 m (3,281 ft)	2,600 km (1,616 miles)
Service ceiling	5,000 m (16,404 ft)
Take-off run	2,400 m (7,874 ft)

Above: A single Tu-4, '23 Red' (c/n 2806702), was converted into the one-off Tu-4T transport/troopship aircraft. This view shows the size of the P-90 cargo pods.

suitability of the underwing cargo pods and the soundness of the idea in general.

On 10th July 1954 the Soviet Council of Ministers issued directive No. 1417-637 ordering the conversion of Tu-4s for transport/paradrop duties, followed two weeks later by MAP order No. 454 to the same effect. The plan was to modify 300 *Bulls* in 1955 to the same standard as the aircraft tested at GK NII VVS. Conversion was to take place in service conditions; the schedule was set forth very explicitly – 30 aircraft in the first quarter of the year, 100 aircraft in the second quarter, 120 more in the third quarter and the final 50 in the fourth quarter. The Tupolev OKB was required to turn over the complete set of working drawings and documents to the Air Force not later than 1st September 1954.

The demands were met; all 300 aircraft were modified to Tu-4Ds and transferred from the strategic bomber command (DA – *Dahl'nyaya aviahtsiya*, Long-Range Aviation) to the Air Force's transport command (VTA – *Voyenno-trahnsportnaya aviahtsiya*, Military Transport Aviation) by the end of 1955. They served on with the VTA until the early 1960s when they were replaced by the purpose-built Antonov An-12 *Cub* medium transport.

Tu-4T military transport/ troopship aircraft (*izdeliye* 4T)

The same CofM directive No. 1417-637 and MAP order No. 454 tasked the Tupolev OKB with developing yet another transport/troopship derivative of the *Bull* designated Tu-4T (*trahnsportnyy* – transport, used attributively). This time the specification was rather more stringent; the aircraft was to deliver and paradrop 40-46 troopers, or two 57-mm

Above: A three-quarters front view of the same aircraft.

This view shows clearly the aerofoil shape of the Tu-4T's underwing cargo pods and the absence of the dorsal and ventral cannon barbettes; unlike the earlier Tu-4D, the Tu-4T had only a single tail barbette.

(2.24-in) ASU-57 self-propelled guns, or a conventional artillery piece with a tractor and a supply of ammunition, or 5,000-6,000 kg (11,023-13,228 lb) of other materiel. The first aircraft thus converted, complete with two sets of underwing cargo pods, was to commence State acceptance trials in December 1955.

The Tu-4T advanced development project was completed in 1955. In preparing it, Tupolev engineers relied heavily on their experience with the Tu-4D, incorporating the same design features, namely troop seats and other appropriate changes to the bomb bays, plus reinforced wings and integral hoists for mounting the cargo pods. The following payload options were possible:

• 42 fully equipped paratroopers seated in the bomb bays and the centre cabin;

• a 57-mm (2.24-in) or 76-mm (3-in) field gun with ammunition and a GAZ-69 jeep in two P-90 paradroppable pods under the wings (the gun crew of eight soldiers was accommodated in the rear bomb bay);

• two ASU-57 SP guns in P-98 paradroppable pods under the wings (the crews were accommodated in the rear bomb bay);

• 3,000 kg (6,614 lb) of cargo (ammunition, engineering troops, materiel, foodstuffs etc.) in four P-85 paradroppable containers;

• 2,500-2,600 kg (5,511-5,732 lb) of cargo in PDMM-47 soft paradropping bags (*parashootno-desahntnyy myahkiy meshok*) provided with PDUR-47 resilient straps (*parashootno-desahntnyy ooproogiy remen'*) and carried in the bomb bays.

The conversion to Tu-4T standard involved deletion of the defensive armament (except the tail gun barbette) and the remote control system for same, the bomb racks and release mechanisms, the bomb sight and Kobal't radar. The pressure floor of the centre cabin, the equipment installed there and the pressurised crawlway from the forward cabin were also removed. Some of the existing equipment items were relocated and the wing structure reinforced at the cargo pod attachment points to absorb the extra loads.

In 42-seat troopship configuration the bomb bays and centre cabin featured easily removable floors incorporating paradropping hatches and equipped with lightweight seats. Control system cables and certain equipment items located in these areas were protected by special covers. Boarding ladders were provided, as were emergency exits enabling the paratroopers to vacate the aircraft in the event of a belly landing. The bomb bays and centre cabin were equipped with duplicated signal lights and horns telling the paratroopers when to jump, an SPU-14 intercom (*samolyotnoye peregovornoye oostroystvo*), oxygen equipment, heating and ventilation systems and cabin equipment.

Special racks with hoists and release mechanisms were installed under the wings for carrying combat vehicles in P-90 and P-98 cargo pods. When configured for carrying P-85 cargo containers the bomb bays were fitted with KD4-248 cassette-type racks and hoists. If PDMM-47 bags and PDUR-47 straps were used, the aircraft was equipped with special containers, loading hoists and release mechanisms. All paradropping equipment could be easily removed and replaced in service conditions, allowing the aircraft to be quickly configured for a specific mission.

The Tu-4T prototype passed its State acceptance trials in 1956. These included verification of the paradropping equipment; the aircraft's performance and handling with underwing cargo pods and in 'clean' configuration were also checked. Still, the Tu-4T remained a one-off because the Antonov An-8 *Camp* and An-12 had appeared by then; these purpose-built transports powered by turboprop engines suited the needs of the VTA much better.

Tu-4R long-range reconnaissance aircraft

Concurrent with the effort to copy the B-29 and put the basic Tu-4 bomber into production the Tupolev OKB worked on a long-range photo-reconnaissance version – the Soviet counterpart of the RB-29. Apart from the recce cameras, the aircraft differed from the bomber version in having extra fuel tanks in both bomb bays holding a total of 10,500 kg (23,148 lb) of additional fuel to extend range. The all-up weight was 65,300 kg (143,962 lb), including 24,500 kg (54,013 lb) of fuel.

The mission equipment consisted of AFA-33 or AFA-33M aerial cameras (*aerofotoapparaht*) with varying focal lengths for daytime photography and NAFA-33S/50 or NAFA-5S/100 night aerial cameras (*nochnoy aerofotoapparaht*) for night missions. In the latter case one of the extra fuel tanks was removed so that the aircraft could carry flare bombs. Otherwise the Tu-4R ([*samolyot-*]*razvedchik* – reconnaissance aircraft), as the aircraft was designated, was identical to the baseline *Bull*. The Tu-4's capacious bomb bays permitted the installation of extremely large film cassettes accommodating enough film for up to 195 300 x 300 mm (11.8 x 11.8 in) frames.

The Tu-4R was not built as such, but a number of *Bulls* were converted into 'Photobulls' in service units as per necessity. These aircraft differed slightly from the original Tupolev OKB project in that the additional fuel tanks (three in all) were all housed in the forward bomb bay while the rear bomb bay housed the cameras.

Later in their service career some Tu-4Rs were equipped with a PR-1 electronic intelligence (ELINT) and electronic countermeasures (ECM) system capable of detecting enemy radars with a pulse rate frequency of 150 to 3,100 MHz; it could also emit D-band (2,600-3,100 MHz) jamming signals, which is why it was sometimes called PR-D. From 1954 onwards the Tu-4R was equipped with SPS-1 wide-band jammers (*stahntsiya pomekhovykh signahlov*); some aircraft which survived into the late 1950s were equipped with the more capable SPS-2 as fitted to the Tu-16.

Additionally, a DOS chaff dispenser could be installed in one of the bomb bays. The ELINT/ECM was operated by two special crewmen – an electronic warfare officer (EWO) and a technician. It has to be said the system was not very popular with Tu-4 crews, especially since the bulky PR-1 deprived the crew of the much-needed rest area.

Tu-4UShS navigator trainer

In the late 1950s several dozen Tu-4 bombers were converted to navigator trainers to fill the needs of the long-range bomber arm (DA). The Soviet equivalent of the TB-29 was designated Tu-4UShS (*oochebno-shtoormanskiy samolyot* – navigator trainer aircraft). The cannon armament was deleted while the Kobal't radar was replaced by an RBP-4 Rubidiy-MM2 radar (NATO *Short Horn*) and OPB-11R bombsight as fitted to the Tu-16 and a limited bombing capability was retained; thus the Tu-4UShS could be used for training not only 'pure' navigators but also bomb-aimers (who doubled as navigators on some Soviet bomber types). The trainees sat in one of the bomb bays, taking turns to man the navigator/bomb-aimer's station. The aircraft remained in service with the Soviet Air Force's navigator schools until the late 1960s when it was replaced by the Tu-124Sh-1, one of two navigator trainer versions of the Tu-124V *Cookpot* twin-turbofan short-haul airliner.

Tu-4 ELINT and ECM versions

In the 1950s the Tu-4 served as the basis for a number of ELINT and passive/active ECM versions designed to support the operations of the basic bomber version. Since Soviet electronic equipment of the time was rather bulky and consumed a lot of power, there was no way the entire mission suite could be crammed into a single aircraft; hence a family of five aircraft working in concert had to be created. Each aircraft carried equipment covering a specific waveband; together they took care of the entire range of the enemy air defence's electronic assets. The equipment was installed in the bomb bays.

No separate designations are known for the five variants; however, each set of equipment had its own code letter in Russian alphabetical sequence (A, B, V, G and D) and a single aircraft invariably carried equipment of a single cipher only. Thus, the ciphers A and G denoted pure ELINT-configured aircraft; the ciphers B and V were aircraft with a mixed ELINT/ECM equipment suite, while the cipher D was for a pure ECM version. The long and short of it was that at least five aircraft representing the five configurations had to escort a bomber armada. This was obviously inefficient, hence no more than ten 'Electric Bulls' were in service and they saw very limited use.

Tu-4 radiation reconnaissance aircraft

In 1951-52 the Tupolev OKB and the Nuclear Physics Research Institute (NIIYaF – *Naoochno-issledovatel'skiy institoot yahdernoy fiziki*) headed by Igor' V. Kurchatov converted a production Tu-4 into a radiation reconnaissance aircraft for gathering intelligence on American nuclear tests in the Pacific. The aircraft was equipped with Geiger counters in the bomb bay and a magnetic anomaly detector (MAD) in the rear fuselage. No separate designation is known. The converted Tu-4 operated from airbases in southeastern China, monitoring the area where the tests were conducted.

Tu-4 communications relay aircraft

In the 1950s at least one Tu-4 was converted into a communications relay aircraft for maintaining radio communication between Soviet Navy ships and submarines and the Navy's shore-based command and control centres. Its main distinguishing feature was a long trailing wire aerial unwound from a drum in the rear fuselage.

Tu-4 escort fighter 'mother ship' (Project *Burlaki*)

When the Tu-4 entered service with the VVS in 1948, it was clear that large bomber formations could not rely on their defensive armament alone and needed fighter escort. The potential adversary had jet fighters capable of flying nearly twice as fast as the Tu-4, and the bomber's prospects of reaching its targets unescorted were limited. This was clearly demonstrated by the Korean War where MiG-15 fighters inflicted heavy losses on USAF B-29s attacking targets in North Korea.

The main problem was that the Soviet Union had no escort fighters compatible with the Tu-4. The Tu-83 long-range escort fighter based on the Tu-82 experimental twinjet tactical bomber of 1949 remained a 'paper aeroplane'. The production MiG-15 *Fagot* was clearly unsuitable; even the MiG-15*bis*S with 600-litre (132 Imp gal) drop tanks had a range of only 2,520 km (1,566 miles). This was adequate for escorting Il'yushin Il-28 *Beagle* tactical bombers with a range of 2,400 km (1,491 miles) but not enough for the Tu-4 with its 5,400-km (3,355-mile) range.

Above: The Tu-4 bombers of the 57th Heavy Bomber Division/17st Guards Heavy Bomber Regiment/3rd Sqn converted under the *Burlaki* captive escort fighter programme.

Above: 46 Black (c/n 221001) was the first Tu-4 modified under the Burlaki programme. As the serial reveals, this was the 46th Kazan'-built example.

Close-up of the rear end of Tu-4 c/n 221001, showing the towing drogue with its holder and external towing cable conduit.

Above: The rear fuselage of Tu-4 '46 Black' with the conduit removed, exposing the towing cable.

Above and below: Close-up of the towing drogue in the stowed position.

One way to crack the range problem was for the bombers to carry captive or 'parasite' fighters with them. This approach had been pursued both in the USSR (by Vladimir S. Vakhmistrov's team which developed seven fighter/bomber combinations called *zveno* (flight, as a tactical unit) in 1931-39) and in the United States where experiments were carried out after the Second World War with B-29s carrying the minuscule McDonnell XF-85 Goblin parasite fighter in the bomb bay or towing Republic F-84 Thunderjet fighters. There were also the FICON (fighter conveyor) and 'Tom-Tom' programmes involving modified Convair B-36 Peacemaker bombers and F-84s. (Created to develop an escort capability, the FICON programme was eventually used for long-range reconnaissance, an RF-84K Thunderflash PHOTINT aircraft being carried in the bay of the B-36.)

A similar programme was conducted in the USSR. In 1950, responding to a Long-Range Aviation headquarters proposal, Aleksandr S. Yakovlev's OKB-115 together with OKB-30 in Tomilino south of Moscow (this became a branch of the Tupolev OKB in 1954) began investigating ways of increasing the range and endurance of escort fighters without resorting to drop tanks. The argument was that a fighter weighed down by drop tanks becomes slow and sluggish, which limits its chances in a dogfight with enemy fighters.

The solution was a system enabling the Tu-4 to tow MiG-15*bis Fagot-B* fighters, with automatic coupling and uncoupling. In theory, it offered two advantages: the bomber would still be able to carry a full payload and the fighter would be 'travelling light', its performance uncompromised by extra fuel. The system was code-named *Burlaki* (pronounced *boorla**kee***). In 19th-century Russia, the *burlaki* were teams of strongmen whose job was to haul barges up rivers by means of ropes; the analogy with the towed fighter concept was obvious.

The Yakovlev/OKB-30 system utilised a drogue deployed by the Tu-4, the towing cable running through an external conduit on the rear fuselage portside to a winch in the fuselage operated by the tail gunner. A pneumatically operated telescopic probe with a barbed tip was installed atop the fighter's nose on the fuselage centreline; it was promptly dubbed 'harpoon' and the appellation found its way into official documents as well. The *modus operandi* was as follows. The bomber paid out 80-100 m (262-328 ft) of cable, the fighter closed in on the drogue and 'fired' the 'harpoon' into it; then the pilot shut down his engine and the fighter was towed by the Tu-4 like a glider. If enemy fighters attacked, the fighter pilot started his engine, broke contact with the bomber and engaged the enemy, subsequently hooking up to the bomber again for the journey home.

(Incidentally, the Lockheed company tested a similar system in mid-1947 on a modified P-80A-1-LO (44-84995/'PN-995'). However, unlike the B-29/Tu-4 story, this was very probably one of those cases when engineers working on the same problem in different parts of the world arrive at the same solution independent of one another.)

Initially the Yakovlev/OKB-30 system was tested on the first prototype of the Yak-25 single-engined straight-wing jet fighter ('15 Yellow', c/n 115001) and a modified North American B-25J Mitchell bomber with a BLK-1 winch and a drogue on a 150-m (492-ft) cable. Stage 1 lasted from 1st June 1949 to 30th September 1950; nine successful contacts were made, with Sergey N. Anokhin flying the bomber and Valentin Chapov flying the fighter.

Stage 2 involved 'the real thing'. The 46th Kazan'-built Tu-4 (aptly serialled '46 Black', c/n 221001) was equipped with a BLI-50E winch and drogue holder 'basket', and a Gor'kiy-built MiG-15*bis* ('408 Red', c/n 53210408) was fitted with a 'harpoon' identical to that of the Yak-25. The bomber was converted by OKB-30, using Yakovlev drawings, and the fighter by Yakovlev's experimental shop (MMZ No. 115; MMZ = *Moskovskiy mashino-stroitel'nyy zavod* – Moscow machinery plant).

Tests began at LII on 2nd February 1951 and were completed on 26th March. The results looked encouraging; the conversion had almost no adverse effect on either aircraft's performance, and reliable and safe contact could be made day and night without any trouble. The MiG-15's engine could be easily restarted at up to 6,000 m (19,685 ft). Contact was so smooth that the bomber's crew hardly felt anything at all, and the bomber's speed was reduced by only 10-12 km/h (6-7 mph) if engine rpm remained constant. Anokhin reported that the MiG-15*bis* handled well under tow and the procedure could be mastered by the average pilot in two or three flights.

Between 28th July and 24th August 1951 the *Burlaki* system passed its State acceptance trials – again with good results. According to the GK NII VVS report, connection and disconnection was possible in level flight at 300-360 km/h (186-224 mph/162-194 kts) IAS and 200-9,000 m (656-29,528 ft), during turns with 15-20° bank and climb/descent at up to 10 m/sec (1,968 ft/min). In clear weather the 'air train' could briefly cruise at its service ceiling of 9,650 m (31,660 ft). The combination's top speed was 392 km/h (243 mph) at sea level and 490 km/h (304 mph) at 9,000 m (29,528 ft); maximum range at 6,000 m (19,685 ft) was 3,920 km (2,436 miles).

Above: One of the five 'production' *Burlaki* conversions (Tu-4 '41 Red', c/n 1840848) was further modified for flight refuelling system tests, with a second drogue and hose using the towing cable as a guide.

Above: The original installation used a relatively slender conduit. Conversion for the tanker role required the conduit to be substantially enlarged.

The tail gunner's station of a *Burlaki*-configured Tu-4. The towing winch control panel, a non-standard item, is marked by a circle.

45

Above: Tu-4 '41 Red' (c/n 1840848) with the towing cable and drogue deployed.

The drogue as seen by the pilot of the captive MiG-15*bis* escort fighter before...

...and at the moment of contact. The fighter's telescopic probe (dubbed 'harpoon') is clearly visible. Curiously, the cable appears to be issuing from the bomber's belly instead of the aft fuselage.

Yet the trials also revealed that the *Burlaki* had serious shortcomings. Firstly, the MiG-15's cockpit heating and pressurization system did not work with the engine inoperative, and sitting for hours in a cockpit which became bitterly cold at 7,000-10,000 m (22,966-32,808 ft), wearing an oxygen mask, was a sore trial for the pilot. Secondly, the drag generated by the towed fighter slowed the Tu-4, and a slow bomber in the formation would inevitably slow down the entire formation, which was unacceptable. Worse, the fighter had no hope of reaching its home base if it became separated from the bombers during a dogfight with enemy fighters.

The trials report contained many suggestions, such as providing a secure telephone link allowing the fighter pilot and the bomber crew to communicate while maintaining radio silence and adapting the system for the new and faster bombers then under development (the Tu-16 and Tu-95). The main proposal, however, was to change the ideology of the system completely; the probe and drogue were to be used for in-flight refuelling rather than towing. This led to the next phase of development described below.

Despite the system's shortcomings, on 30th October 1951 the Council of Ministers issued a directive ordering the conversion of five more Tu-4s and five more *Fagot-Bs* to *Burlaki* standard for service trials. The bombers (c/ns 1840848, 2805003, 2805005, 2805110 and 2805203) were indeed modified by Plant No. 18 in Kuibyshev; in contrast, the fighters were actually built with the system in place by Plant No. 153 in Novosibirsk. They were serialled '2170 Red', '2175 Red', '2176 Red', '2190 Red' and '2204 Red' (c/ns 2115370, 2115375, 2115376, 2115390 and 2215304 respectively).

The trials were held in the 50th VA (*vozdooshnaya armiya* – Air Army, ≅ air force) at Zyabrovka AB in the Belorussian Defence District between 9th July and 8th September 1952. The Tu-4s were flown by five crews of the 57th *Smolenskaya* TBAD/171st *Smolensko-Berlinskiy* GvTBAP/3rd AE, while the MiG-15s were operated by ten crews (ie, pilot and technicians) of the 144th IAD/439th IAP/1st AE.

(**Note:** TBAD = *tyazhelobombardeerovochnaya aviadiveeziya* – heavy bomber division (≅ bomber group (heavy)); GvTBAP = *gvardeyskiy tyazhelobombardeerovochnyy aviapolk* – Guards heavy bomber regiment (≅ bomber wing (heavy)); AE = *aviaeskadril'ya* – air squadron; IAD = *istrebitel'naya aviadiveeziya* – fighter division (≅ fighter group); GvIAP = *gvardeyskiy istrebitel'nyy aviapolk* – Guards fighter regiment (≅ fighter wing).

The Guards units are the elite of the Soviet (Russian) armed forces; this appellation was given for gallantry in combat, thus being an indication that this is a WW II-vintage unit. The *Smolensko-Berlinskiy* honorary appellation was given for the unit's part in liberating Smolensk and taking Berlin. The 57th TBAD and the 171st GvTBAP also bore the *Krasnoznamyonnaya* (*Krasnoznamyonnyy*) title respectively, ie, they had been awarded the Order of the Red Banner of Combat.

The objective was to evaluate the system's reliability and 'user-friendliness', fighter/bomber rendezvous techniques and formation flying techniques. The trials involved 142 hook-ups (including 17 at night) and went without incident. The manoeuvring envelope was slightly narrower than during the State acceptance trials, with bank angles up to 15° and rates of climb/descent up to 7 m/sec (1,378 ft/min). The longest towed flight lasted 2 hours 30 minutes, including 2 hours 27 minutes with the engine shut down.

Before making contact the fighters zeroed in on the bombers, using their ARK-5 automatic direction finders which worked with the bomber's 1RSB-70 radio used as a short-range navigation system. During landing approach the fighters stayed connected right down to 300 m (984 ft). After extending the landing gear and lowering the flaps 20° the fighter pilot waited for the signal from the bomber crew or the tower to break contact; receiving the go-ahead, he disengaged the 'harpoon' at 2-3 km (1.2-1.8 miles) from the runway threshold and landed.

The system was ultimately put to the test in two sessions of mock combat on 5th August 1952. A flight of fighter-towing Tu-4s was 'attacked' by four MiG-15s representing enemy fighters. The attackers were guided to their target by a ground-controlled intercept (GCI) station using target information from an air defence radar.

On the first occasion, the towed fighters lost; paraphrasing the system's 'strongman' name, the *Burlaki* turned out to be strong in the arm but weak in the head. The bombers' flight leader spotted the 'enemy' fighters at 12-15 km (7.5-9.3 miles) range as they were making their first attack and gave the order to start the engines, disengage and repel the attackers. However, as the towed fighters did so the attackers managed to make a second 'firing pass'. If this had been for real, the bombers would have been shot down – probably taking their captive protectors with them!

The second try was more successful; two pairs of MiGs took turns patrolling (flying top cover) and resting (ie, being towed). This time one pair of escort fighters was ready to repel an incoming attack; yet again the 'enemy' fighters were discovered a little too late and the protective pair just couldn't cope with them. Still, the 'bad guys' did not manage to repeat the attack before they found themselves counterattacked. The conclusion was that incoming enemy fighters needed to be spotted at least four minutes before they got within firing range so that the towed escort fighters could get ready. This could be done by fitting the bomber with a search radar, enabling the crew to spot enemy fighters at 60-80 km (37-50 miles) range.

Technology quickly made the *Burlaki* system obsolete and it never entered service. Firstly, the Tu-4 was replaced by the Tu-16 jet bomber capable of cruising at 1,000 km/h (621 mph), equalling the speed of many fighters. Its heavy defensive armament and ECM equipment gave it a good chance of reaching its target. Secondly, experiments began with flight refuelling systems for fighters; some of them are described later in this chapter.

Tu-4 airborne command post conversion

A small number of Tu-4s stripped of all armament were converted into 'flying headquarters' or airborne command posts (ABCPs). The headquarters room was located in the centre pressure cabin which was suitably outfitted and provided with extra windows to admit some light.

Tu-4 modified for 360° movie shooting

Believe it or not, the Tu-4 also had altogether civil applications. In the late 1950s the Tupolev OKB received a request from the Soviet Union's Central Documentary Film Studios to develop a system enabling 360° film shooting from the air by means of several remote-controlled cine cameras installed under an aircraft's belly on an extendable mount. A special term, *tsirkorama* ('circorama' – a contraction of 'circle' and 'panorama'), was coined for such 360° movies.

Basically the customer's demands were that the camera mount was to be extended pretty far into the slipstream in order to create a total 'eye in the sky' effect (ie, to prevent parts of the aircraft from getting into the picture). Also, the surface of the mount was to remain parallel to the fuselage waterline at all times and the whole structure was required to be adequately stiff. The Tu-4 turned out to be the best camera platform for the job.

The OKB's Tomilino branch considered several possible locations for the camera mount, alternative ways of attaching it to the fuselage and alternative actuation system designs. When the optimum design had been chosen this unusual installation was manufactured by the OKB's experimental facility in Moscow (MMZ No. 156 'Opyt'; the name translates as either 'experiment' or 'experience'). The installation was a long externally mounted truss whose rear end was hinged to the fuselage underside. The camera mount was hinged to the front end and maintained in horizontal position by means of mechanical linkages as the truss tilted; extension and retraction was done by means of cables and pulleys. The cameraman operated the cine cameras from the cabin by means of a remote-control system.

After completing its flight test programme the modified aircraft (identity unknown) was turned over to the Central Documentary Film Studios. The 'circorama' movies shot with the help of this aircraft were demonstrated in a purpose-built cinema at the Soviet Union's prime showground, the National Economy Achievements Exhibition (VDNKh – *Vystavka dostizheniy narodnovo khoziaystva*) in Moscow, and Tupolev OKB employees were among the first spectators. (As a point of interest, two helicopter types – the Mil' Mi-4 *Hound* and the Yak-24 *Horse* – were also used for making such movies.)

Tu-4 long-range ice reconnaissance aircraft conversion

In 1957, when the Long-Range Aviation began phasing out the *Bull*, the Polar Aviation (or, to be precise, the Main Directorate of the North Sea Route responsible for ship traffic in the polar regions and support of Soviet Arctic research) started taking delivery of demilitarised Tu-4s which were adapted for ice reconnaissance. The centre pressure cabin of these aircraft was converted into a researchers' bay and also served as an onboard canteen. Two such aircraft – CCCP H-1139

Projected performance of the 'aircraft 94' bomber

Maximum all-up weight	63,300 kg (139,555 lb)
Fuel load	22,050 kg (48,612 lb)
Bomb load	2,000 kg (4,409 lb)
All-up weight over the target	47,800 kg (105,380 lb)
Top speed:	
at 6,000 m (19,685 ft)	676 km/h (420 mph)
at 10,000 m (32,808 ft)	650-680 km/h (404-422 mph)
Cruising speed	550-600 km/h (342-373 mph)
Range	5,400-6,300 km (3,355-3,914 miles)
Cruising altitude over the target	11,000-12,000 m (36,089-39,370 ft)
Take-off run	1,000-1,200 m (3,281-3,937 ft)

Above: Tu-4 c/n 2805204 was converted into a two-point hose-and-drogue tanker for MiG-15 fighters.

Tiksi and Amderma, flying long-range ice reconnaissance missions over the Greenland Sea between the coast of Greenland and Spitsbergen (Svalbard) Island, over Greenland itself, the Franz-Joseph Land archipelago and the North Pole in the direction of Canada. Such missions typically lasted 20-25 hours, so the aircraft carried as much fuel as it could hold and the take-off weight usually exceeded 60,000 kg (132,277 lb). These aircraft were also used as fuel tankers, landing on ice floes to deliver precious fuel to Soviet drifting ice stations in the Arctic Ocean.

(ie, SSSR N-1139 in Cyrillic characters; c/n 2805710) and CCCP-92648 – are known.

(**Note:** In 1922-1959 the CCCP- country prefix was followed by a code letter denoting the aircraft's owner plus up to four digits. N stood for the Main Directorate of the North Sea Route; strictly speaking, the abovementioned registration should have been painted on as CCCP-H1139. Under the new five-digit registration system introduced in 1959 which remains in use to this day, the first two digits are a code denoting the aircraft type – for flight safety reasons, allowing quick identification by air traffic controllers, – though some registration blocks correspond to no specific type and are a 'mixed bag' of various aircraft.)

Polar Aviation Tu-4s were based near Murmansk and occasionally operated from

'Aircraft 94' long-range bomber project

In 1950 the Tupolev OKB began project studies aimed at re-engining the existing Tu-4 fleet with turboprops. This led the Council of Ministers to issue directive No. 3653-1519 on 22nd August 1950, ordering the OKB to develop a version of the Tu-4 powered by four TV-2 or TV-022 turboprop engines (TV = *toorbovintovoy* [*dvigatel'*] – turboprop).

Developed by Nikolay D. Kuznetsov's OKB-276 from the TV-022 (a direct copy of the captured 5,000-ehp Junkers Jumo 022 turbo-

Above: This view of Tu-4 c/n 2805204 on a practice refuelling mission with MiG-15*bis* '342 Blue' and '17 Red' shows the hoses streaming from the wingtips.
Below: The same tanker on the ground. Note how the drogues were stowed in the wingtip fairings.

prop), the basic TV-2 delivered 5,163 ehp for take-off during trials, with an SFC of 297 g/hp·hr versus the progenitor's 300 g/hp·hr. Nominal power and SFC were 4,409 ehp and 313 g/hp·hr, while cruise power and SFC were 3,740 ehp and 328 g/hp·hr (versus 3,000 ehp and 210 g/hp·hr for the TV-022). With accessories installed the engine had a dry weight of 1,700 kg (3,748 lb); it drove AV-41B four-bladed contra-rotating propellers of 4.2 m (13 ft 9 in) diameter. (**Note:** The above SFC figures for the TV2 are as per 'aircraft 94' project documents; the real engine showed a much better SFC of 257 g/hp·hr for take-off and198 g/hp.hr in cruise mode.)

Calculations made by the Tupolev OKB showed that at maximum all-up weight the Tu-4 re-engined with TV-2 turboprops (or 'aircraft 94', as the projected bomber was known in-house) would have a performance as detailed in the table on page 47.

The normal bomb load was set at 1,500 kg (3,307 lb) and the maximum bomb load at 6,000-12,000 kg (13,228-26,455 lb).

As can be seen from the figures in the table, the performance of 'aircraft 94' with TV-2 engines was only some 15-20% higher than that of the standard Tu-4. This was definitely not good enough for the Soviet Air Force, and the project was shelved. Later the OKB came back to it, proposing that Kuznetsov TV-4 turboprops (later redesignated NK-4) be installed on the Tu-4; the NK-4, which ran for the first time in April 1956, delivered 4,000 ehp for take-off and 2,300 ehp in cruise mode, had an SFC of 207 g/hp·hr and a dry weight of 970 kg (2,138 lb). Yet again the NK-4 powered version remained a 'paper aeroplane'; there was no point in pursuing this project further because 'clean sheet of paper' designs of long-range bombers were being developed around new powerful Soviet turbojets and turboprops. These advanced aircraft featuring swept wings were expected to significantly outperform the Tu-4.

Still, a version of the *Bull* powered by turboprops **did** appear eventually – albeit in China, not in the Soviet Union; these aircraft will be described in more detail later.

'Aircraft 79' long-range bomber project

Back in 1947 the Tupolev OKB considered the possibility of fitting the Tu-4 with M-49TK liquid-cooled engines; the result would have looked rather similar to the Boeing YB-29 powered by Allison V-3420 12-cylinder Vee engines. Designated 'aircraft 79', this version was included in the work plan of the OKB's preliminary design (PD) projects section; however, it never got beyond the technical proposal stage due to the unavailability of the intended engines.

Above: Another view of the Tu-4 tanker with *Fagot-B*s '17 Red' and '342 Blue'. A third MiG-15*bis* serialled '618 Red' was also involved.

Above: A fairing with side-looking cine cameras supplanting the tail guns was fitted for capturing the refuelling sequence.

The 'wing-to-wing' in-flight refuelling system devised by Shelest and Vasyanin found use on the Tu-4. Illustrated here is the receiver aircraft (c/n 221901), seen from the tanker during trials of the system.

Above: The tanker-configured Tu-4 (c/n 222202) seen from the receiver aircraft.

This view shows how the tanker and receiver kept formation during the refuelling procedure.

Tu-4 flight refuelling tanker versions

As noted earlier, the Tu-4 belonged to the long-range bomber class. With a normal bomb load it could reach targets in Europe, northern Africa, the Middle East and Japan from bases on the vast territory of the USSR. Yet the Soviet military leaders had even bigger appetites; they wanted an aircraft with intercontinental range which could hit targets in North America. Hence no sooner had the Tu-4 entered production than the Soviet aircraft industry started work on a new intercontinental bomber. One of the steps towards this goal was an attempt to give the Tu-4 longer 'legs' by giving it an in-flight refuelling (IFR) capability.

The first Soviet experiments in this area dated back to the 1930s when attempts were made to extend the range of the Tupolev TB-3 heavy bomber. A sister aircraft equipped with an additional fuel tank acted as the tanker. Since the TB-3's airspeed was low, a hose could be paid out by means of a hand-driven winch as the tanker flew directly above the receiver aircraft; a crewman would then catch it and connect it manually to the fuel

filler, whereupon transfer of fuel by gravity could begin. This method was most inconvenient and, in consequence, the work did not progress beyond the experimental stage.

a) 'system of crossing cables'

The development of in-flight refuelling techniques resumed after the Second World War, when the designers were armed with new technologies and faced new requirements. The Tu-4 bomber was the prime candidate for receiving an efficient IFR system, but tactical fighters were not left out either – at this stage anyway.

In 1948 the design team headed by Vladimir S. Vakhmistrov developed the so-called 'system of crossing cables' based on a system developed by the British company Flight Refuelling Ltd. Before making contact both aircraft would deploy cables; the receiver's cable terminated in a stabilising drogue, stretching out almost horizontally, while the tanker's cable was provided with a weight incorporating a snap lock. The tanker would fall into echelon port formation with the receiver aircraft, keeping 8-10 m (26-33 ft) behind

and 3-4 m (10-13 ft) above it, and move into echelon starboard formation so that the cables crossed and the lock engaged. Then the receiver rewound the cables, the tanker paying out a hose attached to its own cable until it connected with a receptacle under the receiver's wing and locked into place automatically, forming a loop. During fuel transfer the tanker stayed 12-15 m (39-49 ft) above the receiver and slightly behind it, with a distance of about 50 m (164 ft) between the fuselages. Fuel was transferred by pumps delivering up to 700 litres (154 Imp gal) per minute. When refuelling was completed the hose would be unlocked and rewound; the tanker then peeled off to starboard, the cables went taut and a special section in one of them gave way, disengaging the aircraft.

The system was flight-tested first on the Second World War-vintage Tu-2 bomber and then on the Tu-4; no pumps were fitted initially and fuel was transferred by gravity on the first attempts. The use of the rather inefficient and outdated 'system of crossing cables' can only be explained by the need to meet stringent deadlines; an operable IFR system had to be demonstrated to the powers that be at all costs, and a better solution could be devised later. After a great deal of testing and refining, the system underwent State acceptance trials – and was rejected as inefficient and obsolescent.

b) adaptation of the *Burlaki* towed fighter concept

As mentioned earlier, the VVS considered using a probe-and-drogue system based on the *Burlaki* towed fighter concept.

Initially OKB-30, OKB-134 and the Yakovlev OKB modified the existing *Burlaki* system by adding new elements. The fighter's 'harpoon' incorporated a valve and was connected to the fuel system. The bomber was equipped with three kerosene tanks, a pump and an inert gas pressurisation system to reduce the risk of fire and explosion if hit by enemy fire. After the fighter had made contact with the tanker's towing drogue, a hose terminating in a smaller drogue was paid out along the towing cable and the fighter accelerated, locking the two drogues together. (The original drogue was modified so as to allow fuel to pass through it into the probe.) 1,210 litres (266 Imp gal) of fuel could be transferred in six minutes. When refuelling was completed the smaller drogue was automatically disengaged and the hose rewound.

Two of the aircraft used for service trials of the *Burlaki* system – Tu-4 '41 Red' (c/n 1840848 – ie, Plant 18, Tu-4, 08th aircraft in Batch 48) and MiG-15*bis* '2204 Red' (c/n 2215304) – were converted for flight refuelling trials which took place at LII between 24th September 1954 and 2nd March 1955. The tanker was piloted by A. Yefimov, with A. I. Vershinin as the refuelling system operator; the fighter was flown by Sergey N. Anokhin and Fyodor I. Boortsev. The programme involved ten flights in the MiG-15*bis*, including five contacts at 2,000 m (6,562 ft) and 4,000 m (13,123 ft); on three occasions fuel was actually transferred. However, an attempt to repeat the performance at 8,500 m (27,887 ft) failed because the system's rubber components froze up, losing their elasticity.

c) two-point probe and drogue system

Generally the 'wet *Burlaki*' system was considered excessively complex, and as early as December 1952 another design bureau, OKB-918 led by Semyon Mikhaïlovich Alekseyev, took on the flight refuelling problem. This bureau, which absorbed the entire Vakhmistrov team, later became the Zvezda (Star) company best known for the K-36 ejection seat fitted to almost all current Russian combat aircraft.

No fewer than 12 Kuibyshev-built Tu-4s, including c/n 2805204 (ie, year of manufacture 1952, Plant No. 18 (the first digit was omitted to confuse would-be spies), Batch 052, fourth aircraft in the batch), were converted for the tanker role at Plant No. 18. The arrangement proposed by OKB-918 differed from the OKB-30/Yakovlev system in two important aspects. Firstly, it was much simpler, with only one drogue and hose (just like the system developed by Flight Refuelling Ltd which is in worldwide use today). Secondly, the aircraft was a two-point tanker. Two hose

drum units (HDUs) were installed in the forward bomb bay, the hoses running on supporting rollers inside the wings and exiting from specially modified wingtips. The refuelling system operator sat in the tail gunner's station; the tail guns were replaced by a fairing housing cine cameras to record the refuelling sequence. The hoses were extended by the drag created by the drogues when the HDUs were set to 'unwind'. Since the tanker was to work with jet aircraft, part of the fuel tankage was isolated and set aside for jet fuel (kerosene).

Three *Fagot-Bs* serialled '17 Red', '342 Blue' (c/n 123042 or 133042) and '618 Red' were fitted with fixed telescopic refuelling probes offset to port on the intake upper lip; the conversion work was done by the Novosibirsk factory in May 1952. Test flights began in 1953, with a considerable delay because of late equipment deliveries for the tanker conversion. The tanker was flown by P. I. Kaz'min, S. F. Mashkovskiy, L. V. Chistyakov and other LII test pilots, while Sergey N. Anokhin and V. N. Pronyakin flew the fighters. At first, Mikoyan OKB engineers were apprehensive about having the probe near the intake, fearing the drogue would generate excessive turbulence at the air intake lip and provoke a compressor stall. These fears were possibly caused by knowing that in the USA, an F-84 fitted experimentally with the probe-and-drogue refuelling system had the probe mounted on the starboard wing, well clear of the air intake. However, trials showed these fears were unfounded.

Several versions of the hose had to be tried before the system was deemed satisfactory. The original hose incorporating a reinforcing wire spiral was not durable enough. On the other hand, a 'soft' hose with no reinforcing wire flexed excessively and fighter pilots found that just a little turbulence made 'hitting the tanker' very difficult. Another problem was the considerable amount of fuel remaining in the hose after the transfer pumps were shut down; immediately after breaking contact with the tanker the fighter was liberally doused with fuel, some of which entered the cockpit. Still, the system was simple, reliable and offered a high fuel transfer rate.

The combination of the Tu-4 tanker and two MiG-15*bis* receivers was presented twice for State acceptance trials but failed both times because of problems with the supporting rollers inside the wings which caused hose oscillation and failure of the fighters' refuelling probes due to the whiplash effect of the hose. Also, unlike the USAF, the VVS had no need to fly its fighters over long distances. However, once again the probe-and-drogue system was used successfully on strategic aircraft – the Myasishchev 3MN/3MS *Bison-B* and 3MD *Bison-C* heavy bombers, most aircraft of the Tu-95/Tu-142 family, the Tu-126 *Moss* airborne warning and control system (AWACS), the Tu-22KD/RD/PD/UD *Blinder* and Tu-22M0/M1/M2 *Backfire-A/B* supersonic long-range bombers and their versions etc. In the mid-1970s the system was finally adapted for tactical aircraft as well.

Another view of a pair of Tu-4s in refuelling formation; the receiver aircraft is just pulling the hose up to its wingtip.

d) wing-to-wing system

Another wing-to-wing refuelling system was developed by LII test pilots Igor' I. Shelest and Viktor S. Vasyanin. They witnessed the testing of the original 'system of crossing cables' and were quick to see its weaknesses. Since both men had received an engineering education, they had no trouble preparing a technical proposal, with drawings and all, which they showed to the institute's top brass. The Shelest/Vasyanin system clearly had major advantages over the 'system of crossing cables': the refuelling process was completely automated, the tanker and receiver aircraft flew on parallel courses and neither had to enter the other aircraft's wake vortex.

Shelest and Vasyanin were allowed to go ahead with the project, working in parallel with Vakhmistrov's team. Initially a pair of Tu-2 bombers was equipped with the new system by LII. On 16th July 1949 test pilot Amet-Khan Sultan and one of the system's inventors successfully performed a fully automatic in-flight refuelling in these aircraft. The process was duly documented on cine film and this was demonstrated to Andrey N. Tupolev, who immediately recognised the soundness of the idea and approached the Government, lobbying for support. He got his way; a few days later LII received an official government assignment to install and test the new IFR system on the Tu-4 bomber. To this end the institute received two brand-new *Bulls* (c/ns 221901 and 222202) for conversion as the tanker and receiver aircraft.

Since Shelest and Vasyanin had developed the system on their own initiative, they had to draw up the system's specifications for themselves, relying on their experience as test pilots, engineering intuition and common sense. Recorded in the official test report, the requirements were outlined as follows:

'1. Making contact and keeping formation during refuelling shall be safe and relatively simple, presenting no problem for first-line service pilots after a few conversion training sessions;

2. Contact shall be established quickly in daytime and at night, given adequate visibility, and in moderate turbulence;

3. The means of contact (the hose and whatever goes with it – Auth.) shall remain stable in flight and present no danger of damage to the aircraft's vital components in the event of an incident;

4. The tanker, not the receiver aircraft, shall perform all the necessary manoeuvres during contact and fuel transfer;

5. The bomber's IFR equipment shall be as lightweight and compact as possible and the bomber crew shall have the smallest possible additional workload during refuelling;

6. The refuelling process shall be automated and the refuelling system shall be remotely controlled from the pressurised cabins;

7. The overall time required, including engagement and disengagement, shall not exceed 20 minutes;

8. The volume of transferable fuel shall be 35-40% of the total fuel capacity if the tanker and receiver aircraft are sister ships;

9. Installation of IFR equipment in the tanker shall not render it unusable in the bomber role and shall not cause deterioration of flight performance.'

Items 4 and 5 of the above are especially noteworthy. Since the bomber is out on a combat mission, it will have to penetrate enemy air defences; then things will really get ugly and all available crew resources will be needed. Therefore it is perfectly natural that the bomber's crew need not waste adrenalin on the refuelling procedure and that the tanker's crew should take care of the whole thing, with the receiver flying in autopilot mode. A few years later, however, when the Shelest/Vasyanin system was adapted to the Tu-16, the Air Force command demanded that the bomber crew should play the active part in the refuelling procedure. The argument in support of this requirement was positively staggering: 'Suppose the bomber crew decides not to fulfil the mission and returns to base, claiming they had not been refuelled. Who will take the blame then?'

Actually, Igor' I. Shelest and Viktor S. Vasyanin proposed three versions of their IFR system. Version 1 (described below) was implemented on the Tu-4 on a small scale; Version 2, designed for fighters, underwent preliminary tests on two modified MiG-19 *Farmer-As* designated SM-10/1 and SM-10/2 but was not adopted for Soviet Air Force service. The third version was used successfully for many years on the Tu-16, the tanker version of the *Badger-A* being designated Tu-16Z (*zaprahvschchik* – refuelling tanker).

In the version used by the *Bull* a hose deployed by the tanker was pulled over to the wing of the receiver aircraft by a special contact cable, forming a loop; this left both aircraft enough room for manoeuvring and allowed refuelling to take place in turbulent conditions. All the principal manoeuvres and actions involved in formating with the receiver aircraft and making contact were performed by the tanker, while the bomber kept its intended course.

The tanker's equipment fit included the fuel transfer hose, a winch and cable for rewinding the hose, a cluster of three booms tipped with rings for capturing the bomber's contact cable, a fuel transfer pump, a sealing chamber for connecting the hose to the fuel delivery pipeline, a hose ejector and a control and indication system. The receiver aircraft featured a winch and cable terminating in a weight equipped with a snap lock and a stabilising drogue, a hose receptacle and fuel transfer pipeline, shutoff valves and a control and indication system. The engagement/disengagement process and fuel transfer were remote-controlled and automated. The entire system was housed inside the airframes of both aircraft, creating no extra drag and having virtually no adverse effect on their performance and handling.

The refuelling procedure was as follows. Maintaining speed, heading and altitude, the receiver aircraft deployed a contact cable 100-120 m (328-394 ft) long from the starboard wingtip fairing. The tanker closed in from behind, falling into echelon starboard formation with the bomber and placing its port wing over the cable. Then the tanker moved away and forward so that the cable slid along the wing undersurface onto a boom at the wingtip, engaging a ring connected by springs to the fitting at the hose's outer end. The ring came off the boom and the bomber's crew member responsible for the refuelling started rewinding the cable; at the same time the outer end of the hose was ejected from the tanker's wingtip. Next, the weight at the end of the contact cable locked into the ring, connecting the cable with the hose; as the cable was rewound further it extracted the hose from the tanker's wing, pulling it up to the receiver aircraft. When the hose was fully extended a fitting at the inner end locked into the sealing chamber; meanwhile the fitting at the other end automatically engaged the receptacle under the bomber's wingtip and a connection was established, whereupon the transfer pump was switched on.

When the bomber's tanks were full the shutoff valves automatically stopped further fuel delivery. After that the fuel lines were scavenged by compressed nitrogen forcing the remaining fuel back into the tanker's fuel tanks and the hose was released. The tanker rewound the hose, the bomber paying out the contact cable at the same time; as the end of the hose disappeared inside the tanker's wingtip the connection was broken, the ring remaining on the weight at the end of the cable which the bomber then rewound.

The system allowed the tanker to make up to three contacts with the bomber during a sortie. Each time a fresh boom and ring would be extended from the tanker's wingtip and a special mechanism would attach the ring to the fitting at the end of the hose.

As a matter of fact, the Tu-4 equipped as the receiver aircraft had a duplicated set of IFR equipment for maximum reliability – two winches with contact cables and two refuelling receptacles. Each cable could be used three times, as there was room for only three contact rings on the weight at the end of the cable; thus the bomber could 'hit the tanker' up to six times in a single sortie, which made for very long range indeed.

Refuelling was done at indicated airspeeds of 320-350 km/h (199-217 mph) with the aircraft cruising at the service ceiling. The fuel transfer rate was 800 litres (176 Imp gal) per minute and a maximum of 10,400 litres (2,288 Imp gal) could be transferred at a time.

Being test pilots, the inventors were concerned about developing an acceptable piloting technique for the tanker crew right from the start. Igor' Shelest took great pains to make sure the system worked OK, testing it over and over again; he was well aware that a single accident could cost both him and his 'co-author' their lives. Reprisal came swiftly in those days, and a death sentence would be more than likely.

The tanker crew ran into a few problems during early test flights. As the aircraft approached the contact cable deployed by the bomber, the tanker pilots tended to look at their port wingtip over the shoulder, which was inadmissible during formation flying as it created a risk of mid-air collision. The problem was fixed by installing a forward-facing light on the tanker's wingtip for night operations; this emitted a narrow beam of light which the tanker pilot could see clearly. Also, the pilots were now assisted by the defensive weapons operator (DWO) who sat in the centre pressure cabin, controlling the dorsal and ventral cannon barbettes. Using the lateral sighting blister, the DWO gave directions over the intercom to the pilot who could now look ahead and left, focusing his attention on the receiver aircraft. He smoothly manoeuvred the tanker into position without bank or sideslip, keeping the required interval by checking the bearing on the bomber and using the bomber's tail to gauge the distance.

As a result, the tanker now 'hooked up' to the bomber flawlessly on the first try.

Later test flights performed by Amet-Khan Sultan and A. P. Yakimov gave interesting results: after making a few successful contacts the tanker pilots no longer needed assistance from the DWO, learning to judge the distance and position relative to the bomber correctly just by watching it. For instance, Mark L. Gallai made contact with the bomber successfully on his first night refuelling mission, even though he had no prior experience of night tanker operations. Later, when the Shelest/Vasyanin IFR system found its way to service units flying the Tu-4, service pilots mastered the knack after undertaking ten training flights.

Since the new system had shown good results during tests, in 1952 the Air Force suggested building a small batch of Tu-4 tankers and IFR-equipped Tu-4 bombers. The Government picked up the ball: on 28th March 1952 the Council of Ministers issued directive No. 1523-530 ordering the Tupolev OKB, Plant No. 18 and a number of other enterprises in the aviation industry to convert three Tu-4s into tankers and equip a further three *Bulls* with refuelling receptacles. The document specified the amount of transferable fuel as 10,000 litres (2,200 Imp gal) and duration of the refuelling as 20 minutes. The aircraft were to be submitted for State acceptance trials in August 1952.

When the trials programme had been completed a small number of Tu-4s retrofitted with the wing-to-wing IFR system (Version 1) entered service with the VVS. Not many *Bulls* were thus upgraded for the simple reason that the far more capable jet-powered Tu-16 featuring Version 3 of the same system was about to enter large-scale production.

Tu-4 fuel carrier

The Tu-4's large fuel tankage rendered it suitable for the 'fuel carrier' role. A number of *Bulls* were adapted for delivering fuel to fighter and tactical bomber bases and refuelling tactical aircraft on the ground. To this end some of the fuel cells were isolated from the bomber's fuel system and used for carrying jet fuel; simple refuelling equipment with hoses, pumps and a control panel was fitted.

Tu-4TRZhK liquid oxygen tanker

Similarly, the need to supply aviation and missile units with liquid oxygen (LOX) spawned a version designated Tu-4TRZhK (*trahnsportnyy rezervouar zhidkovo kisloroda* – LOX transportation reservoir). Heat-insulated LOX tanks and associated equipment were installed in the bomb bays of the otherwise standard *Bull*. Normally the equipment was only fitted during military exercises when units scattered far and wide had to be supported.

Tu-4NM drone launcher aircraft

In 1952 six late-production Kazan'-built Tu-4s, including '29 Red' (c/n 2207510; the aircraft actually carried a seven-digit c/n instead of the normal six-digit presentation), were converted intto Tu-4NM drone launchers (*nositel' misheney*) carrying a pair of Lavochkin La-17 (*izdeliye* 201) jet-propelled target drones under the outer wings for training air defence missile crews. The aircraft were suitably lightened by removing all armament and some equipment items; still, they climbed awfully slowly, requiring two hours to reach 8,000 m (26,247 ft) and guzzling fuel at a horrible rate. Hence the air launch idea was abandoned and in service the La-17 used a ground launcher, taking off with the help of two solid-fuel rocket boosters.

Tu-4 c/n 230322 was converted into the ShR-1 bicycle landing gear testbed for the Myasishchev M-4 bomber. The extensively modified landing gear is well illustrated in this view.

Above and below: One of the three Tu-4LL engine testbeds (c/n 230214) used for testing turbojet engines. The nacelle of the development engine was mounted under the former forward bomb bay.

Tu-4 target drone conversion

Also in 1952 the decision was taken to convert time-expired aircraft, including Tu-4s, into remote-controlled target drones. After taking off and climbing to the required altitude the pilots would bale out and the bomber flew on towards destruction, controlled by an onboard computer or a ground control station.

Tu-4 'mother ship' for DFS 346 experimental aircraft

A Moscow-built Tu-4 with no serial (c/n 230503 – ie, Plant No. 23, fifth aircraft in Batch 03) was converted for carrying the '346' (DFS 346) rocket-powered experimental aircraft – probably in accordance with the aforementioned MAP order No. 210 of 16th April 1948. As was the case with B-29 '256 Black', the '346' was carried aloft on a special pylon mounted between the Nos. 3 and 4 engines. Tu-4 c/n 230503 served in the 'mother ship' role until the termination of the '346' programme in 1951 when the third prototype (346-3) crashed on its third powered flight.

ShR-1/ShR-2 bicycle landing gear testbed

When the newly organised OKB-23 led by Vladimir Mikhaïlovich Myasishchev began development of the M-4 (*izdeliye* M) *Bison-A* long-range heavy bomber in March 1951, the

engineers chose the bicycle landing gear arrangement from the outset. The twin-wheel nose unit envisaged originally and the main unit equipped with a four-wheel bogie absorbed 30% and 70% of the aircraft's weight respectively. This arrangement was not totally new to Soviet aircraft designers by then, as the I-215D experimental fighter designed by Semyon M. Alekseyev and featuring a bicycle landing gear had successfully flown in October 1949. However, there was as yet no experience of using the bicycle landing gear arrangement on a heavy aircraft (the 'aircraft 150' twinjet medium bomber designed by the captive German designer Brunolf Baade did not make its first flight until 5th September 1952), and the need arose to verify the novel arrangement on a suitably converted bomber.

Hence OKB-23 developed a testbed version of the Tu-4 for studying the behaviour of a heavy aircraft with a bicycle landing gear during take-off, landing and taxying and for training flight crews. The aircraft was designated **ShR-1**, the Sh denoting *shassee* (landing gear) and the R referring to the Tu-4's in-house product code (*izdeliye* R).

A brand-new *Bull* manufactured by the co-located production plant No. 23 (no serial, c/n 230322) was delivered to the Myasishchev OKB for conversion into the ShR-1

testbed. The standard nose gear unit was replaced by a new twin-wheel levered suspension strut with larger 1,450 x 520 mm (57 x 20.4 in) wheels. The scratchbuilt main gear unit consisted of two stock Tu-4 main gear oleos mounted in tandem and rigidly connected; to these was hinged a four-wheel bogie with 1,450 x 520 mm wheels. The entire assembly was attached to a hefty steel frame installed near the aft bomb bay; it could be installed in three different ways so that the main gear absorbed 72%, 85% or 90% of the total weight. This unusual design feature was introduced to see how the changing weight distribution and wheelbase affected the aircraft's field performance and manoeuvrability on the ground (the reason was that different versions of the M-4's preliminary design project featured an aft-retracting or forward-retracting nose gear unit, with attendant changes in wheelbase and weight distribution). The nosewheels and mainwheels were equipped with hydraulic brakes.

The outrigger struts installed a short distance outboard of the Nos. 1 and 4 engines consisted of stock Tu-4 nose gear units mated with special truss-type mountings which allowed the length of the outriggers to be adjusted. Interestingly, the non-retractable experimental landing gear could be removed and the normal gear reinstalled for positioning flights.

The conversion job was completed in January 1952; Stage 1 of the test programme began in April, lasting until June. The ShR-1 made 50 taxy runs and 34 flights to check the aircraft's stability and controllability, the operation of the nose gear steering mechanism and the optimum position of the main gear and outrigger struts. As the main gear was moved aft the load on the nose gear gradually increased from 10.6% to 20.8% to 28.6%. Test data were recorded automatically.

Meanwhile the M-4's twin nosewheels had been rejected in favour of a four-wheel bogie with electrically steerable nosewheels. Hence the Tu-4 testbed was modified accordingly and redesignated **ShR-2**. In this guise the aircraft underwent further tests in 1953, making 24 taxy runs and 17 flights; the nose gear bogie absorbed 20% of the weight versus 40% on the actual *Bison*. These tests showed that the bicycle landing gear offered excellent ground handling and simplified the take-off technique – the M-4 required no rotation to get unstuck, taking off almost of its own accord.

UR-1/UR-2 control system testbed

The bicycle landing gear was not the only novel feature of the M-4. For the first time in Soviet aircraft design practice the *Bison* incorporated fully powered controls with reversible and irreversible hydraulic actuators in the aileron, rudder and elevator control circuits, plus an artificial feel mechanism.

Of course, testing these features on a ground rig ('iron bird', to use Boeing terminology) was not enough and the actuators had to be put to the test in flight. Hence a Tu-4 (identity unknown) was converted into the UR control system testbed by the Myasishchev OKB; the U stood for [*sistema*] *oopravleniya* – control system and the R was again a reference to the Tu-4.

The first version designated **UR-1** featured reversible actuators; tests in this configuration were completed in March 1952, involving 12 flights totalling about 20 hours. The test flights showed that the powered controls worked acceptably, even though a few failures did occur; incidentally, the powered controls improved the *Bull's* handling dramatically. Later the aircraft was refitted with irreversible actuators and tested in April 1952 as the **UR-2**. The test results obtained on this aircraft enabled OKB-23 engineers to simplify the M-4's control system, utilising a simple spring-loaded artificial feel mechanism instead of a complex automatic device. Still, further tests with a pneumatically operated automatic artificial feel system were conducted on the UR-2 in September 1952.

KR crew rescue system testbed

Later on, the UR-2 control system testbed was modified for testing the M-4's crew rescue system and redesignated KR, the K denoting *katapool'teeruyemoye kreslo* (ejection seat). Its *raison d'étre* was the *Bison's* unconventional crew rescue system with movable ejection seats, the captain and co-pilot ejecting consecutively through a common hatch.

The KR was equipped with ejection seats for the pilots, navigator, flight engineer and dorsal gunner (DWO). Between October 1952 and January 1953 it performed 12 test flights in which 20 ejections were made, including seven with live parachutists. As a result, some changes had to be introduced into the ejection seat's design.

Tu-4LL (also DR-1/DR-2, '94/1' and '94/2') engine testbeds

The Tu-4 was also used for testing new piston, turboprop and turbojet engines. Actually the first *Bull* of this kind was not a Tu-4 but a B-29 – specifically, the aforementioned B-29-5-BW '256 Black' which served as a testbed for the Shvetsov ASh-73TK radial (the development engine was fitted instead of the starboard inner Wright R-3350 Twin Cyclone). After passing a rigorous test programme the ASh-73TK was used successfully for many years on the Tu-4 and the Beriyev Be-6 *Madge* flying boat.

In 1950 the ninth Kazan'-built Tu-4 (c/n 220204), appropriately serialled '9 Black',

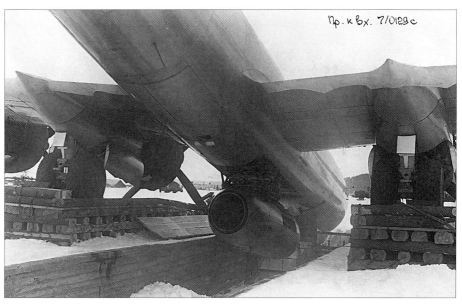

The photos on this page depict another Tu-4LL (c/n 230113) in its early configuration with a Mikulin AM-3 turbojet (known as the DR-1). The aircraft is parked over a concrete-lined trench for ground-running the engine; note the foreign object damage (FOD) prevention screen ahead of the turbojet in the lower photo.

Above: One of the 'turboprop' Tu-4LLs known as the 'aircraft 94/2'. The No. 3 nacelle houses a 2TV-2F coupled turboprop engine with contra-rotating propellers as fitted to Tupolev's '95-1' - the first prototype of the *Bear-A*. Note the air data boom mounted on the flight deck glazing.

Above: This Tu-4LL was used to test the Ivchenko AI-20 and Kuznetsov NK-4 turboprops with AV-68 propellers. The portside overwing installation is an AI-20 as fitted to the Il'yushin IL-18 airliner while the underwing installation on the starboard wing is an NK-4 as fitted to the Antonov An-10 airliner!

One more Tu-4LL (c/n 221203), apparently coded '22 Red'. This aircraft is equipped with two AI-20 turboprops in the Nos. 1 and 4 nacelles (both installed in the underwing position).

Above: Tu-4LL '9 Black' (c/n 220204) was fitted with two Dobrynin VD-3TK radial engines driving AV-28 contra-rotating propellers.

Above: Another view of Tu-4LL '9 Black', showing to advantage the shape of the new nacelles housing the development engines.

Tu-4 '29 Red' (c/n 2207510) was one of six converted in 1952 to Tu-4NM drone launcher aircraft carrying La-17 target drones on underwing pylons. The results proved disappointing and the La-17 was adapted for ground launch.

The No. 4 NK-4 engine of the Tu-4LL shown on page 56. Note the aft position of the oil cooler.

was modified for testing of the 2,000-hp Dobrynin VD-3TK; this liquid-cooled engine was intended for the Alekseyev I-218 attack aircraft which in the event never materialised. Two VD-3TKs driving AV-28 four-bladed contra-rotating propellers were fitted in place of the outer ASh-73TKs. Like most Tu-4s filling this role, the aircraft was designated **Tu-4LL** (*letayuschchaya laboratoriya* – literally 'flying laboratory'. **Note:** In Russian the term *letayuschchaya laboratoriya* is used indiscriminately to denote any kind of testbed or research aircraft.)

In the second half of the 1950s the Tupolev OKB converted two *Bulls* (c/ns 221203 and 225402) into engine testbeds. Initially these two aircraft were used to test the engines intended for the Tupolev 'aircraft 80' and 'aircraft 85' long-range bombers – the 4,000-hp Shvetsov ASh-2TK and 4,700-hp ASh-2K 28-cylinder four-row air-cooled radi-

als and the 4,300-hp Dobrynin VD-4K 24-cylinder water-cooled radial engine driving an AV-44 four-bladed propeller. (The ASh-2TK never flew on anything except a testbed, but the other two engines subsequently powered the two prototypes of the '85'.) Once again the development engine was installed in the No. 3 position.

When turboprop engines came on the scene these two aircraft were further modified for testing early Soviet turboprops – the 5,163-ehp Kuznetsov TV-2, the 6,250-ehp TV-2F (*forseerovannyy* – uprated), the 7,650-ehp TV-2M (*modifitseerovannyy* – modified) and the 12,500-ehp 2TV-2F coupled engine (the Tu-4LL with the latter engine was also known as the '**aircraft 94/2**'). The '**aircraft 94/1**' had the entire forward fuselage of 'aircraft 91' (Tu-91) *Boot* naval strike aircraft with a single TV-2F turboprop supplanting the starboard inner ASh-73TK radial. An air data

boom looking like a tripod was installed on the fuselage nose.

In most cases the development engine was again installed in the No. 3 position. Tu-4LL c/n 225402 (serial unknown) was an exception, with a pair of TV-2 engines (c/ns 16 and 17) replacing both outer ASh-73TKs. In this configuration it made 27 test flights totalling 72 hours 51 minutes. Unfortunately the aircraft was lost on 8th October 1951 when the No. 4 engine caught fire during a planned in-flight restart attempt. The fire was caused by a leak of burning fuel into the turboprop's nacelle through the joint between the engine and the extension jetpipe. The crew managed a forced landing, escaping from the burning aircraft which was destroyed by the fire.

After completing their trials programmes on the Tu-4LL the TV-2M and the 2TV-2F went on to power two aircraft designed by the Tupolev OKB – the '91' (Tu-91) naval strike aircraft and the '95-1' heavy bomber (the first prototype of the Tu-95 *Bear-A*) respectively. Both aircraft had an unhappy fate, the '91' falling victim to a whimsical head of state (Nikita S. Khruschchov's predilection towards missiles was the bane of the Soviet aircraft industry's existence) while the '95-1' was lost in a crash caused by an engine fire which necessitated a change of powerplant.

One peculiarity of the turboprop testbeds was that the power of the development engine exceeded that of the original ASh-73TK by a factor of 2 to 5. This required major structural changes; in particular, the engine bearer(s) had to be designed anew to convey the much higher forces. Also, the development engine(s) ran on kerosene instead of aviation petrol, which meant a separate fuel system had to be provided for the turboprop(s).

In 1954 one more *Bull* was urgently converted into a Tu-4LL in the wake of the crash of the '95-1' bomber. This aircraft served as a testbed for the 12,500-ehp Kuznetsov TV-12 driving AV-60 four-bladed contraprops of 5.6 m (18 ft 4½ in) diameter. The massive engine was again installed in the No. 3 position, the nacelle protruding far ahead of the wing leading edge so that the propeller rotation plane was almost in line with the flight deck. After passing its test programme the TV-12 was installed in the second prototype of the *Bear* (the '95-2'), subsequently entering production as the NK-12. To this day it remains the world's most powerful turboprop (later versions, starting with the NK-12M, deliver 15,000 ehp for take-off!) and has done sterling service on the Tu-95, Tu-142 *Bear-F* long-range anti-submarine warfare aircraft, Tu-114 *Cleat* long-haul airliner, Tu-126 *Moss* AWACS, An-22 Antey (Antheus; NATO code name *Cock*) heavy-lift transport aircraft and Alekseyev A-90 Orlyonok (Eaglet) transport *ekra-*

Tu-4 '4114 Red' (c/n 2806501) was one of several *Bulls* re-engined with locally manufactured AI-20 copies in China. Later it was further modified to become an AWACS testbed with a conventional rotodome.

noplan (wing-in-ground effect craft) for more than 40 years now.

The next Tu-4LL converted by LII for testing turboprop engines in the mid-1950s (identity unknown) was a most unusual testbed. Like the ill-fated Tu-4LL c/n 225402, it had two development engines – initially 4,000-ehp Kuznetsov NK-4s and then identically rated Ivchenko AI-20s driving AV-68 four-bladed propellers – in the Nos. 1 and 4 positions. Both engines had been developed for the An-10 Ookraina (the Ukraine; NATO code name Cat) and the Il'yushin IL-18 Moskva (Moscow, the 'second-generation' IL-18 of 1957; NATO code name Coot-A) and the AI-20 was eventually selected to power both types. The unusual part was that the port turboprop was installed above the wing as on the IL-18, while the starboard turboprop was mounted below the wing as on the An-10! This 'lop-sided' installation served to check the behaviour of the engine in different operating conditions.

Tu-4LL testbeds with experimental turboprop engines were operated by the Tupolev OKB and LII in 1951-60. Interestingly, LII sources state that three, not four, examples (including the crashed one) were equipped with turboprops.

Three other Tu-4LLs were used to test new jet engines. Among other things, the Myasishchev OKB together with LII converted a Moscow-built Tu-4 (c/n 230113) into a testbed for the 5,000-kgp (11,023-lb st) Lyul'ka AL-5 turbojet which was considered as a possible powerplant for the M-4 at an early development stage. In this guise the aircraft was known in the Myasishchev OKB as the **DR-1**; D stood for dvigatel' (engine, a reference to the engine testbed role) while the R was the Bull's product code. Later, when the much more powerful Mikulin AM-3 turbojet rated at 8,700 kgp (19,180 lb st) for take-off was selected for the M-4, this replaced the AL-5 development engine on Tu-4LL c/n 230113 in January 1952 and the in-house designation at OKB-23 was changed to **DR-2**.

The turbojet was installed in the forward bomb bay in a special nacelle which could move up and down on a system of levers. It was semi-recessed in the fuselage for take-off and landing to give adequate ground clearance, extending clear of the fuselage into the slipstream before start-up; it was also possible to extend the engine on the ground when the aircraft was parked over a special trench with concrete-lined walls and a jet blast deflector for ground runs. When the nacelle was retracted the air intake was blanked off by a movable shutter to prevent windmilling and foreign object damage. In an emergency (for instance, if the hydraulic retraction mechanism failed) the development engine could be jettisoned to permit a safe landing, special pyrotechnical guillotines cutting the fuel and electric lines. The test engineer and his assistant sat in the centre pressurised cabin; the cabin floor incorporated a glazed window for inspecting the nozzle of the development engine.

The testing of the AM-3 involved a lot of defining and refining, but it was worth the effort as it enabled the M-4 and the Tu-16 to quickly complete their test programmes and enter production.

Later two more Bulls (one of them was probably c/n 230314) were converted into Tu-4LLs for testing jet engines. Apart from the two types mentioned above, the three aircraft had been used to test a wide range of engines by 1962 – the 2,700-kgp (5,952-lb st) AM-5F, the 3,300-kgp (7,275-lb st) Mikulin RD-9B afterburning turbojet, the 5,110-kgp (11,266-lb st) Tumanskiy R11-300, the 900-kgp (1,984-lb st) Tumanskiy RU19-300, the 6,830-kgp (15,057-lb st) Lyul'ka AL-7 turbojet and its versions – the 7,260-kgp (16,005-lb st) AL-7P and the 9,200-kgp (20,282-lb st) afterburning AL-7F, the 8,440-kgp (18,607-lb st) Klimov VK-3 afterburning turbofan, the 6,270-kgp (13,823-lb st) VK-7 turbojet, the Dobrynin VD-5, the 11,000-kgp (24,251-lb st) VD-7 afterburning turbojet and the 5,400-kgp (11,905-lb st) Solov'yov D-20P turbofan. The method of installation and the testing techniques were basically the same as on the DR-1/DR-2 testbed, except in the case of the VD-5 and VD-7; these bulky turbojets were positioned too low even when stowed in the bomb bay, necessitating a special non-retractable landing gear with lengthened struts.

In addition to the M-4 and Tu-16, the jet engines tested on the Tu-4LL powered the '98' (Tu-98) experimental bomber; the Tu-110 Cooker medium-haul and Tu-124 short-haul airliners; the Mikoyan/Gurevich SM-1, SM-2, SM-9, MiG-19 Farmer, Ye-5, Ye-6, Ye-7, I-1, I-7 and MiG-21F Fishbed-A fighters; the Sukhoi Su-7 Fitter-A fighter-bomber/Su-7U Moujik trainer, Sukhoi T-3, S-1, Su-9 and Su-11 Fishpot-A/B interceptors; the Yakovlev Yak-25 Flashlight, Yak-27 Mangrove and Yak-28 Brewer/Firebar tactical aircraft family and the Yak-30 advanced trainer; the Il'yushin IL-40 attack aircraft and IL-46 tactical bomber; the Myasishchev 3M/3MS/3MN/3MD Bison-B/C which passed manufacturer's flight tests and State acceptance trials in the 1950s and early 1960s. Many of these aircraft entered production, forming the backbone of the Soviet Air Force and (in the case of the Tu-124) the Soviet airline, Aeroflot, in the 1960s.

Avionics and weapons testbeds

The Tu-4 was also used extensively for verifying various new (mostly military) avionics systems. These included the Rym-S targeting system, a remote guidance/targeting system for torpedo boats and the PRS-1 Argon gun ranging radar for the tail gunner's station (PRS = pritsel rahdiolokatsionnyy strelkovyy – 'radio gusight'). The latter programme was especially intensive – a small batch of Tu-4s was actually built with PRS-1 gun ranging radars; the model later became a standard fit for Tupolev and Myasishchev bombers.

The Tu-4 served as the testbed for the DISS-1 Doppler speed and drift indicator (doplerovskiy izmeritel' skorosti i snosa), the ARK-5 automatic direction finder (avtomaticheskiy rahdiokompas), the RSIU-2 and RSIU-3 communication radios, the Booivol-Kod (Buffalo-Code) blind landing system, short-range radio navigation (SHORAN) slot antennas built into the fin, very low frequency trailing wire aerials (TWAs) and many other avionics items which became a standard fit for Soviet aircraft.

Additionally, the Bull was used for testing new weapons systems. In 1948-49 the Soviet Air Force considered the possibility of equipping the Tu-4 with cruise missiles developed by V. N. Chelomey's OKB. Also, in the late 1940s a minelayer and torpedo-bomber version of the Tu-4 for the Soviet Navy was under consideration.

In 1950 the OKB-2 weapons design bureau led by A. D. Nadiradze (renamed GosNII-642 in December 1951) developed the UB-2000F and UB-5000F guided bombs (UB = oopravlyayemaya aviabomba) aimed by means of an OPB-2UP optical sight and a radio command channel. During trials in 1953 a modified Tu-4 carried two such bombs on underwing pylons. The results proved disappointing and the UB-2000F had to undergo a redesign, eventually being included in the VVS inventory two years later as the UB-2F Chaika (Seagull, aka izdeliye 4A22). The UB-5000F tested in 1954 was of similar design but featured a TV command guidance system, a TV camera in the nose transmitting a 'bomb's eye view' to a screen at the bomb-aimer's station; the bomb-aimer then manually corrected the weapon's flight path. Pretty soon, however, the Soviet Union discontinued work on guided bombs and the weapons system was never introduced on the Tu-4.

Perhaps the most unusual weapon carried by the Bull was the RS-2-U air-to-air missile (NATO code name AA-1 Alkali), fitted in an attempt to enhance the bomber's defensive capability in the rear hemisphere. Guidance was effected by means of the suitably modified Kobal't radar; the missiles were carried on launch rails under the aft fuselage and launched by the radar operator.

A few Tu-4s modified in this fashion even saw operational service with the 25th NBAP (nochnoy bombardirovochnyy aviapolk – night bomber regiment). Generally, however, the system proved unsatisfactory and did not gain wide use. Target lock-on was unstable, the launch range was rather short and the missiles were expensive, not to mention the fact that they were intended for the Air Defence Force, not the bomber arm.

Chinese turboprop conversions

In the 1970s the few Tu-4s remaining in service with the Chinese People's Liberation Army Air Force (PLAAF) were re-engined with 4,250-ehp Shanghai WJ-6 turboprops (Wojiang-6, 'Turboprop Type 6', Chinese derivatives of the Ivchenko AI-20K) driving locally made copies of the AV-68 four-bladed reversible-pitch propeller. The new engines were markedly smaller in diameter but much longer than the original ASh-73TK radials; this meant that new fairings had to be made, resulting in weird-looking nacelles with a pronounced bottle shape. The jetpipes were located on the outer or lower surfaces of the nacelles. To compensate for the destabilising effect of the extra area ahead of the cg, small pentagonal endplate fins were mounted at the tips of the horizontal tail.

The 'Turbo Bulls' remained in service with the PLAAF until the 1980s. At least two such bombers were further converted into special mission aircraft described below.

Chinese drone launcher version

One of the Tu-4s thus modified, a Kazan'-built example serialled '4134 Red' (c/n 225008), was converted into a drone launcher which could perhaps be described as the Chinese counterpart of the Lockheed DC-130 Hercules. Two simple cradles were fitted under the outer wing panels for carrying Chang Hong-1 reconnaissance drones. The Chang Hong-1 was a reverse-engineered version of the Ryan BQM-34A Firebee, a number of which had been captured in reasonably good condition by the Chinese in the late 1960s.

Tu-4 '4134 Red' is now preserved at the PLAAF Museum at Datangshan airbase north of Beijing.

Chinese AWACS testbed

Another 'Turbo Bull', this time a Kuibyshev-built Tu-4 ('4114 Red', c/n 2806501), was converted into an aerodynamics testbed for a prospective airborne warning and control system (AWACS) aircraft. A conventional rotodome with two dielectric segments was mounted above the wing centre section on two N-struts with bracing wires in between; however, no radar was ever installed in it. Additionally, a fairly large dielectric canoe fairing was added aft of the nosewheel well, with a smaller canoe fairing and two thimble fairings aft of the wings. A small ventral fin was added to improve directional stability.

The AWACS testbed is likewise on display at the PLAAF Museum. Interestingly, it has been reported that neither of the two *Bulls* at Datangshan had any non-standard equipment when they were first noted there in 1990 and that they were active aircraft involved in research and development programmes when not on display!

Above and below: Turboprop-powered Tu-4 '4134 Red' (c/n 225008) was converted into a drone launcher aircraft carrying two Chang Hong-1 drones under the wings. It is seen here at the PLAAF Museum in company with an An-12, a Mil' Mi-8 and a de Havilland DH.121 Trident; note the stabilizer endplate fins.

Chapter 4

The Tu-4 in Detail

The following structural description applies to the standard production Tu-4.

Type: Four-engined long-range heavy bomber designed for day and night operation in visual meteorological conditions (VMC) and instrument meteorological conditions (IMC).

Fuselage: All-metal semi-monocoque stressed-skin structure of streamlined cigar shape and circular cross-section with stamped frames (61 in all) and stringers. Near cutouts the structure was reinforced by additonal structural members (eg, the bomb bay aperture was flanked by beams). The fuselage skin was made of D16AT duralumin sheets of mostly 0.8 to 1.8 mm (0.03 to 0.07 in) thickness increasing to 2 mm (0.078 in) at the most stressed locations; it was attached to the internal structure by mostly flush rivets. Fuselage length was 30.18 m (99 ft 0 in), maximum diameter 2.9 m (9 ft 6 in).

Structurally the fuselage consisted of six sections: the flight deck glazing frame (Section F-1), the forward pressure cabin (Section F-2, frames 2 through 13), the centre fuselage (Section F-3, frames 13 through 37), the centre pressure cabin (Section F-4, frames 37 through 46), the aft fuselage (Section F-5, frames 46 through 57), and the rear fuselage or tail section (Section F-6, frames 57 through 61) which was the tail gunner's pressurised compartment. All sections were assembled in

The forward fuselage of a typical late-production Tu-4.

separate jigs and mated by means of flanges. The forward and centre pressure cabins were connected by a pressurised crawlway passing along the top of Section F-3.

The fuselage housed the greater part of the systems and equipment (some of which was housed in the pressurised sections), the offensive and defensive armament and, of course, the crew. The centre fuselage incorporated two bomb bays closed by hinged clamshell doors and separated by the wing carry-through box (centre section).

The *forward pressure cabin* accommodated six persons: the crew captain, the co-pilot, the bomb-aimer, the flight engineer, the navigator and the radio operator. The centre pressure cabin was occupied by the three gunners working the remote-controlled barbettes and the bomb-aiming radar operator, while the tail gunner had the rear pressure cabin (rear fuselage) all to himself.

The *flight deck glazing frame* was a dome-shaped casting made of magnesium alloy. Some glazing panels were made of triplex sil-

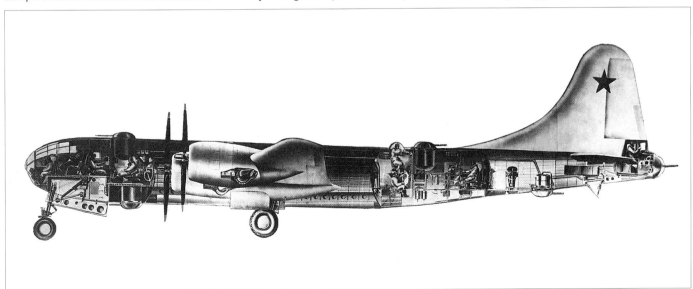
This cutaway drawing shows the location of the crew, defensive armament, bomb bays and equipment in the Tu-4's fuselage.

Above and below: The flight deck glazing consisted of numerous small panels and blended smoothly into the fuselage contour.

icate glass and the remainder of Plexiglas. Additionally, part of the forward pressure cabin roof was glazed (again both silicate glass and Plexiglas being used), while the centre pressure cabin featured three Plexiglas sighting blisters (two lateral and one dorsal). The tail gunner's station glazing was mostly Plexiglas, with silicate glass panels at the rear.

The crew was protected against bullets and cannon shell fragments by steel armour and bulletproof glass. The pilots enjoyed the protection offered by triplex bulletproof glass panels, forward armour plates, armoured seat backs and hinged rear armour screens. The gunners and radar operator in the centre cabin were protected by an armoured door and an armoured box housing the weapons control system processors, while the tail gunner was protected by a steel plate and triplex bulletproof glass panels.

Wings: Cantilever mid-wing monoplane; sweepback 0°, aspect ratio 11.5, taper 2.36. The wings utilised an airfoil similar to the RAF-34 airfoil.

The wings were of all-metal, two-spar stressed-skin construction; they were built in three sections (centre section and outer wings). The *centre section* comprised a centre portion (consisting of two halves joined at the fuselage centreline), a detachable leading edge and a trailing-edge portion incorporating flaps; it featured 32 ribs and 24 stringers. The thickness of the duralumin skin varied from 1.0 to 2.5 mm (0.039 to 0.098 in on the lower panels and 4 to 5 mm (0.157 to 0.196 in) on the upper panels. The spars, ribs, stringers and heavy-gauge skin formed a tough torsion box carrying the engine nacelles and main landing gear units; it also housed the main fuel tanks. The wing centre section was mated to the centre fuselage (Section F-3).

Each *outer wing* was built in four pieces – the torsion box, a detachable leading edge, a detachable tip fairing and an aileron incorporating a servo tab. The outer wings were joined to the wing centre section at ribs No. 14L/14R and the upper/lower spar caps.

The two-section slotted flaps were of all-metal single-spar construction. They occupied the entire trailing edge of the wing centre section (up to ribs No. 14L/14R), making up 19% of the wing area. Flap settings were 25° for take-off and 45° for landing.

The ailerons were one-piece single-spar structures with a rear false spar, 32 ribs and fabric skin, except for the leading edge which was skinned with duralumin. The trailing edge incorporated an all-metal trim tab.

Tail unit: Cantilever conventional tail surfaces of all-metal stressed-skin construction. The tail unit comprised a fin, a fin root fillet, a stabilizer assembly, a rudder and two elevators; the fixed components were joined to each other and to the fuselage by bolts. The rudder and elevators were both aerodynamically balanced and mass-balanced.

The *vertical tail* utilised a symmetrical aerofoil section. The fin was a two-spar structure with a front false spar, 23 ribs, a forward bulkhead and duralumin skin 0.6 mm (0.023 in) thick. The fin root fillet had 24 frames, a number of stringers, a 'false spar' along the leading edge and duralumin skin.

The one-piece rudder had an all-metal framework with a single spar, a rear false spar for trim tab attachment, 16 ribs, leading-edge and trailing-edge fairings and fabric skin.

The *horizontal tail* featured an asymmetrical inverted aerofoil section and zero dihedral. The fixed-incidence stabilizers were built as a one-piece riveted structure with two spars, 27 ribs, 22 stringers and duralumin skin. The horizontal tail was attached to fuselage frame No. 53.

The interconnected elevators were symmetrical single-spar riveted structures with 20 ribs, a rear false spar for trim tab attachment and fabric skin.

Landing gear: Electrically retractable tricycle type, with twin wheels on each unit; wheel track 8.68 m (28 ft 5 in), wheelbase 10.44 m (34 ft 3 in). A retractable tail bumper was provided to protect the rear fuselage in the event of overrotation on take-off or a tail-down landing.

The nose unit retracted aft, the main units forward into the rear portions of the inboard engine nacelles. All three landing gear struts and the tail bumper were actuated by electrically powered screwjacks featuring auto-brake mechanisms, with back-up electric actuators for emergency extension and, in case of need, emergency retraction.

The main units had 1,450 x 520 mm (57.08 x 20.47 in) wheels with hydraulic brakes. The steerable nose unit was equipped with 950 x 350 mm (37.4 x 13.77 in) non-braking wheels and a shimmy damper. All of the landing gear units were fitted with oleo-pneumatic shock absorbers.

The nosewheel well was closed by twin lateral doors, the mainwheel wells by twin lateral doors and a small rear door hinged to the oleo leg. All doors remained open when the gear was down.

Powerplant: Four Shvetsov ASh-73TK air-cooled 18-cylinder two-row radial engines delivering 2,400 hp at 2,600 rpm for take-off and 2,000 hp at 2,400 rpm in cruise mode (at nominal power). The engine had a planetary reduction gearbox with a ratio of 0.375.

The ASh-73TK had a length of 2.29 m (7 ft 6 in), a diameter of 1.37 m (4 ft 6 in) and a dry weight of 1,339 kg (2,951 lb). Specific fuel consumption was 350 g/hp·hr (0.77 lb/hp·hr) at take-off power and 315-335 g/hp·hr (0.69-0.74 lb/hp·hr) at nominal power.

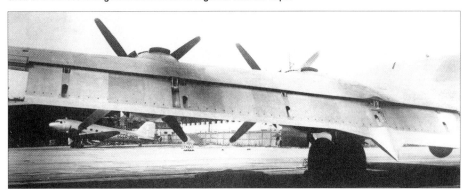

The wing trailing edge with the flaps fully retracted (above) and fully deployed (below). Note how the rear ends of the inboard engine nacelles moved together with the flaps.

Above: An overall view of the tail unit, showing the rubber de-icer boots.

The tail unit, looking aft. This view shows well that the Tu-4 had zero dihedral on the horizontal tail.

The nose landing gear unit (left) and the port main landing gear unit.

The engine had a two-stage supercharging system to improve its high-altitude characteristics. The first stage consisted of two TK-19 exhaust-driven turbochargers (*toorbokompressor*) operating in parallel; they were automatically controlled by an electronic governor and could be selected on or off from the flight deck. After passing through an intercooler the air was fed to the second stage, a PTsN single-speed engine-driven centrifugal blower (*privodnoy tsentrobezhnyy nagnetahtel'*).

Engine starting was electrical by means of an electrically actuated inertia starter known as 'unit 263'. If electric power was unavailable, the starters could be spun up and engaged manually.

Each engine drove a V3-A3 or V3B-A5 four-bladed variable-pitch propeller (V = [*vozdooshnyy*] *vint* – airscrew) of 5.06 m (16 ft 7 in) diameter. Constant engine rpm was automatically maintained by an R-18V or R-18A engine governor (R = *regoolyator*) which was also responsible for propeller feathering.

The engines were mounted on welded truss-type engine bearers in individual nacelles; the latter were attached to the front spar of the wing centre section and to the wing skin by gussets. The nacelles were of stressed-skin semi-monocoque construction.

The port outboard (left) and starboard inboard engine nacelles, showing details of the V3B-A5 propellers.

Each engine bearer was attached to the nacelle structure by six fittings and the engine was attached to the bearer via nine vibration dampers. Electrically actuated multi-segment flaps were located at the trailing edge of each engine cowling for controlling the cooling airflow.

The powerplant controls were located on both pilots' control consoles and the flight engineer's console. All control inputs were transmitted by means of cables.

An M-10 auxiliary power unit was installed on the port side of the unpressurised aft fuselage (Section F-5) for providing emergency power. The M-10 was a 10-hp two-stroke engine driving a GS-5000 generator.

Control system: Conventional mechanical flight control system with full dual controls, a control column and rudder pedals being provided for both pilots. Control inputs were transmitted to all control surfaces, including trim tabs, by cables and pulleys.

The flight controls were manual (ie, unpowered). The system included an AP-5 electric autopilot.

Fuel system: 22 flexible fuel cells (bag tanks) holding a total of 20,180 litres (4,439 Imp gal) in the wing centre section torsion box. The tanks were divided into four groups, one for each engine. Fuel was fed to the engines by electric transfer pumps or by gravity. For long-range missions three auxiliary fuel tanks holding 2,420 litres (532 Imp gal) each could be installed in the forward bomb bay.

Oil system: Each engine had its individual oil system housed inside the respective engine nacelle. Five bag-type oil tanks (four main tanks and one auxiliary tank) held a total of 1,540 litres (339 Imp gal). Type 729A oil coolers were located in the lower portions of the nacelles, the airflow and hence oil temperature being controlled by a flap at the rear of the oil cooler air duct. Oil temperature was adjusted by an ARTM-46 controller (*avtomaticheskiy regoolyator temperatoory mahsla* – automatic oil temperature governor, 1946 model).

Electrical system: The Tu-4 featured more than 150 electric servo systems and actuators; 28V DC power for these was supplied by six engine-driven 9-kilowatt GS-9000M generators (two on each outer engine and one on each inner engine), replaced by GSR-9000 generators on Kazan'-built aircraft from c/n 225301 onwards, Kuibyshev-built aircraft from c/n 184132 onwards and all Moscow-built aircraft from c/n 230101 onwards. Back-up 28V DC power was provided by a 12A-30 (28 V, 30 A·h) silver-zinc battery and a 5-kilowatt GS-5000 generator driven by the M-10 APU. A ground power receptacle was also fitted, allowing a starter cart to be connected to the aircraft.

Above: This view of a decommissioned and sadly dilapidated Tu-4 ('08 Red', c/n 226002) gives details of the engines' cooling flaps and access panels.

The Tu-4's flight deck, showing the captain's (above) and co-pilot's (below) control columns, the two banks of throttles, the rudder pedal hinges and the large elevator trim tab handwheels.

Above: The tail gunner's station of Tu-4 '22 Red' with a DK-3 tail barbette. Note the gunner's entry/escape hatch on the port side.

Above: The dorsal and lateral sighting blisters in the centre pressure cabin. The rear dorsal barbette with two 23-mm NR-23 cannon is also visible.

The rear ventral remote-controlled barbette.

26V/400 Hz and 115V/400 Hz AC power for some equipment items was supplied by two PK-750F converters and two MA-1500K converters (one of the latter served the IFF system and the other powered the radar set).

The electrical system used single wiring throughout, with BPVL type wire or BPVLE type shielded wire. There were three electrical circuits: main DC (powered by the engine-driven generators), emergency DC (powered by the storage battery and the APU) and AC (powered by the PK-750F combined AC converters).

Interior lighting included overhead dome lights, fluorescent lights, PS-45 and PSG-45 directional lamps, an ARUFOSh ultraviolet light system for illuminating the instrument panels, and cabin wander lights. *Exterior lighting* comprised BANO-45 port and starboard navigation lights (*bortovoy aeronavigatsionnyy ogon'*), retractable LFSV-45 landing lights in the undersurface of both outer wings, VBSOS-45 and KOS-45 identification lights and PSSO-45 formation lights.

Hydraulic system: Two hydraulic systems (main and back-up) worked the wheel brakes and the nosewheel steering mechanism. Hydraulic pressure for normal braking was supplied by a hydraulic accumulator charged by an electrically driven pump ('unit 265M'); a hand-driven hydraulic pump was used in an emergency. Hydraulic pressure was 56-70 bars (800-1,000 psi). The systems used GMTs-2 grade hydraulic fluid.

Fire suppression system: An OSU fire suppression system using carbon dioxide as an extinguishing agent (hence OSU for ogne-tooshitel' statsionarnyy ooglekislotnyy – 'stationary CO_2 fire extinguisher') was used to fight engine fires. The system's two bottles charged with CO_2 were installed in the nosewheel well. Three portable fire extinguishers were provided in the pressure cabins for combating any fires breaking out there.

Armament: The *offensive armament* consisted of free-fall bombs carried internally in two bomb bays; depending on the mission the bombs were loaded into the rear bay or both bays (for extra-long range missions the forward bomb bay was occupied by auxiliary fuel tanks). Initially a mixed complement of bomb racks was fitted, but from Kazan'-built Tu-4 c/n 225701 onwards a standardised set of bomb racks was introduced; this allowed FAB-250M46 and FAB-500M46 bombs to be suspended on two rows of shackles, doubling the number of 250- and 500-kg (551- and 1,102-lb) bombs carried by the Tu-4.

Possible payload options are detailed in the tables on the opposite page. (**Note:** the bombs were suspended in two rows for options 1-9 and in one row for options 10-13.)

Normal and emergency bomb release could be performed by the bomb-aimer, the captain or the radar operator. The bombs could be dropped singly, in series of one, two or four, or in a salvo by means of the ESBR-45 electric bomb release mechanism (*elektrosbrahsyvatel'*). A special signal light was provided, allowing the lead aircraft in a formation to give the 'bombs away' signal to the wingmen while maintaining radio silence. The bomb bay doors were actuated electromechanically and operated by the bomb-aimer.

In VMC the bomb-aimer used an OPB-4S optical bombsight (*opticheskiy pritsel bombardirovochnyy*) installed in the foremost part of the forward pressure cabin. This was superseded by the OPB-5SN model from c/n 221901 onwards in Kazan' and from c/n 184402 onwards in Kuibyshev, whereas all Moscow-built Tu-4s had the new bombsight. Data from the bombsight were fed to the AP-5 autopilot, enabling the bomb-aimer to take over control of the aircraft during the bombing run. In IMC bombing was done using the display of the Kobal't radar for targeting, the bomb-aimer and the radar operator working together; the radar operator could also perform the entire operation himself if necessary.

The *defensive armament* of early Tu-4s consisted of the PV-20 system (*pushechnoye vo'oroozheniye* – cannon armament) comprised four pairs of 20-mm (.78 calibre) Berezin B-20E cannon in remote-controlled barbettes (two dorsal barbettes and two ventral barbettes) and a tail barbette with three B-20 cannon. From c/ns 223201, 184309 and 230102 onwards the Tu-4 featured the PV-23 defensive armament system with two 23-mm (.90 calibre) Nudel'man/Rikhter NR-23 cannon in each station (a DK-3 tail barbette was used). The five barbettes were positioned so as to give 360° coverage, excluding 'blind spots' in the sectors of fire.

The cannon barbettes were located outside the pressurised areas of the airframe and were remote-controlled by an electric servo system using synchros. Aiming was done by means of five PS-48 sighting stations (*pritsel'naya stahntsiya*): forward (in the forward pressure cabin), dorsal, port and starboard (at the three sighting blisters in the centre pressure cabin) and rear (at the tail gunner's station). All sighting stations except the tail gunner's had two barbette control modes (primary and auxiliary), allowing the gunners to operate barbettes other than those they were assigned to if one of the crew was incapacitated. In primary mode the bomb-aimer operated both dorsal barbettes and the forward ventral barbette; the rear dorsal barbette was operated by the dorsal gunner, the rear ventral barbette by the lateral gunners and the tail barbette by the tail gunner. In auxiliary mode the forward dorsal barbette could be operated from the dorsal sighting station, the

The Tu-4's offensive weapons options

a) mixed set of bomb racks

Payload option	Rack type	Bomb type	Quantity of bombs fwd bay	aft bay	Warload, kg (lb)
1	KD4-546A KD3-246A	FAB-250M43	12	12	6,000 (13,228)
2	KD4-546A KD3-246A	FAB-250M46	12	12	6,000 (13,228)
3	KD4-546A	FAB-500M43	6	6	5,830 (12,853)
4	KD4-546A	FAB-500M44 FAB-500M46	6	6	6,000 (13,228)
5	KD4-546A	FAB-1000M44 (shortened)	4	4	7,120 (15,697)
6	KD4-248	FAB-1000M44 (shortened)	4	4	7,120 (15,697)
7	KD4-248	FAB-1500M44	4	4	11,840 (26,103)
8	KD4-248	FAB-3000M44	2	2	11,930 (26,301)

b) standard set of bomb racks

Payload option	Rack type	Bomb type	Quantity of bombs fwd bay	aft bay	Warload, kg (lb)
1	K34-547 SD3-248	FAB-50	20 4	20 4	2,000 (4,409)
2	KD3-547 SD3-248	FAB-100	20 4	20 4	5,000 (11,023)
3	KD3-547 SD3-248	FAB-250M46	20	20	10,600 (23,369)
4	KD4-547 SD3-248	FAB-250M46	10 4	10 4	12,000 (26,455)
5	KD4-547 SD3-248	FAB-250M43 or FAB-250M44	10 2	10 2	6,000 (13,228)
6	KD4-547 SD3-248	FAB-500M43 or FAB-250M44	6 1	6 1	6,800 (14,991)
7	KD4-248	FAB-1000M44	4	4	7,120 (15,697)
8	KD4-248	FAB-1500M46	4	4	11,840 (26,103)
9	KD4-248	FAB-3000M46	2	2	11,930 (26,301)
10		FAB-6000M46	2	2	11,930 (26,301)
11		FAB-250M44	12	12	6,000 (13,228)
12		FAB-500M44	7	7	6,802 (14,996)
13		FAB-1000M44	4	4	7,120 (15,697)

tail barbette and the forward ventral barbette from the lateral stations.

The weapons control system included electric barbette actuators and the aforementioned servo system which controlled these actuators by means of servo amplifiers and amplidyne generators. The system featured processors which automatically introduced target lead and compensated for parallax (caused by the distance between the gunner and the barbette) and shell ballistics.

The ammunition was stored in ammo boxes located inside the dorsal and ventral barbettes or, in the case of the tail barbette, in the rear fuselage. The total ammunition complement was 3,150 rounds. The cannon were cocked by an electrically controlled pneumatic mechanism and then recharged by recoil action, which allowed the heavy-calibre weapons to have a high rate of fire and be rel-

atively lightweight. The NR-23 weighed 39 kg (85 lb) and fired 200-gram (7.06-oz.) projectiles (the complete rounds weighed 340 g/12 oz); the rate of fire was 800-950 rounds per minute and muzzle velocity was 680 m/sec (2,231 ft/sec). The ammunition belts to the dorsal and tail turrets were fed electrically.

Avionics and equipment:

a) navigation equipment: ARK-4 or ARK-5 Amur automatic direction finder (ADF – *avtomaticheskiy rahdiokompas*), RV-2 *Kristahl* (Crystal) low-range radio altimeter (*rahdiovysotomer*), RV-10 high-range radio altimeter, MRP-45 marker beacon receiver (*markernyy rahdiopreeyomnik*) replaced by the MRP-48 *Dyatel* (Woodpecker) from c/ns 221401, 184402 and 230101 onwards. Tu-4s from c/ns 225501 and 230101 onwards, as well as c/ns 184232 and 184133, featured the SP-50 *Materik* (Continent) instrument landing

The radio operator's workstation.

system (ILS) comprising the SD-1 *Shipovnik* (Dog rose) distance measuring equipment (DME – *samolyotnyy dahl'nomer*), the KRP-F localiser receiver (*koorsovoy rahdiopreeyomnik*) and the GRP-2 glideslope beacon receiver (*glissahdnyy rahdiopreeyomnik*).

b) communications equipment: 1RSB-70 two-way communications radio with fixed and extendable aerials, SCR-274N two-way HF command radio (the American model was replaced by a Soviet RSB-5 radio from c/ns 222101, 184505 and 230101 onwards), 12RSU-10 VHF command radio with blade aerial (replaced by the RSU-5 radio from c/ns 221901, 184301 and 230101 onwards and then by the RSIU-3 radio), AVRA-45 emergency radio (*avareeynaya rahdiostahntsiya*). Early aircraft had an SPU-14 intercom replaced by the SPU-14M from c/ns 225501, 184430 and 230105 onwards.

c) flight instrumentation: US-7-OO airspeed indicator (ASI, *ookazahtel' skorosti*), VD-15A altimeter indicators, AGK-47B artificial horizons (*aviagorizont kombineerovannyy*), UPE-46 electric turn and bank indicator (*ookazahtel' povorota elektricheskiy*), VAR-30-3 vertical speed indicators (VSI – *variometr*), GPK-46 pneumatic directional gyros (*gheeropolukompas*), AB-52 drift sight, AK-53P astrocompass, KI-11 magnetic compasses, DIK-46 remote flux-gate compass (*distantsionnyy indooktivnyy kompas*), NK-45 co-ordinate indicator (*navigatsionnyy ko'ordi-*

nahtor), AP-5 electric autopilot, UVPD-3 cabin altitude/pressure indicator (*ookazahtel' vysoty i perepahda davleniya*), TP-49 pitot heads, AVR-M and AChKhO clocks, TNV-45 outside air thermometer (*termometr naroozhnovo vozdukha*) and TV-45 cabin air thermometer, UZS-46 wing flap position indicators, UYuZ-4 cowling flap position indicators, MG manometers, TE-2 engine tachometers, 2MB-2 fuel pressure indicators, 2MM-15 oil pressure indicators, 2MV-18-P vacuum meters, 2TUE-46 multi-purpose electric thermometers, 2TTsT-47 cylinder head thermometers, ME-4 electric oil meter (*maslomer elektricheskiy*) and BE-4 electric fuel meter (*benzinomer elektricheskiy*).

d) IFF equipment: Magniy (Magnesium) IFF interrogator (replaced by the Magniy-M from c/ns 224501, 184121 and 230103 onwards) and SRO-1 Bariy-M (Barium) IFF transponder (*samolyotnyy rahdiolokatsionnyy otvetchik*).

e) radar equipment: Kobal't (Cobalt) or Kobal't-M bomb-aiming radar with a 360° field of view installed in a hemispherical retractable radome under the centre fuselage.

f) photo equipment: For post-attack reconnaissance duties the basic bomber version initially featured an AFA-33/100 aerial camera for vertical photography, an AFA-27/T hand-held camera for oblique photography and a KS-50B cine camera. From c/ns 223001 and 184309 onwards the bomber version

could be equipped with one of three still cameras: an AFA-33/100, an AFA-33/75 with a shorter focal length for daytime photography or an NAFA-3S/50 for night photography, plus an AKS1-50 cine camera. The cameras were installed in an unpressurised bay in the aft fuselage.

g) interior equipment: Apart from crew seats, the Tu-4 featured a crew rest area with bunks. The flight deck glazing and other windows were provided with curtains (for blind flying training and for eye protection) and stained glass filters. Toilet buckets were provided for the crew.

Crew rescue equipment: All crew members were provided with PLK-45 parachutes. Two inflatable dinghies were provided to save the crew in the event of ditching.

Air conditioning and pressurization system: Three ventilation-type pressure cabins; the forward and centre cabins were connected by a pressurised crawlway and the centre and aft cabins by an air duct. The cabins were pressurised by air bled from the inner engines' superchargers; a variable pressure differential depending on the flight altitude was maintained by an RDK-47 pressure regulator (*regoolyator davleniya v kabinakh*). Cabin air temperature was controlled by RTVK temperature regulators which opened or closed the flaps of the air/air heat exchangers as necessary. Additionally, Model 900A electric heaters installed in the forward and centre cabins, plus a Model 1010 electric heater in the tail gunner's station, were provided to warm the air and demist the glazing.

Oxygen system: The permanent oxygen system comprised 15 individual oxygen supply stations, each with a KP-16 breathing apparatus, an IK-15 oxygen flow meter, an MK-13 manometer, indicators and a connector for charging a portable breathing apparatus. Eighteen oxygen bottles were connected by a system of piping; the nominal pressure was 30 kg/cm^2 (428.5 psi) and the oxygen supply was sufficient to keep a 15-man crew alive in totally decompressed cabins at 7,000-8,000 m (22,966-26,247 ft) for 4 hours 12 minutes. Additionally, 14 KP-19 portable breathing apparatus (*kislorodnyy preebor*) were provided; finally, each crewman's parachute pack included a KP-23 breathing apparatus enabling the crewman to survive a descent from high altitude after baling out.

De-icing system: B. F. Goodrich-type rubber de-icer boots on the wing, fin and stabilizer leading edges; compressed air for operating the de-icer boots was supplied by engine-driven vacuum pumps. The system worked automatically after being selected on. Alcohol de-icing for each of the propeller blades, with the alcohol contained in a 90-litre (20 Imp gal) tank; two filters and two SN-1 pumps.

Chapter 5

In Service

In late 1948 Iosif V. Stalin endorsed with his personal signature the report on the completion of the State acceptance trials; as mentioned earlier, by that time the first batch of ten bombers intended for service units of the Air Force was ready at Plant No. 22. After the successful demonstration of the 20 initial production machines at the November parade over the Red Square, Stalin personally endorsed the 'Report on State acceptance trials', which was a unique event in the aircraft industry. Conversion of Long-Range Aviation crews to the Tu-4 had begun as early as 1946 when the first production B-4 was still under construction. Training of flight personnel for the Tu-4 was started at the 203rd Guards Regiment. The first crew to have undertaken and completed training was that comprising first pilot V. V. Ponomarenko, navigator K. P. Ikonnikov, flight engineer Kishchenko and radio operator Daniuk. Several more crews were trained later; they subsequently took part in the joint testing of the Tu-4.

The 13th DBAD (*dahl'nebombardiro-voch-naya aviadiveeziya* – Long-Range Bomber Division) was chosen as the unit to be re-equipped with the Tu-4s, and the leading role was assigned to the 185th GvDBAP (*Gvardeyskiy dahl'nebombardiro-vochnyy aviapolk* – Guards Long-Range Bomber Regiment) based at Poltava. Pilots of this regiment underwent training in Kazan' under the auspices of the 890th DBAP which was turned into a training unit. Pilots of this regiment had accumulated much experience in flying the American Boeing B-17 Flying Fortress and Consolidated B-24 Liberator heavy bombers, which enabled them to be the first service pilots to convert to the Tu-4. The B-24s were widely used for mastering the technique of piloting heavy aircraft with a tricycle undercarriage. The regiment catered for training Tu-4 crews until 1955 when the jet-powered Tu-16 began to reach service units. The first *Bulls* arrived at Poltava in April 1949, and re-equipment of the 185th DBAP was completed in May.

Mastering of the Tu-4 by service pilots was not a simple matter, even though a regiment of Tu-4s had made a fly-past over the Red Square as early as May 1948. Deliveries of the Tu-4s *en masse* to service units started in 1949, after the endorsement of the report on State acceptance trials by Stalin. In first-line service the *Bull* came to supersede the IL-4s, B-25s and Pe-8s that had survived the war, as well as a few dozen restored B-17s and B-24s recovered from all parts of Eastern Europe that had been occupied by the Red Army and where American machines damaged over Germany made emergency landings. The first to receive the Tu-4s were the western defence districts; that was the usual practice in the USSR at that time when introducing new combat materiel. The aircraft were delivered to regiments based at Nezhin, Poltava, Priluki in the Ukraine, Lodeinoye Pol'e near Leningrad, as well as in Karelia, in the vicinity of Narva in Estonia and in Belorussia. In the course of military exercises the Tu-4s were redeployed to forward airfields in Eastern Europe and were thus ready to make bombing raids against the NATO troops stationed in Europe. Regiments re-equipping with the Tu-4 were renamed Heavy Bomber Air Regiments. They were tasked with destroying priority military and industrial targets on the enemy's territory and dealing massive strikes against political and economic centres and directly against enemy troops. The use of bases in Eastern Germany and in the countries of Eastern Europe was envisaged for this purpose.

As was the case with the American B-29s, the Soviet Tu-4s would scramble on alert and fly towards the borders of the Eastern Bloc. Single machines or groups of the Tu-4s were sent to patrol the borders of the presumed adversaries in the future Third World War. The options of armament carried by the Tu-4s included 3,000-kg (6,614-lb) FAB-3000 and 1,500-kg (3,307-lb) FAB-1500 heavy bombs. Weapons of mass destruction included 500-kg (1,102-lb) KhAB-500-280S M-46 and 250-kg (551-lb) KhAB-250-150S M-46 chemical warfare bombs whose charge was a jellified mixture of mustard gas and lewisite with a durability period of no less than 72 hours. But the main weapon was to be the nuclear bomb, development of which was soon to be completed. The aircraft that were on strength with Naval Aviation regiments were armed with 500-kg and 1,000-kg (1,102-lb and 2,204-lb) BRAB armour-piercing bombs intended for destroying large warships and heavily protected installations, and with moored or bottom-placed mines. Bombs were dropped singly, in series of one, two or four bombs, or in a salvo with the help of the ESBR-45 electric release mechanism. The OPB-48 automatic bombsight made it possible to deliver the bombs at any speed or altitude, and in cases when visibility was nil the Kobal't radar was brought into play.

The onboard radar was derived from the American AN/APQ-13 by the design bureau of the Leningrad Electromechanical Plant (currently the Leninets Holding company) led by A. I. Korchmar' and Ya. B. Shapirovskiy. It radically altered the tactics of bomber aviation, making it possible to undertake bombing in adverse weather and at night from altitudes between 3,000 m (9,842 ft) and the aircraft's service ceiling. The Kobal't detected big industrial premises at a distance of 100 km (62 miles) and determined the target's co-ordinates with an accuracy margin of $\pm 2°$ with regard to direction and ± 100 m (328 ft) with regard to distance; its maximum detection range was 400 km (248 miles). The radar could also be used for determining the aircraft's location by comparing the image on the screen to a map.

Deployment of the Tu-4 necessitated equipping the airbases with radio beacons (two such beacons were placed in each direction along the extended runway centreline), with relay stations for distance control, and light beacons and well-equipped air traffic control towers. The crews of the 52nd GvTBAP were the first to master the OSP-48 instrument landing system in late 1949; the system permitted landings with the cloudbase at 200 m (656 ft) and 2,000 m (6,560 ft) horizontal visibility. As early as 1950, however, the regiments began to receive Tu-4s equipped with the more advanced SP-50 Materik (Continent) ILS which made it possible to reduce the weather minima to 100 x 1,000 m (328 x 3,280 ft). The onboard equipment was supplemented by the Litiy (Lithium) radio altimeters (albeit, according to the official version, that the first production Tu-4s were presumed to be already fitted with the Materik ILS).

The plethora of complicated equipment created difficulties of its own. It was thus necessary to radically improve the training level of the personnel, especially of the radio operators. Just learning the work procedures was

Above: A line-up of 20 Kazan'-built Tu-4s, including '32 Black' (c/n 220702), '39 Black' (c/n 220804) and '37 Black' (c/n 220802), at the LII airfield in Zhukovskiy during trials.

not enough, the operator had to become a practised hand – sometimes literally. For example, the adjustment of the radar receiver was effected by pinpointing the maximum level of the current in the Kristall detector; if the operator turned the vernier just a little too briskly he slipped past the optimum value and the reception quality suffered. To comment on this situation, a phrase was coined: 'Kristall current is too weak – operator's fault I seek'.

Fire control of the aircraft's defensive weapons was also organised along new lines. Now it was possible to open fire from any of the barbettes, using just one of the PS-48 sighting stations. On the other hand, adjustment and ranging of the system was a complicated and labour-consuming matter.

The maintenance personnel also had to shoulder more than their fair share of hard work when servicing the aircraft and the

engines. For example, many of the bolts designed to sustain high stresses were screwed in under substantial pressure and, in consequence, could be removed only by drilling them out; no simple task because they were made of extremely hard chrome-molybdenum steel alloy. When the skin panels of the wing centre section were removed, it was necessary to prop up the outer wing panels by special jacks, otherwise the wings could

Another view of the Tu-4 line-up at LII, showing Bulls '19 Black' (c/n 220404), '24 Black' (c/n 220504) and '23 Black' (c/n 220503).

collapse under their own weight. One can also imagine the trouble involved in putting in place the extremely heavy canvas covers using high and flimsy stepladders.

However, there were not only difficulties in store for those who mastered the Tu-4s. Most of the instruments and equipment items were conveniently placed and could be easily accessed. Pressurised cabins afforded a degree of comfort that had been unheard of previously; the cabins were even provided with Thermos bottles for warm food and with sleeping bunks for the crew. Due care was also taken of the crew's need to relieve themselves – there were three buckets and a little tank, all provided with tight covers ensuring that the air in the cabins remained reasonably fresh. On the whole, the aircraft immediately evoked a feeling of genuine respect.

Several interesting episodes from the service career of the Tu-4 can be related here.

On 3rd August 1947 three heavy bombers (they were still designated B-4s at that time) made a fly-past at the Air Display in Tushino. Th crews were captained by N. S. Rybko (aircraft R-01), M. L. Gallai (aircraft R-02) and by A. G. Vasil'chenko (aircraft R-03). A curious episode occurred involving these aircraft. Aboard the R-01 was Chief Air Marshal Aleksandr Ye. Golovanov, who had been Commander of the Long-Range Aviation during the war. This brilliant pilot possessing a perfect command of instrument flying and navigational calculations 'was in command of the parade' on board the aircraft. Nevertheless, a

Above: A pair of Tu-4s, including '93 Black' (c/n 221903?), in echelon starboard formation.

A flight of Tu-4s in Vee formation cruises over the desolate countryside somewhere in the eastern regions of the USSR.

Above: A line of in-service Tu-4s at a Soviet tactical airbase (note the unpaved parking area), with '21 Black' (c/n 220501) and '66 Black' (c/n 221401) nearest to the camera.

Above: Flight lines in units equipped with Tu-4s were very long, primarily because of the bomber's huge wing span.

A still from a cine film showing two *Bulls* in cruise flight.

mistake in calculations amounting to just about one minute compelled the three bombers to literally dive under a formation of fighters flying ahead of them in order to avoid a collision; thus, to quote the later wisecrack from the airfield personnel, for the first time an air display featured a fly-past in 'sandwich formation'. Nevertheless, all the top government officials were of the opinion that 'the overall impression was favourable' and the incident entailed no reprisals. Quite different was the impression produced by these aircraft on foreign observers – notably the Americans. They could not even imagine that the Soviet aircraft industry had mastered the manufacture of such machines, and believed that the Russians had repaired the three B-29s interned in the Far East during the war and were displaying them now.

After the war, documentary films were shot during the Tushino Air Displays; these films were later widely shown all over the country. The **Ves'nik voz*doosh*novo *flot*a** (Air Fleet Herald) magazine (later terminated but now reborn) published a detailed account of the parade and a detailed review of the film. According to some memoirs, the first such documentary was shot in black and white and Stalin ordered the film shooting to be repeated in colour. So the Air Display had to be 'repeated' over Kubinka, Monino and Tushino. For the film to have the 'true ring', the film sequences had to include 'enthusiastic crowds of spectators' at Tushino. They had been assembled using a sale of some short supply goods as a pretext.

Organisation of air displays and parades in the 1940s was invariably connected with the name of Air Lieutenant-General Vasiliy I. Stalin, Commander of the Air Force of the Moscow Defence District. Promoted to the rank of General at the age of 25, the Soviet leader's son was not easy to deal with, being endowed with a bad temper, and had a drinking problem.

At the end of 1946 Major-General V. I. Stalin was appointed deputy of N. Sbytov, then Commander of the Air Force of the Moscow DD. Shortly thereafter Sbytov was forced into retirement and Vasiliy became the commander. His first 'undertaking' designed to enhance the combat efficiency of the Air Force was the construction of a new building for the headquarters of the Moscow Military District air force at the Central Airfield (Moscow-Khodynka). A constant stream of trains from Germany brought construction materials and costly equipment (marble, sculptures, carpets, etc.). Built from scratch within six months, the headquarters was rather more reminiscent of a palace.

When inspecting air units and formations of the district in Kalinin (now Tver'), Kubinka, Torzhok, Tyoplyy Stan and other garrisons,

Vasiliy Stalin flew there in a Tu-4 (or in one of the remaining airworthy B-29s) converted to a command post of the Moscow Defence District Air Force. As related by the son of his aide-de-camp V. Polianskiy, the fuselage housed a lounge, a study and a bedroom, all richly decorated. Outwardly the aircraft was in no way different from production Tu-4s; it flew as a flagship at Air Displays in the late 1940s and early 1950s. Press correspondents often photographed V. I. Stalin, commander of the Air Display, sitting at the controls of this aircraft. In his capacity of Commander of the district's aviation, he conducted 14 parades over the Red Square; as a rule, nearly 200 aircraft took part in these parades – several fighter regiments, two bomber regiments and one long-range aviation regiment. The fly-past was usually concluded by Tu-4 bombers, but during the last 'parade' years they immediately followed the flagship.

After having flown over Moscow all the aircraft returned to their bases, and the flagship landed at the Central Airfield; from there Vasiliy Stalin sped in a car to the Kremlin where he ascended to the right wing of Lenin's Mausoleum and reported to the Commander-in-Chief of the Air Force about the completion of the fly-past. On the evening of that day the Government gave a reception in the Kremlin in honour of the parade's participants (mainly the parade's commanders).

As related by V. Polianskiy, in his later years V. Stalin almost stopped flying, with his alcoholism going from bad to worse. He was, in the opinion of many, quite a skilled pilot, but sometimes he tried to pilot his Tu-4 in a state of intoxication (though not during preparations for parades). He gave full throttle to all the engines and sharply gained altitude or entered a dive, forgetting that it was no fighter he was piloting. If reasoning was to no avail, other crew members used brute force to remove him from the pilot's seat, wisely considering that it was better to suffer punishment from the 'boss' than to be killed in a crash.

Many people have a vivid remembrance of the story told by Hero of the Soviet Union, test pilot I. Ye. Fyodorov about a 'demonstration flight' over the Kremlin that he had performed together with Vasiliy. One fine day, Vasiliy Stalin arrived in his aircraft at the LII airfield and, prompted by the desire to show off his flying skill to his father, suggested to Fyodorov that he should fly over the Kremlin at very low altitude. Being well aware of the possible consequences, Fyodorov asked Vasiliy to write a flight document stating the particulars of the forthcoming flight – the route, the altitude etc. Vasiliy Stalin did so, and they set out for the flight. Barely half an hour passed after their landing when 'appropriate authorities' made their appearance at the airfield; they quickly found out who was the pilot, took

Above: A line of parked Tu-4s at a Soviet airbase.

Above: The flight and ground crew of a Moscow-built Tu-4 coded '35 Red' (c/n 230317) receives instructions prior to a mission.

Landing gear caught in mid-extension and flaps fully deployed, this Tu-4 is seen during landing approach.

73

Above: Vasiliy I. Stalin in his days as Commander of the Moscow Defence District Air Force and a Tu-4 pilot. He was removed from office by Iosif V. Stalin himself after a bungled 1952 May Day parade flypast.

Above: A formation of Tu-4s flies over the Red Square in Moscow, with the Historic Museum in the background.

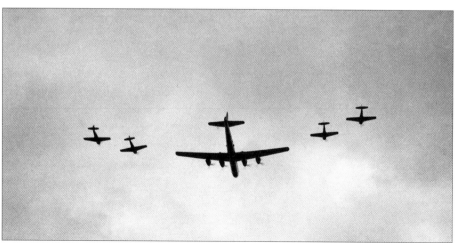

A scene from another parade over the Red Square, showing a Tu-4 escorted by four Lavochkin La-11 fighters.

hold of Fyodorov, put him into a special room and set about extracting from him the 'evidence' as to who had masterminded an attempt against the leader's life. The 'flight document' failed to convince them and was promptly torn into pieces; in fact, it added more zeal to their interrogation. Fyodorov was saved only because Vasiliy Stalin was still at the airfield. The pilot's friends gave him a hint about what was going on. He came into the room, asked Fyodorov 'what he was doing there', half-embraced him by the shoulders and led him away. The State security officers did not dare to disagree.

Unlike the majority of his subordinates, Vasiliy Stalin failed to earn the coveted decoration – the Gold Star that went with the Hero of the Soviet Union title. As for his simple human 'guiding star', it eclipsed during the May Day Parade of 1952. The weather report was absolutely prohibitive – dark thick clouds were hanging low and it was drizzling. The weather was just as beastly at the airfields where the regiments and divisions taking part in the parade were based (equipped with Tu-4s, IL-28s and MiG-15s). The Commander-in-Chief of the Air Force cancelled the flying display, but V. Stalin telephoned him from his command post, requesting permission to undertake the fly-past should the weather turn to the better. The Commander-in-Chief transferred to him full responsibility, permitting him to act at his own discretion. As a result, without waiting for the weather to improve, Vasiliy Stalin took a risk and ordered all the units to take to the air and head for Moscow in instrument flying mode. That was a decision unprecedented in peacetime.

The result was deplorable. Some units missed the Red Square altogether, others flew across it instead of lengthwise, still others received a message from the flagship aircraft ordering them to turn away from Moscow and return to base. Spectators on the Red Square did not see the aircraft at all, they could only hear the roar of jet engines. Here is the story of this 'parade' as related by chief of the Main Command Post Colonel B. A. Morozov and test pilot Lieutenant-General Stepan A. Mikoyan, retold by S. Gribanov: *'Vasiliy Stalin himself was the first to take off; he made a pass exactly over the Red Square,'* Morozov recalls. *'He was followed by a division of Tu-4s. But the bombers' formation stretched out during the approach pattern: the last regiment was some 30 seconds late and it was difficult to catch up with those that were ahead. They were flying very low, just some six hundred metres* (1,970 ft). *At that moment […] a group of Il'yushins* (IL-28 *Beagle* twinjet tactical bombers – *Auth.*) *led by General Dolgooshin put in an appearance. What do we do now? If I let them fly on, collision is imminent – the Il'yushins have a higher speed. I took the* decision to stop the Dolgooshin group. I ordered, "Turn to port!" and directed the group towards Monino...' As a result, the formation broke up, one of the *Beagles* scraped the top of a pine tree at low altitude and brought home some twigs, another one broke its pitot tube. Worst of all, two IL-28s collided near Migalovo airfield and crashed, killing their crews (according to other sources, the collision caused one of the bombers to crash; the other one was damaged but landed safely).

The 'post-flight briefing' conducted in the study of N. Boolganin, the Minister of Defence, ended in a slight fright for Vasiliy Stalin, as well as for all the others involved – he earned nothing more than a reprimand. But at the reception held after the parade the leader, in everybody's presence, called Vasiliy 'a fool, a snotty kid' in very vivid expressions of which the 'great leader and teacher of all times and all peoples' (an oft-cited description of Iosif V. Stalin) was a past master. Then he ordered him to leave the study and instructed the C-in-C of the Air Force to dismiss him from the post of Commander of the Moscow Defence District air force.

Apart from the Air Force, Tu-4 heavy bombers were operated by the Naval Air Arm (AVMF – *Aviahtsiya voyenno-morskovo flota*). The AVMF units stationed at the Baltic Sea were the first to convert to the new bomber. In February 1955 the 57th Bomber Division comprising two regiments equipped with Tu-4s was transferred to the Red Banner Baltic Fleet air arm. It was renamed the 57th MTAD (*minno-torpednaya aviadiveeziya* – Minelayer and Torpedo-Bomber Division). The flying personnel was well trained, but the Naval Aviation was not particularly in need of the Tu-4 – the aircraft had already became obsolete by then. Therefore it was decided that the division should become the first to convert to new aircraft. Some of the Tu-4s were transferred to the 33rd Combat and Conversion Training Centre in Nikolayev on the Black Sea, others were struck off charge, and the command staff was sent to production plants to study the Tu-16.

Some of the exercises that took place during the 1950s involved the few Tu-4s that had been modified into Tu-4A nuclear weapon carriers. To give the crews instruction in the handling of nuclear bombs, dummy bombs were used which emulated the weight and dimensions of the real Soviet nukes.

The crews of the Tu-4As were involved in the tests of the Soviet nuclear weapons conducted at nuclear test ranges near Semipalatinsk and on the Novaya Zemlya archipelago. During these tests, Tu-4 bombers were used as camera ships and air-sampling platforms. The Tu-4 had the distinction of being the first Soviet aircraft on which studies were made of problems associated with pro-

Above: A Tu-4 on short finals.

Centre and above: A flight of Tu-4s seen during a military exercise.

Above: A Tu-4 seen shortly after take-off.

Above: A Tu-4 cruises at high altitude over thick clouds.

tecting the aviation hardware and crews from the impact of the shock wave, the light emission and the radiation. Thus, on 24th September 1951, one Tu-4 took part in the testing of the *izdeliye* RDS-2 nuclear bomb, conducted as a ground level explosion and accompanied by the destructive impact inherent in a nuclear explosion. The first mid-air test of an RDS-3 nuclear bomb, conducted on 18th October of the same year, involved the use of a Tu-4A (crew captain Konstantin I. Oorzhuntsev) as the carrier aircraft from which the bomb was dropped. In 1952, check-up flight tests of the RDS-3 and of the Tu-4A carrier aircraft took place, as well as the training of the first group of aviation specialists from service units of the Air Force for the operation of the RDS-3 and of the special equipment fitted to the carrier aircraft. The year 1953 saw the continuation of flight tests for the purpose of evaluating the safety of take-offs and landings of the Tu-4A carrier aircraft with the RDS-3 on board; also, three experimental releases of the RDS-5 atomic bomb from a Tu-4A were conducted (the crews were captained by V. Ya. Kutyrchev and F. P. Golovashko).

In 1954 an all-arms exercise was held at the 71st test range in Totskoye in the Orenburg Region involving the use of the RDS-3 nuclear bomb dropped from a Tu-4A (14th

September, crew captain Kutyrchev). That year, tests were conducted to check the safety of take-offs and landings of the Tu-4A carrier aircraft and measure the radiation levels in the tell-tale mushroom clouds at a long distance from the same aircraft.

The exercise at the Totskoye test range merits a few more details.

The successful testing of Soviet nuclear weapons and the active efforts pursued in the USA to prepare the armed forces and the civil defence for operations in a nuclear environment, prompted a decision to conduct in the USSR an all-arms exercise involving the use of nuclear weapons. Such an exercise, as mentioned earlier, took place on 14th September 1954. Within the scenario of this exercise the 71st test range was tasked with conducting an atomic bomb drop from a Tu-4A carrier against a target replicating exactly the defensive positions of a US Army battalion. The nuclear attack would be followed by an assault by strike aircraft and finally an assault by a mechanised infantry regiment. Numerous invited guests from 'friendly nations' were going to watch from a command post located 2 km (1.2 miles) from the 'Americans' first line of defence'.

The original intention was to drop the bomb from the brand-new Tu-16 but the *Bad-*

ger showed disappointing results: dummy bombs missed the target by as much as 700 m (2,297 ft), creating a considerable danger that the invited guests could be caught by the blast. Hence the proven Tu-4 offering greater accuracy was chosen. The 71st test range assigned to this task two first-rate crews on the Tu-4A aircraft, led by Lieutenant-Colonel V. Ya. Kutyrchev and Captain K. K. Liasnikov. These crews boasted not only excellent piloting skills; they had accumulated much experience of flying with dummy nuclear bombs on board during their testing at the 71st test range, and the crew captained by Kutyrchev had participated in aerial nuclear tests at the Semipalatinsk test range, having performed two live drops from a Tu-4A in 1953. Concurrent with the preparation of the two carrier aircraft, two nuclear bombs were being prepared. A few days prior to the exercise, academician Igor' V. Kurchatov arrived at the airfield. He checked the readiness degree of the bombs and the carrier aircraft, as well as the readiness of the crews. Later the pilots recollected warmly the meeting with him, his good humour and his parting words with good wishes for a successful mission.

On the day of the exercise, 14th September, each of the two carrier aircraft had one bomb on board (a nuke on the primary aircraft and an HE bomb of the back-up aircraft) and each crew was ready to perform the task. By the time of the scheduled take-off both Tu-4As were in stand-by readiness with the engines running and their crews on alert for the expected order. The order to take off was issued to the crew captained by Lieutenant-Colonel V. Ya. Kutyrchev. He performed his mission successfully: the bomb released by navigator/bomb-aimer Kokorin from the Tu-4A carrier aircraft at 8,000 m (26,247 ft) – the minimum altitude at which the bomber could escape the blast wave – exploded at 09:33 hours Moscow time, above the target at the stipulated height of 350 m (1,148 ft).

When reviewing and summing up the results of the exercise, Marshal of the Soviet Union Gheorgiy K. Zhookov gave high praise to the work of the crew of the carrier aircraft. As a reward for the successful mission, the crew captain was promoted to the rank of Colonel and awarded the Order of Lenin by a decree of the Presidium of the USSR Supreme Soviet. The other crew members were also awarded State decorations.

Not only nuclear weapon carriers constituted the power of the Soviet Air Force in the early 1950s. The Tu-4KS equipped with the Kometa weapons system posed a real threat to the Western allies' sea convoys. The system was quickly mastered in operational service and used successfully during naval exercises with the participation of Tu-4KS missile strike aircraft.

Tu-4D transports/troopships were placed on the strength of the Air Force's airlift regiments; until the early 1960s they were actively used for carrying troops and combat materiel. This was probably the only version of the *Bull* actually used in combat by the VVS, namely during the suppression of the Hungarian anti-Communist uprising which started in late October 1956. It was Tu-4Ds that delivered small units of Soviet paratroopers to Hungary, operating from the town of Chop near the Soviet-Romanian border; on 4th November these troops were the first to break their way into the rebellious Budapest on their ASU-57 self-propelled guns and then set about restoring 'revolutionary order'.

There were cases when the Tu-4Ds were fired upon by the rebels, and the gunners fired back; many aircraft were damaged by small arms fire but none were lost. On the return trip the Tu-4Ds carried the bodies of Soviet soldiers killed in the fighting. One can only imagine the psychological impact the sight of coffins being offloaded at Chop had on paratroopers waiting their turn to board the aircraft. 'See Budapest and die.'

In fact, on the night of 4th November several standard Tu-4s, each carrying two FAB-500 bombs and eight FAB-250s, took off from Borispol' airbase (now Kiev's main international airport) on a mission to bomb Budapest, where the rebels had their headquarters. Fortunately, wiser counsels prevailed and the mission was aborted when the

bombers were passing over the Romanian city of Moreni.

Tu-4 operations in the Soviet Air Force were not altogether without incident. On 1st November 1956, a few days before the abortive raid on Budapest, a Tu-4 was lost when the pilot of a MiG-15 fighter making a practice attack misjudged his speed and collided with the bomber, all 13 airmen in the two aircraft losing their lives. On 2nd November an armourer hooking up an FAB-500 to a Tu-4 forgot to activate the safety mechanism of the bomb hoist and the 500-kg (1,102-lb) bomb fell on top of him, crushing the luckless man to death.

Several fatal accidents were caused by the tail gunners whose responsibilities included operating the M-10 APU. To start up the 'putt-putt' before landing the gunner had to get up, which was anything but easy in the cramped conditions of the gunner's station. In so doing he would often accidentally grab hold of the trim tab control cables, causing uncommanded elevator deflection and an abrupt nose-down movement. When this came to light the cables were closed by protective covers.

In the early 1950s twenty-five Tu-4 long-range bombers capable of carrying nuclear weapons were turned over to China (Stalin and Mao Tse-tung reached an agreement in principle providing for the transfer of such weapons to China). The situation in the region was taking an alarming turn. The war in Korea

was continuing, and the conflict around Taiwan showed no prospect of ending. Conversion of Chinese crews had not yet been completed when the Tu-4s started their combat operations, dealing strikes against the 'breakaway' island. Interestingly, entries in the flight documents read 'training flight with a live bomb release over the bombing range – the island of Taiwan'. Initially the crews were captained by Soviet pilots.

The Chinese rewarded the Soviet instructors for their contribution – for example, instructor Balenko was given a personal car (no small reward by the day's standards), and upon return to the home country in 1954 he was awarded the Order of the Red Banner, ostensibly 'for prolonged meritorious service' (he had no less than four combat missions against Taiwan to his credit).

In China the Tu-4s were intended for the role of nuclear weapon carriers, but this was beset by frustrations. In 1957 the Soviet Union began transferring the manufacturing documents for the Tu-16 bomber to China, and it seemed that the days of the Tu-4 were numbered. However, shortly thereafter a wind of change unsettled the Sino-Soviet relations, and the 'great leap forward' policy had a detrimental effect on the mastering of new technology; as a result, the operational career of the *Bull* proved to be unexpectedly long.

The Chinese set about updating the bomber: they installed the SRO-2 Khrom-Nikel' (NATO *Odd Rods*) IFF system, the Sire-

Clad in winter uniform, the officers of a Soviet long-range bomber regiment pose for a group photo in front of Tu-4 '02 Red' (c/n 2806101).

Above: A demilitarised Tu-4 (c/n 223204); note the lack of cannon barbettes. Though still in Soviet Air Force markings, this is a Polar Aviation aircraft.

na-2 (Siren) radar homing and warning system (RHAWS) and other pieces of equipment copied from Soviet models. Although China did not obtain a nuclear bomb from the USSR, the Tu-4 soldiered on in the Chinese People's Liberation Army Air Force (PLAAF) for more than 40 years; the *Bulls* were used not only as bombers but also for long-range maritime reconnaissance and as transport aircraft.

The shortage of ASh-73TK engines proved to be the biggest problem. However, as already recounted, an unorthodox solution

was found: in the mid-1970s the remaining airworthy aircraft were re-engined with the powerplant borrowed from the Shaanxi Y-8, which was a 'Chinese' (in a double sense) copy of the Soviet An-12BK. The powerplant comprised four Dongan WJ-5 turboprops (copies of the Ivchenko AI-20M), with a take-off rating of 4,250 ehp and driving Chinese copies of the AV-68 propeller.

However, the Tu-4 could no longer be used as a bomber; yet it found other uses. In 1978 several machines were converted into

carriers for air-launched Chang Hong-1 (Ryan BQM-34A copy) drones, and one aircraft ('4114 Red', c/n 2806501) became a testbed for developing an AWACS/electronic counter-measures system. In 1991 no fewer than 15 Tu-4s were listed in the PLAAF inventory. Two *Bulls* – a drone carrier ('4134 Red', c/n 225008) and the abovementioned AEW&C aircraft – are now exhibits at the PLAAF Museum at Datangshan AB near Beijing.

From 1954 onwards the Tu-4 was gradually supplanted in the Soviet Air Force's Long-

This early-production Kuibyshev-built Tu-4D coded 28 Blue (c/n 184218) was used to carry a team of skydivers into the stratosphere.

Range Aviation units by the Tu-16, and from 1956 onwards the first regiment in the Ukraine began to receive the Tu-95 possessing intercontinental range as a replacement for its Tu-4s. By the early 1960s the Tu-4s were retained only in transport units of the Air Force, in training institutions and as flying testbeds in the system of the Air Force and the Ministry of Aircraft Industry.

Unfortunately only one example of the Tu-4 survives in Russia nowadays; it is a Kuibyshev-built example coded '01 Red' (c/n 2805103) and manufactured in 1952. This was one of the bombers that took part in the famous 'raid that never was' against Budapest; later it was used by GK NII VVS as a testbed for the PRS-1 Argon gun ranging radar. In 1958 the aircraft was donated to the Soviet Air Force Museum (now the Central Russian Air Force Museum) in Monino near Moscow. At the time of writing, the bomber's flight engineer Yevgeniy Podol'nyy was alive and well, and a nostalgic meeting took place in 2002.

As a rule, the Tu-4s were rolled out of the assembly shops unpainted; they were sprayed with clear dope and had the colour of natural metal. A red, blue or black serial or tactical code the size of about one-third of the fuselage diameter was painted on the fuselage sides behind the forward cannon barbettes. The tactical codes in a given air formation ran in sequence; the colour of the numbers could be different for different regiments or squadrons. The c/n was painted in the same colour and was applied in quite large figures on both sides of the forward fuselage and at the base of the fin. The c/n had six or seven digits and carried information about the production plant, the batch number and the number of the aircraft in the batch; sometimes the c/n included digits denoting the aircraft type and the year of manufacture. The decoding of the c/ns depended on the production plant and the time of manufacture.

Propeller blades were painted black with yellow tips. Until 1954, red stars with a red outline were applied to the aft fuselage, the underside of the wings and the fin. After 1954 the star insignia were removed from the fuselage but applied to the wing upper surfaces. Sometimes the stars had a white or yellow stripe between the star itself and the outline.

In the 1960s the tactical code painted on the fuselage was repeated in small digits at the top of the fin for quick identification on the flight line. The final change occurred at the end of 1980s and concerned only the example of the Tu-4 preserved at Monino. In common with all the other combat aircraft of the Soviet Air Force it had its c/n removed from the outer surfaces to enhance security! (Damn stupid notion, considering the status of the aircraft… – translator's note.)

A retired but still intact Tu-4 ('08 Red', c/n 226002) sits on a snow-covered airfield, awaiting scrapping. Sadly, nearly all VVS Tu-4s were destroyed as target drones or reduced to scrap.

Known Tu-4 production and operational details

a) Kazan' production (Plant No. 22)

C/n	Serial/reg'n	Version	Notes
220001	none	Tu-4	F/F 19-5-47; pilots N. S. Rybko/A. G. Vasil'chenko, later Rodionov/Piskunov; flight engineers (F/Es) P. S. Shestkov, Andreyev, radio operator (R/O) Krasnov
220002	'202 Black'	Tu-4	F/F 2-7-47; pilots M. L. Gallai, N. N. Arzhanov, radio operator Tyagoonov
220101	none	Tu-4	C/n painted on as '101'. F/F 31-7-47; pilots A. G. Vasil'chenko, B. G. Govorov, F/E N. I. Filizon, R/O Somushkin. Crashed near Kolomna 18-9-47
220102	none	Tu-4	C/n painted on as '102'. F/F date unknown, pilots V.P. Maroonov, A. Ye. Smolovich, R/O Ivannikov
220103	none	Tu-4	F/F 6-9-47; pilots A. P. Yakimov, Ryabchenko, F/E R. K. Kotoorin, R/O Trooshin
220201	not known	Tu-4	F/F 13-9-47; pilots B. G. Govorov, K. A. Soldatkin, lead navigator Zhdanov, F/Es I. N. Grishko, D. V. Anduyev, R/O Ignatov
220202	none	Tu-4	C/n painted on as '202'; later serialled '7 Black' Pilots S.F. Mashkovskiy, Pal'chikov; F/Es Antonov, K. Bogoveyev, R/O Glookhan'kov
220203	not known	Tu-4	F/F 10-10-47; pilots I. Sh. Vaganov, K. N. Toropov, navigator A. N. Sidorov, F/Es Gorshkov, Shoovalov, R/O K. I. Malkhasian
220204	'9 Black'	Tu-4	F/F 19-10-47; pilots M. M. Gromov, K. A. Soldatkin, navigator S. V. Vitebskiy, F/Es L. Yu. Nookhlin, Booyanov, R/Os Karevich, Dorofeyev. Converted to (see next line)
		Tu-4LL	Dobrynin VD-3TK development engines (Nos. 1 & 4)
220205	'10 Black'?	Tu-4	F/F 19-10-47; pilots A. D. Perelyot, M. L. Mel'nikov, F/Es G. A. Nefyodov, R/O Mayorov
220301	'11 Black'?	Tu-4	F/F date unknown; pilots A. G. Vasil'chenko, P. S. Yakovlev, F/E N. I. Filizon, R/O Sovooshkin
220302	'12 Black'?	Tu-4	
220303	none?	Tu-4	Serial '13 Black' unlikely. Pilots M. V. Rodnykh, G. I. Kondratov, navigator V. Ya. Mayanskin, F/Es N. I. Bannikov, Bogoveyev; R/O V. P. Bulatov. Crashed ?-10-47
220304	'14 Black'?	Tu-4	F/F 3-7-48
220305	'15 Black'?	Tu-4	Pilots A. Kh. Romanov, K. N. Malooyev, navigator G. S. Frenkel', F/E V. Ye. Vlasov, R/O V. K. Barbashin
220401	'16 Black'?	Tu-4	F/F 3-7-48
220402	'17 Black'?	Tu-4	Pilots N. N. Arzhanov, Pal'chikov, F/E Shoovalov, R/O Krasnov
220403	'18 Black'?	Tu-4	Crew captain A. G. Vasil'chenko
220404	'19 Black'	Tu-4	Pilots K. K. Rykov, Vaoolin, F/Es A. P. Khlynov, Shoovalov; R/O M. N. Volkov
220405	'20 Black'?	Tu-4	F/F date unknown, pilots M. L. Gallai, A. Ya. Vernikov, F/E Vedeshkin, R/O Laikin
220501	'21 Black'	Tu-4	Pilots V. P. Maroonov, A. Ye. Smolovich, F/E Chernov
220502	'22 Black'?	Tu-4	
220503	'23 Black'	Tu-4	
220504	'24 Black'	Tu-4	
220505	'25 Black'?	Tu-4	
220601?	'26 Black'	Tu-4	C/n not 100% confirmed but probable
220602	'27 Black'?	Tu-4	
220603	'28 Black'?	Tu-4	
220604	'29 Black'?	Tu-4	

C/n	Serial/reg'n	Version	Notes	C/n	Serial/reg'n	Version
220605	none	Tu-4				
220701	'31 Black'?	Tu-4				
220702	'32 Black'	Tu-4				
220703	'33 Black'?	Tu-4				
220704	'34 Black'?	Tu-4		220705	'35 Black'?	Tu-4
220801	'36 Black'?	Tu-4				
220802	'37 Black'	Tu-4				
220803	'38 Black'?	Tu-4				
220804	'39 Black'	Tu-4				
220805	'40 Black'?	Tu-4				
220901	'41 Black'	Tu-4				
220902	'42 Black'?	Tu-4		220903	'43 Black'?	Tu-4
220904	'44 Black'?	Tu-4				
220905?	'45 Black'	Tu-4	C/n not 100% confirmed but probable *Burlaki* system testbed			
221001	'46 Black'	Tu-4				
221002	'47 Black'?	Tu-4				
221003	'48 Black'?	Tu-4				
221004	'49 Black'?	Tu-4				
221005	'50 Black'?	Tu-4				
221101	'51 Black'?	Tu-4				
221102	'52 Black'?	Tu-4				
221103	'53 Black'?	Tu-4				
221104	'54 Black'?	Tu-4				
221105	'55 Black'?	Tu-4		221201	'56 Black'?	Tu-4
221202	'57 Black'?	Tu-4				
221203	'58 Black'?	Tu-4	Converted/recoded to (see below)			
	'22 Red'?	Tu-4LL	Ivchenko AI-20 development engines (Nos. 1 & 4)			
221204	'59 Black'?	Tu-4				
221205	'60 Black'?	Tu-4				
221301	'61 Black'?	Tu-4				
221302	'62 Black'?	Tu-4				
221303	'63 Black'?	Tu-4				
221304	'64 Black'?	Tu-4				
221305	'65 Black'?	Tu-4				
221401	'66 Black'	Tu-4				
221402	'67 Black'?	Tu-4				
221403?	'68 Black'	Tu-4	C/n not 100% confirmed but probable			
221404	'69 Black'?	Tu-4				
221405	'70 Black'?	Tu-4				
221501	'71 Black'?	Tu-4				
221502	'72 Black'?	Tu-4				
221503	'73 Black'?	Tu-4				
221504	'74 Black'?	Tu-4				
221505	'75 Black'?	Tu-4				
221601	'76 Black'?	Tu-4				
221602	'77 Black'?	Tu-4				
221603	'78 Black'?	Tu-4				
221604	'79 Black'?	Tu-4				
221605	'80 Black'?	Tu-4				
221701	'81 Black'?	Tu-4				
221702	'82 Black'?	Tu-4				
221703	'83 Black'?	Tu-4				
221704?	'84 Black'	Tu-4	C/n not 100% confirmed but probable			
221705	'85 Black'?	Tu-4				
221801	'86 Black'?	Tu-4				
221802	'87 Black'?	Tu-4				
221803	'88 Black'?	Tu-4				
221804	'89 Black'?	Tu-4				
221805	'90 Black'?	Tu-4				
221901	none	Tu-4	Equipped with refuelling receptacle			
221902	'92 Black'	Tu-4				
221903?	'93 Black'	Tu-4	C/n not 100% confirmed but probable			
222101	not known	Tu-4				

1. (Kazan production) — continued

c/n	code	type	notes
222202	none	Tu-4	Converted to refuelling tanker
222402	none	Tu-4	Converted to refuelling tanker
222903	not known	Tu-4	
223001	not known	Tu-4	
223002	not known	Tu-4	
223201	not known	Tu-4	
223204	none	Tu-4	Demilitarised/cvtd to ice reconnaissance aircraft
223701	not known	Tu-4	
224203	none	Tu-4	Converted to (see next line)
		Tu-4KS	Prototype, Tupolev OKB
224501	not known	Tu-4	
224506	not known	Tu-4	
225002	not known	Tu-4	
225008	not known	Tu-4	Transferred to China; see next line
	'4134 Red'	AP-1?	Re-engined with WJ-6A turboprops; converted to drone launcher aircraft. Preserved PLAAF Museum, Datangshan AB, Beijing
225301	not known	Tu-4	
225303	not known	Tu-4	
225402	not known	Tu-4	Converted to (see next line)
		Tu-4LL	Kuznetsov TV-2 development engines (Nos. 1 & 4). Crashed 8-10-51
225501	not known	Tu-4	225502 not known Tu-4
225701	not known	Tu-4	
225801	not known	Tu-4	
226001	not known	Tu-4	
226002	'08 Red'	Tu-4	
226110	not known	Tu-4	
226305	none	Tu-4	Converted to, see below
		Tu-4KS	Prototype, Tupolev OKB
226601	not known	Tu-4	
227209	not known	Tu-4	
227506	not known	Tu-4	
2207510	'29 Red'	Tu-4	Converted to (see next line)
		Tu-4NM	Drone carrier aircraft

Note: Initially Kazan'-built Tu-4s were serialled consecutively, the serial indicating the number of the aircraft on the production line. Some aircraft, though, had no serials; therefore the probable serials of the aircraft in between those with known serials are given in italics. Red markings are presumably post-1955 tactical codes which were not related to the production sequence, being simply the aircraft's number in the unit operating it.

2. Kuibyshev production (Plant No. 18)

a) System 1

c/n	code	type	notes
184301	not known	Tu-4	
184402	not known	Tu-4	
184304	not known	Tu-4	
184505	not known	Tu-4	
184107	not known	Tu-4	
184209	not known	Tu-4	
184309	not known	Tu-4	
184115	not known	Tu-4	
184218	not known	Tu-4	Converted to (see next line)
	'28 Blue'	Tu-4D	
184121	not known	Tu-4	
184430	not known	Tu-4	
184132	not known	Tu-4	
184232	not known	Tu-4	
184133	not known	Tu-4	
1840136	not known	Tu-4	
1841039	not known	Tu-4	
1840140	not known	Tu-4	
1840841	not known	Tu-4	Converted to (see next line)
	'18 Red'	Tu-4D	

c/n	code	type	notes
1840347	'26 Red'	Tu-4	
1840348?	not known	Tu-4	C/n quoted as 1803048 but this does not make sense
1840848	'41 Red'	Tu-4	Converted to *Burlaki* system testbed; later converted to refuelling tanker

Note: Initially Kuibyshev'-built Tu-4s had five aircraft to a batch (eg, 184218 = Plant No. 18, Tu-4, 2nd aircraft in Batch 18). After Batch 33, however, the number of aircraft per batch was increased to ten, which is why an extra digit was added after the type designator.

b) System 2

c/n	code	type	notes
2805001	not known	Tu-4	
2805002	'22 Red'	Tu-4	
2805003	not known	Tu-4	Converted to *Burlaki* system testbed
2805005	not known	Tu-4	Converted to *Burlaki* system testbed
2805009	not known	Tu-4	
2805103	'01 Red'	Tu-4	Preserved Central Russian AF Museum, Monino
2805110	not known	Tu-4	Converted to *Burlaki* system testbed
2805203	not known	Tu-4	Converted to *Burlaki* system testbed
2805204	none	Tu-4	Converted to (see next line)
		Tu-4D	Further converted to (see next line)
		Tu-4*	Two-point refuelling tanker, designation unknown
2805710	not known	Tu-4	Demilitarised and registered as (see next line)
	CCCP H-1139	Tu-4	Polar Aviation, transport/ice reconnaissance aircraft
2805901	'21 Red'	Tu-4	
2806101	'02 Red'	Tu-4	
2806303	'28 Red'	Tu-4	
2806501	not known	Tu-4	Transferred to China; see next line
	'4114 Red'	AP-1?	Re-engined with WJ-6A turboprops; converted to AWACS testbed. Preserved PLAAF Museum
2806702	not known	Tu-4	Converted to (see next line)
	'23 Red'	Tu-4T	Prototype, Tupolev OKB

3. Moscow-Fili production (Plant No. 23)

c/n	code	type	notes
230101	not known	Tu-4	
230102	not known	Tu-4	
230103	not known	Tu-4	
230503	none	Tu-4	LII, 'mother ship' for DFS 346 experimental aircraft
230104	not known	Tu-4	
230105	not known	Tu-4	
230205	not known	Tu-4	
230307	not known	Tu-4	
230407	not known	Tu-4	
230109	not known	Tu-4	
231012	not known	Tu-4	
230113	not known	Tu-4	Converted to (see next line)
		Tu-4LL	LII/Myasishchev OKB, aka DR-1 testbed, Lyul'ka AL-5 development engine; later DR-2 testbed, Mikulin AM-3 development engine
230314	not known	Tu-4	Possibly converted to (see next line)
		Tu-4LL	Type of development engine (turbojet) not known
230115	not known	Tu-4	
230217	'35 Red'	Tu-4	
230219	not known	Tu-4	
230320	none	Tu-4	Converted to (see next line)
		Tu-4D	
230322	none	Tu-4	Myasishchev OKB, ShR-1/ShR-2 landing gear testbed
230123	not known	Tu-4	

4. Aircrafft with unknown c/ns

c/n	code	type	notes
?	'207 Black'	Tu-4	Possibly the 207th Kazan'-built aircraft
CCCP-92648		Tu-4	Polar Aviation, transport/ice reconnaissance aircraft

This fine air-to-air shot of a Tu-4 (probably a Soviet Navy aircraft) cruising over international waters was taken by an intercepting NATO fighter in the mid-1950s.

Chapter 6

Transport Derivatives

'Aircraft 70' airliner (Tu-12, Tu-70)

In early 1946 the Tupolev OKB began development of a four-engined airliner which received the in-house designation 'aircraft 70'. The B-4 (Tu-4) bomber, which had just entered production, was chosen as the starting point. The idea of creating an airliner derivative of a combat aircraft then in first-line service seemed extremely appealing in the 1940s and 1950s, especially in the Soviet Union where operating economics did not enjoy the highest priority at the time. (Later the Tupolev OKB pursued this approach with the Tu-104 *Camel* twinjet medium-haul airliner and the Tu-114 *Rossiya* (Russia; NATO code name *Cleat*) four-turboprop long-haul airliner which were spin-offs of the Tu-16 *Badger* and the Tu-95 *Bear-A* respectively.)

Experience gained with the 'donor' bomber in the process of its development, testing and operational use made it possible to develop and put into service an airliner based on the said bomber with minimum technical risk and a very high degree of operational safety. Structural commonality was another important factor; this meant that no drastic changes of manufacturing technology and tooling at the OKB's experimental plant and eventually at the production factory would be required, which in turn reduced production costs and helped keep unit costs down. Finally, skilled flight crews which had trained in earnest on the bomber were available to crew an airliner development, which again enhanced flight safety.

Construction of a full-scale mock-up started in February 1946. In mid-March the Soviet Council of Ministers issued directive No. 472-191 followed by MAP order No. 159 on 27th March; these documents tasked the Tupolev OKB with designing and building a passenger aircraft based on the B-4 bomber and officially designated Tu-12. (This designation would later be re-used for a twinjet experimental bomber ('aircraft 77') based on the Tu-2.) A single prototype was to be completed and submitted for State acceptance trials not later than 1st May 1947; the decision on whether to proceed with series production would depend on the test results.

To speed up prototype construction it was decided to use, inasmuch as possible, the components of B-29-15-BW '365 Black' (42-6365) which had been dismantled com-

pletely for studying the design and also some of the usable parts salvaged from the wreckage of B-29A-1-BN 42-93829. By early 1946 the Tupolev OKB's experimental plant (MMZ No. 156) and the OKB's Kazan' branch had completed the task of reassembling the structural components of '365 Black'. Thus, B-29 subassemblies used in building the Tu-12 prototype included the outer wings, engine nacelles, flaps, main gear units and tail surfaces. The wing centre section was new, however, since the Tu-12 was a low-wing aircraft as opposed to the mid-wing B-29/Tu-4, and featured an increase in wing span of 0.81 m (2 ft 8 in).

The fuselage was also new, with a maximum diameter of 3.6 m (11 ft 10 in) versus the bomber's 2.9 m (9 ft 6 in). Unlike Boeing, which developed the Model 377 Stratocruiser from the same basic design, the Tupolev OKB opted for a conventional circular-section fuselage, not a 'double-bubble' structure. For the first time in Soviet aircraft design practice the fuselage was completely pressurised, with a pressure differential of 0.57 kg/cm² (8.14 psi); flush riveting was used, with sealed rivets and Thiokol rubber strips to seal the manufacturing joints. We may as well say at this stage that upon completion the fuselage was tested for leaks by pressurising it to the design pressure differential – again for the first time in the Soviet Union.

The mock-up was completed by June 1946 and duly approved by the mock-up review commission of the Civil Air Fleet (GVF – *Grazhdahnskiy vozdooshnyy flot*, the official name of the airline doing business as Aeroflot). In October of the same year MMZ No. 156 completed the 'aircraft 70' (Tu-12) prototype; following comprehensive systems checks the outer wings and tail unit were detached and the aircraft was trucked to Moscow's Central airfield, named after Mikhail V. Frunze (Moscow-Khodynka), where it was reassembled and then underwent further checks. Interestingly, the aircraft wore Soviet Air Force insignia (but no serial) and 'Tu-12' nose titles. By the time 'aircraft 70' arrived at Khodynka the B-29 pattern aircraft ('358 Black') was already parked there, having flown in from Izmaïlovo airfield a while earlier; thus any snags associated with the airliner's equipment and systems could be

resolved on site by simply checking up against the B-29.

The advanced development project was officially completed on 21st October 1946. According to ADP documents the Tu-12 was a four-engined airliner designed for international air routes (including intercontinental ones) and for long-haul domestic air routes. The ability to carry a large number of passengers in comfort over long distances at high speeds made the Tu-12 a first-rate heavy airliner.

Comfortable conditions for the passengers and crew were ensured by the pressurised cabin and flight deck which enabled the aircraft to cruise at up to 10,000 m (32,808 ft) above the clouds and turbulence. The cabin was furnished with comfortable seats and couches, featuring a heating/ventilation system and a galley. Three interior configurations were offered; one was a VIP aircraft for government use, with the rear cabin configured as an office and conference room for the 'main passenger' (ie, the head of an official delegation). The second version was a mixed layout with normal first class seating in the rear cabin while the forward cabin was divided into two de luxe compartments. The aircraft could be configured with either 48 seats for day flights or 40 seats, six of which could be transformed into sleeping bunks, for overnight flights. Finally, the third version seated 72, featuring four-abreast first class seating in both cabins. The latter version was selected as the standard one; however, it was decided that the Tu-12 would be used for 'special' (ie, VIP and other non-scheduled) flights during the initial production stage.

The Tu-12 had a crew of seven or eight comprising two pilots, a navigator, a flight engineer, a radio operator and two or three flight attendants, one of which was the 'ship's cook' (!). The flight crew sat on a flight deck featuring a two-level arrangement, the navigator sitting sideways, slightly below the others, in the extreme nose which was extensively glazed, like a bomb-aimer's station on a heavy bomber. This arrangement (used on subsequent Tupolev airliners up to the Tu-134 *Crusty* of 1963) allowed Air Force crews trained on the Tu-4 to fly the Tu-12 during special operations or if the airliner was requisitioned by the Air Force in times of war

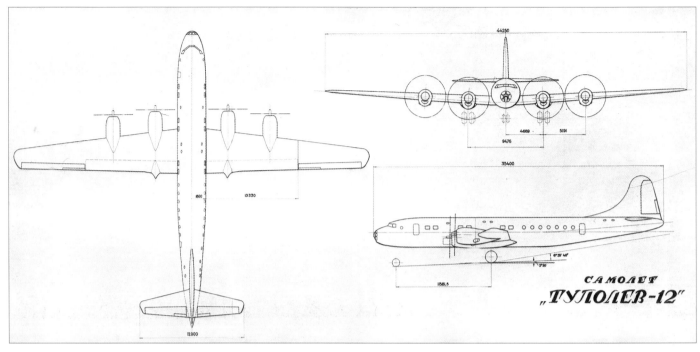

Above: A three-view drawing of the Tu-12 airliner featured in the advanced development project documents.

for use as a troop and cargo transport. The flight engineer and radio operator sat behind the pilots (to starboard and port respectively).

A crew rest area with a tip-up sofa and two bunks was located aft of the flight deck; it was accessible via the forward entry door and a ventral hatch with a ladder for access via the nosewheel well (the latter would be used for entering and exiting the aircraft at remote locations where normal airstairs were unavailable). Further aft was the forward passenger cabin, separated from the aft cabin by the galley compartment located over the wing centre

section and a 'cafeteria' (dining area) for eight with two tables (folding tables built into the seat backs had not been invented yet). The galley featured a sink for washing dishes – the days of disposable plastic tableware were still very far away. In the 40-seat mixed-class configuration the forward cabin was divided into two compartments, with toilet facilities in between. The forward compartment featured a pair of sofas for two persons each on the starboard side which could be slid towards each other and folded down to make a comfortable bed; a foldaway bunk was located above

these. On the opposite side was a table and two revolving seats (or rather, armchairs!) facing each other. The toilet compartment included a washroom, a lavatory and a wardrobe with a built-in strongbox for keeping valuables. The second compartment was similar to the first one, except that a second pair of transformable sofas and fold-away bunk were located to port in lieu of a table and two seats. The entire forward cabin could be isolated from the crew rest area and the galley by internal doors when a delegation was carried – presumably to prevent the crew from

These drawings show the interior layout of the 40-seat version, with three isolated compartments and basically four-abreast seating in the rear cabin. Interestingly, there were separate toilet facilities for gents and ladies. Of equal interest is the 'cafeteria' just ahead of the rear cabin (there were no integral tables yet).

Above and below: Final assembly of the 'aircraft 70' (Tu-12) prototype at the Tupolev OKB's experimental shop (MMZ No. 156) in Moscow.

Above: One of the Tu-12's main landing gear units. Like some other airframe components and equipment items, the main gear was borrowed from B-29-15-BW 42-6365.

Above: The Tu-12's tail unit.

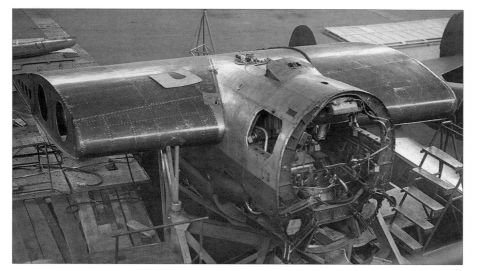

The Tu-12 differed from the Tu-4 in the position of the wings' production breaks. Illustrated here is one of the inner wing sections complete with the inboard engine nacelle.

eavesdropping! Aft of the wings was the rear passenger cabin with four/three-abreast first class seating for 26, a service compartment and the rear lavatories. Interestingly, there were separate men's and ladies' rooms.

The flight deck and passenger cabins formed a single pressure cabin occupying almost the entire fuselage. Air for the pressurisation/ventilation system was supplied by six turbochargers mounted on the engines; before entering the cabin it was heated or cooled as per requirement in air/air heat exchangers. Warm air was distributed in the cabins by overhead ducts, excess air exiting via automatic bleed valves under the cabin floor; this ensured that the cabins were evenly heated and ventilated. Two automatic pressure regulators maintained a constant cabin air pressure from 2,500 m (8,208 ft) right up to 9,000 m (29,528 ft); if these failed the flight engineer could still control the air pressure by means of a manual regulator and an emergency bleed valve. The system's maximum air delivery rate of 2,000 m³/sec (70,630 cu ft/sec) made it possible to prevent total decompression even if a sizeable air leak developed. A self-contained heater and blowers powered by the emergency generator/APU served for pre-heating the cabins in winter prior to passenger embarkation.

In all other aspects the Tu-12 was identical to the B-4, utilising many of the bomber's airframe components, the same powerplant and much the same equipment fit. The wings, for instance, were stock B-4 subassemblies, save for the centre section which was designed from scratch. Interestingly, the wing root ribs were flush with the fuselage sides, which facilitated final assembly considerably. In contrast, the B-4's huge centre section/inner wing assembly, built integrally with the fuselage, resulted in large 'stub wings' which hindered the fuselage's transportation to the final assembly line where the outer wings were attached.

The entire trailing edge of the inner wings and centre section was occupied by slotted flaps which moved on curved tracks when deployed. The flaps were electrically actuated.

Despite having a larger diameter and different contours, the fuselage of the Tu-12 made use of the same production technologies and design features as those of the B-4 – right down to the use of certain structural components, the same fuselage frame cross-sections etc. The tail surfaces were again borrowed from the B-4; stabilizer incidence could be adjusted on the ground by using interchangeable fittings.

The main landing gear units with twin 1,422 x 508 mm (56 x 20 in) wheels were identical to those fitted to the B-4. Conversely, the nose gear unit with twin 914 x 333 mm

(36 x 13.1 in) wheels was specially designed for the Tu-12, even though some stock B-4 components, including the shimmy damper, were used.

The Tu-12 was powered by four ASh-73TK engines. A total of 22 main fuel tanks in the wings held 22,000 litres (4,840 Imp gal) of fuel; they were divided into four groups, one for each engine, with a cross-feed system. Provision was made for four auxiliary tanks in the wing centre section holding an additional 6,000 litres (1,320 Imp gal) of fuel.

Six GS-9000 nine-kilowatt DC generators supplied electric power, with two 12A-30 DC batteries as a back-up. AC power was provided by four PK-750F converters. When the engines were shut down DC power was supplied by a 5-kW GS-5000 generator driven by the M-10 APU.

The pneumatic de-icing system was taken straight from the B-4. It enabled the airliner to operate in adverse weather, enhancing operational reliability and despatch regularity.

Apart from the usual complement of avionics and flight instrumentation, the Tu-12 was to feature an AP-5 electric autopilot, a high-range radio altimeter and an RV-2 low-range radio altimeter, an RUSP-45 blind landing system, an MRP-45 marker beacon receiver, two ARK-45 ADFs (main and back-up), a gyro-flux gate compass, a drift sight and a co-ordinate indicator. Just in case, however, an astrodome was provided for the navigator who could plot the aircraft's course, using an astrosextant and an astrocompass if all else failed.

Two-way communication with air traffic control (ATC) centres was catered for by a 1RSB-70 radio set; two further radios – a Soviet 12RSU-10 HF radio and a reverse-engineered American SCR-274N VHF radio – were provided for communication with the airport tower and other aircraft. An SPU-BS-36 intercom was fitted for communication between the crew members (including the cabin crew). The Tupolev OKB intended to equip the Tu-12 with an indigenous Gneys-5S (Gneiss) radar, a Ton-3 (Tone) radar warning receiver and an SCh-3 IFF transponder.

The real prototype did not exactly conform to the ADP specifications as far as the equipment was concerned. For instance, larger wheels were fitted to all three landing gear units – 1,450 x 520 mm (57.08 x 20.47 in) on the main units and 950 x 350 mm (37.40 x 13.77 in) on the nose unit. An SPU-14 intercom and a Bariy (Barium) IFF were installed; the Gneys-5S radar was missing etc. Later, as the flight tests progressed and the aircraft underwent repairs, some equipment items gave way to newer ones which had just been mastered by the Soviet aircraft industry – a process which paralleled the upgrading of the production Tu-4.

Above and below: Roll-out of the Tu-12 at Khodynka. The type is marked on the nose in the Tupolev OKB's 'trademark' typeface. Note also the Yermolayev Yer-2, Il'yushin IL-4 and DC-3s on the apron.

Close-up of the Tu-12's landing gear as the aircraft sits on the apron at Khodynka.

This page: Three views of the 'aircraft 70' (Tu-12) during manufacturer's flight tests. The rectangular windows are for the sleeper compartments and dining area while the circular ones are for the rear cabin; the small windows located higher up are for the galley and lavatories.

Three more views of the prototype. Apparently the 'Tu-12' nose titles were carried on the port side only. Note the crew access ladder in the nosewheel well in the centre photo. Curiously, despite its civil nature, the aircraft wore Air Force markings throughout its flying career.

Tu-12 specifications as per ADP documents

Wing span	44.25 m (145 ft 2 in)
Length overall	35.4 m (116 ft 2 in)
Height on ground	9.75 m (31 ft 11 in)
Wing area	166.1 m² (1,788 sq ft)
Empty weight	37,140 kg (81,880 lb)
All-up weight:	
normal	50,000 kg (110,231 lb)
maximum	59,000 kg (130,072 lb)
Top speed:	
at sea level	465 km/h (289 mph)
at 10,000 m (32,808 ft)	582 km/h (362 mph)
Service ceiling	10,400 m (34,121 ft)
Climb time to 5,000 m (16,404 ft)	17.3 minutes
Maximum range:	
with normal AUW	2,500 km (1,553 miles)
with maximum AUW	5,000 km (3,107 miles)
Take-off run	960 m (3,150 ft)
Take-off distance	1,800 m (5,905 ft)

Officially, Stage A of the manufacturer's flight tests lasted from 19th October 1946 to 16th February 1947. On 25th November the reassembled and checked aircraft was taken on charge by the OKB's flight test facility, making its maiden flight two days later with F. F. Opadchiy in the captain's seat and A. D. Perelyot as co-pilot; M. M. Yegorov was the engineer in charge of the test programme.

The first three flights from Moscow-Khodynka proceeded normally but the fourth (on 16th February 1947) nearly ended in disaster. The day's task was to check the airliner's stability and handling at maximum speed, and as 'aircraft 70' accelerated at 4,000 m (13,120 ft), flying over the suburbs of Moscow near Chkalovskaya airbase, the No. 2 engine disintegrated. Bits and pieces of the engine flew in all directions and a fire erupted, quickly burning through the engine cowling. The crew managed to extinguish the flames, using the fire suppression system, but then another problem manifested itself as the propeller of the stricken engine started to overspeed. Try as they might, the crew could not feather it.

A loud bang resounded through the aircraft and the propeller froze violently as the No. 2 engine's reduction gearbox failed and jammed. As a line from a song by Rod Stewart goes, 'Act One is over without costume change'. But the drama kept unfolding: even as Yegorov advised the captain that now they could head back to Khodynka, the three good engines started losing power inexplicably and the aircraft could no longer maintain altitude. All attempts to restore normal engine operation failed and the Tu-12 continued descending slowly but surely.

Realising he would not make it to Khodynka, Opadchiy opted for a wheels-up landing at the Medvezh'yi Oziora ('Bear Lakes')

airfield located about halfway between Chkalovskaya AB and the Moscow city limits. In fact, the aircraft did not even make it that far, putting down in a snow-covered field short of the runway, 1.5 km (0.9 miles) from the highway that runs east from Moscow to the town of Schcholkovo. With the engines cut and the fuel fire shut-off valves closed, the airliner was still slithering fast and a high-voltage power line was directly ahead.

Still, the prototype and the crew were miraculously saved at the last moment. Mercifully the port flap hit a large snow-covered mound; the aircraft swung 90° to port and came to rest directly under the power line, the starboard wing pointing between two power line pylons. Jumping clear of the aircraft, the crew quickly ascertained there was no fire and immediate danger of an explosion and then set about assessing the damage. When the cowlings of the three ailing engines were opened the cause of the trouble was immediately apparent: all of the inlet pipes had become separated from the cylinder heads (!) and the engines were simply not getting enough air.

On learning of the crash-landing Andrey N. Tupolev and the top officers of GK NII VVS rushed to the scene; the area was promptly cordoned off by security police. Apart from the investigation of the accident, the OKB was now facing the task of returning the airliner to

Andrey Nikolayevich Tupolev in the forward luxury compartment of the Tu-12 intended for the head of an official delegation.

airworthy condition as soon as possible, since the Tu-12 was slated to participate in that year's May Day parade in Moscow. After defuelling, the aircraft was lightened as much as possible by removing the engines and engine nacelles, flaps and all equipment items. Then the Tu-12 was removed from under the power line and towed on its undercarriage along a specially built dirt road to the Medvezh'yi Oziora airfield. There it was trestled, a heated temporary shed was erected around the wings and centre fuselage where the engine nacelles and flaps had been, and an AOG (aircraft on ground) team took charge and set about making field repairs.

Two months later, on 20th April 1947, the aircraft (which in the meantime had received the new designation Tu-70 and appropriate nose titles) made its first post-repair flight. This marked the beginning of Stage B of the manufacturer's flight tests which lasted until 10th October 1947. The mission was accomplished: on 1st May 1947 the Tu-70 prototype led a large formation of Il'yushin IL-12 airliners – an equally new type – in a low-level pass over Moscow's Red Square. This spectacular move is perfectly understandable, since the Tu-70 was regarded as Aeroflot's future flagship at the time. In August 1947 the aircraft participated in the traditional Tushino fly-past along with the first production Tu-4 bombers.

Meanwhile, both the Tupolev OKB and Arkadiy D. Shvetsov's OKB-19 were trying to determine the cause of the accident. A special accident investigation board was set up to find out why the port inboard engine had disintegrated and what had caused the mysterious damage to the remaining engines. Three areas then came under close scrutiny: the wrecked No. 2 ASh-73TK engine, the quality of the fuel and the design of the copied American supercharger control system.

Examination of the No. 2 engine revealed that severe scoring had occurred on all 18 pistons; this had caused several pistons to jam and the connecting rods to break, smashing the crankcase. As the engine came apart, flying debris ruptured the oil line for the propeller feathering system pump and damaged the supercharger controls.

Analysis of the fuel showed thing were not all well here either. Sloppy work practice at Moscow-Khodynka's fuel depot often caused different grades of aviation gasoline to get mixed inside the fuel bowsers; as a result, aircraft would often be serviced with 70-72 octane avgas instead of the required 92-93 octane fuel.

Finally, it turned out that the supercharger governing system copied straight from the B-29 had a serious design flaw. The supercharger control circuits of all four engines were connected to a common potentiometer, which was a bad idea. If any of the super-

The rear cabin of the Tu-12, looking aft...

charger control circuits shorted, the system would automatically shut all the superchargers' air bleed valves, which is exactly what happened when the No. 2 engine of the Tu-70 failed. All three good engines were immediately overpressurised, the inlet pipes breaking away violently from the cylinder heads like a cork popping out of a champagne bottle.

(Quite possibly Boeing had encountered the same problems during the B-29's flight test programme when the reliability of the Wright R-3350 still left a lot to be desired. The Superfortress had several instances of uncontained engine failure and in-flight fires which paralleled the scenario of the Tu-70's 16th February 1947 accident; one of these resulted in the

...and looking forward, with the dining area visible beyond. This photo was taken at a later date, judging by the embroidered seat covers (no comment on the artistic design) and the addition of window curtains.

Above left: The entrance to the navigator's station; note the astrodome. The notice reads: 'WARNING! Replace L/G retraction fuse before take-off'; apparently it was removed to prevent accidental retraction on the ground! Above right: The co-pilot's seat, control column and instrument panel; the wheel is marked 'Tu-70'.

Left: The flight engineer's workstation on the left side with engine instruments, throttles (on the left) and propeller pitch control levers (on the right).
Right: The navigator's instrument panel on the left side. Note that some of the instruments are American-made and some positions on the panel are vacant.

Above: The forward luxury compartment featured two sofas and a table to starboard (left) and two revolving armchairs with a table in between to port (right).

Above left: A view of the second luxury compartment.
Above right: The sofa and table in the forward luxury compartment.

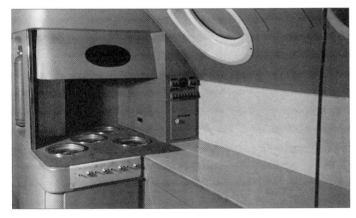 

Above left: The galley compartment.
Above right: The first-class seats in the rear cabin. Note that the headrest covers are stamped 'Tu-70'.

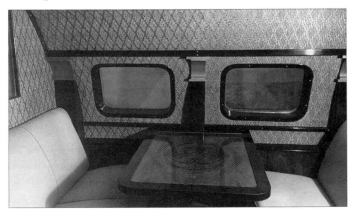 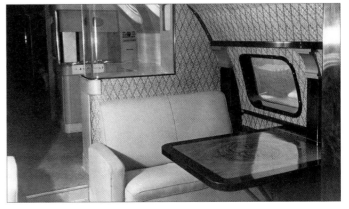

The 'cafeteria' (dining area) where up to eight people could eat at a time; the bar is visible in the background in the right-hand photo. Note the high-quality upholstery.

Above: The Tu-12 came to grief on 16th February 1947, belly-landing in a field after a multiple engine failure. The trail shows how the aircraft swung to starboard before coming to rest; note the wires in the background.

Above and below: The cowlings and bent propellers of the starboard engines. Note the Hamilton Standard badges on the propeller blades.

fatal crash of the first XB-29. Apparently the Americans had never discovered the bug in the system – especially since the Wright Aeronautical Company quickly brought the Twin Cyclone up to an adequate reliability level. No more investigative effort was spent on this design aspect and all B-29s left the production lines with a flawed and potentially dangerous supercharger control system.

When the findings of the accident investigation board had been formulated the Shvetsov OKB made a promise to improve the ASh-73TK by introducing adequate manufacturing tolerances for the pistons. As an interim measure it was decided to exercise strict control of the octane number of the gasoline used by the ASh-73TK, in order to ensure better working conditions for the engines. It was further decided to modify the supercharger governing system by introducing individual potentiometers (one for each engine) and upgrade all existing Tu-4s forthwith. Within a short time the engine had been brought up to scratch, the Tu-4 fleet equipped with the new system and everything was back to normal. Meanwhile, on the wrong side of the Pacific, the B-29 fleet continued operating successfully with the old system and pretty soon no one – except the manufacturers, of course – remembered (or cared) how many potentiometers there were.

In October 1947 the Tu-70 completed its manufacturer's flight tests which involved 35 flights totalling 36 hours. The following performance figures were obtained at this stage:

Empty weight	38,290 kg (84,415 lb)
All-up weight:	
normal	51,400 kg (113,317 lb)
maximum	60,000 kg (132,277 lb)
Top speed:	
at sea level	424 km/h (263 mph)
at 9,000 m (29,530 ft)	568 km/h (353 mph)
Service ceiling	11,000 m (36,089 ft)
Climb time to 5,000 m (16,400 ft)	21.2 minutes
Take-off run	670 m (2,198 ft)
Landing run	600 m (1,968 ft)

Between October 1947 and 2nd July 1948 the Tu-70 was laid up, sitting engineless pending the delivery of improved ASh-73TKs with an engine life extended to 100 hours. Equipping the airliner with off-the-shelf ASh-73TKs having a 50-hour service life, as fitted to the Tu-4, was out of the question: the Civil Air Fleet refused to admit the Tu-70 for State acceptance trials with these engines. On 6th August 1948 the aircraft was finally submitted for State acceptance trials; these officially began on 11th September, lasting until 14th December. The trials report said the Tu-70 met the requirements stated in the Council of Ministers directive in accordance with which it was designed.

A short while earlier, on 16th June 1948, the Council of Ministers and MAP had released directive No. 2051 and order No. 424 respectively, ordering the Tu-70 into production. Eventually, however, production never commenced. For one thing, the government order for the Tu-4 was so large that the three production plants building the type were not in a position to build any Tu-70s due to lack of capacity. Secondly (and even more importantly), the Civil Air Fleet really was not interested in such a large airliner at the time; the relatively cheap and abundant, if less luxurious, Lisunov Li-2 *Cab* (a derivative of the Douglas DC-3 built under licence) and IL-12 twin-engined airliners could cope with the existing passenger traffic. The need for a Soviet airliner seating 50 to 100 passengers did not arise until seven or ten years later, by which time gas turbine engines had appeared on the commercial scene, powering the twin-jet Tu-104 and the four-turboprop An-10 and IL-18 *Coot-A*. The Tu-70 and the original 'first-generation' IL-18 (incidentally, powered by the same ASh-73TK radials) were first victimised by bad timing and then rendered obsolete by new technology; yet they generated valuable experience to be used in designing future Soviet commercial aircraft.

Still, this was not the end of the road for the Tu-70. On 17th October 1949 it was submitted for checkout tests which continued until 20th January 1950. Then it caught the eye of Vasiliy I. Stalin, the Soviet leader's son and Commander of the Moscow Defence District air force, who wanted the Tu-70 for himself as a staff transport. In preparation for the planned transfer to the Air Force, the aircraft underwent a lengthy refurbishment at MMZ No. 156 which was completed in the summer of 1950, but it was never delivered. The OKB managed to keep the prototype; Andrey N. Tupolev proved that the aircraft had experimental status and was powered by development engines (a rumour was even spread that the Tu-70 was fitted with Wright R-3350 engines removed from a B-29) and hence he could not put the precious life of Stalin Jr. at risk. Thus the Tu-70 was saved from the ignominy of carrying football players, horsies and dames, to all of which the generalissimo's son was more than partial.

In 1949 the Tupolev OKB considered the possibility of re-engining the Tu-70 with 4,000-hp ASh-2TKs, but the proposal was not proceeded with.

In December 1951 the Tu-70 was turned over to GK NII VVS for checkout tests with a view to determining the type's suitability for the military transport role. After that the aircraft was used in various test and development programmes and for regular passenger/cargo transport duties, until finally struck off charge and scrapped in 1954.

Above: With the engines removed to save weight and the nacelles covered by tarpaulins, the Tu-70 (formerly Tu-12) is evacuated from the crash site.

Above and below: Stuck in the middle of a house? No indeed! These pictures show the Tu-70 undergoing repairs at Medvezh'yi Oziora airfield, with a shed built around it to ensure comfortable working conditions.

Above: The Tu-70 after arriving by road at Medvezh'yi Oziora in late February 1947 minus engines and flaps.

The Tu-70 starts up the engines before a test flight.

Above: This drawing shows the structural components which the Tu-70 and the B-4 (Tu-4) had in common. It also illustrates the difference in fuselage cross-section and the position of the fuselage relative to the wings.

A rare air-to-air shot of the Tu-70.

Three views of the Tu-75 military transport. The kinship between the Tu-75 and the Tu-70 is obvious; what is not obvious is that the Tu-75 was actually not just a simple adaptation of the airliner.

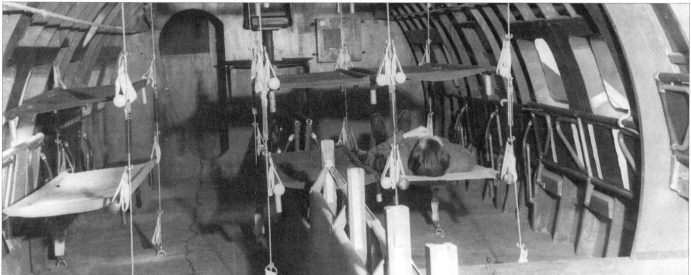

Top to bottom: The Tu-75's cargo cabin in troopship configuration with lightweight paratroop seats installed along the centreline and cabin walls; the same aircraft in medevac configuration with stretchers; and the ventral cargo loading/paradropping hatch (note the folded troop seats along the walls).

A full load of paratroopers in the cabin of the Tu-75 during trials.

Tu-75 military transport ('aircraft 75', Tu-16 – first use of designation)

In September 1946 the Tupolev OKB started work on a military transport derivative of the Tu-70 (Tu-12). The initiative was supported by the Soviet government: the Council of Ministers directive No. 493-192 of 11th March 1947 and MAP order No. 223 of 16th April tasked OKB-156 with developing a military transport based on the Tu-70 airliner. A single prototype was to be submitted for State acceptance trials in August 1948.

The advanced development project was completed by 1st December 1947. Again the Soviet approach differed from the American one: unlike the C-97 (Model 367)/Model 377 Stratocruiser, which were almost identical in airframe design, the new transport was **not** a simple adaptation of the Tu-70, even though it used many of the latter's airframe components and equipment items. The wing span and wing area were increased, and the fuselage was stretched while its maximum diameter was marginally reduced to 3.5 m (11 ft 5 in). The height on the ground was reduced by a modified landing gear design (the aircraft sat lower over the ground due to the need to facilitate loading). The 'aircraft 75' was to be powered by improved ASh-73TKVN engines.

The fuselage of 'aircraft 75' featured a ventral loading/paradropping and a hinged cargo ramp forming the rear part of the cargo cabin floor. Additionally, side doors were introduced aft of the wings for dropping paratroopers. A tail gunner's station and two remote-controlled gun barbettes mounted dorsally ahead of the wings and ventrally aft of the wings were envisaged; the defensive armament was borrowed completely from the Tu-4.

The cargo hatch was the most interesting design feature. The hatch was closed by a downward-opening cargo ramp and a rear door segment which hinged upwards into the fuselage. The ramp could be used for loading paratroopers or vehicles and permitted paradropping of same. Thus 'aircraft 75' presaged the cargo-handling system used later by the Antonov OKB on the An-8 and An-12 military transports.

'Aircraft 75' was the Soviet Union's first succesful attempt to create a fully capable military transport carrying heavy and bulky vehicles internally. The aircraft was to operate in three configurations to suit different missions – transport, troopship and medevac – and be readily convertible to any of these configurations.

Typical payload options for the basic transport configuration included two OSU-76 SP guns, or two ST-3 caterpillar tractors, or up to seven GAZ-67B army jeeps, or five 85-mm (3.34-in) field guns without tractors, or two artillery pieces with tractors, or other fighting and transport vehicles and weaponry in various combinations. The maximum payload was 12 tonnes (26,455 lb). A cargo hoist with a 3-tonne (6,614-lb) lifting capacity, moving along rails on the cargo cabin roof, was provided to facilitate loading and unloading.

When configured as a troopship the aircraft could carry 120 fully armed troops or 90 paratroopers. Alternatively, small cargo items could be paradropped in 64 PDMM flexible bags suspended under the cargo cabin roof. The medevac version accommodated 31 stretcher patients and four medical attendants.

A full-scale mock-up was built in December 1947 and presented to the mock-up review commission in January 1948. In June the Ministry of Aircraft Industry issued an order postponing the beginning of the State acceptance trials until June 1949. Concur-

rently the transport received the provisional official designation Tu-16. Prototype construction began at the Tupolev OKB's Kazan' branch located at the production Plant No. 22. Once again bearing Air Force insignia but no serial number, the aircraft was completed in November 1949, making its first flight on 21st January 1950. Manufacturer's flight tests contin- ued until May 1950, with I. Kabanov and M. Mel'nikov as project test pilots; the aircraft was test flown with a crew of six. By then the transport aircraft had received its final designation: Tu-75.

Contrary to the ADP documents, the actual aircraft had only the tail gunner's station, the upper and lower gun barbettes being omitted, and the apertures for the envisaged sighting blisters on the aft fuselage sides were blanked off; no armament was ever installed. Some other airframe design features also differed slightly from the project.

The following data were recorded for the Tu-75 during manufacturer's flight tests:

Wing span	44.83 m (147 ft 1 in)
Length overall	35.61 m (116 ft 10 in)
Height on ground	9.05 m (29 ft 8 in)
Wing area	167.2 m² (1,798 sq ft)
Empty weight	37,810 kg (83,357 lb)
All-up weight:	
normal	56,660 kg (124,914 lb)
maximum	65,400 kg (144,182 lb)
Top speed	545 km/h (339 mph)
Service ceiling	9,500 m (31,168 ft)
Maximum range	4,140 km (2,572 miles)
Take-off run	1,060 m (3,478 ft)
Landing run	900 m (2,953 ft)

Despite its advanced features and fairly high performance in its day, the Tu-75 did not enter production because the VVS opted for a 'quick fix', converting several hundred *Bulls* into Tu-4D transports, which was cheaper. At the same time the Air Force placed an order for the development of modern military transport aircraft powered by turboprops. Additionally, the VVS demanded that new airliner designs be provided with quick-install medical and paradropping equipment and that alternative rear fuselage sections be designed for these airliners, allowing military transport versions to be built on the same production lines! These requirements proved to be largely impracticable and were not complied with.

Upon completion of the trials programme the sole Tu-75 was used by the Tupolev OKB for several years as a cargo transport, operating from the OKB's flight test facility in Zhukovskiy, and occasionally participated in the testing of new paradropping systems. Sadly, the aircraft was lost in a fatal crash in 1954.

Chapter 7

The Final Development

'Aircraft 80' (Tu-80) long-range heavy bomber

Possessing a range of some 6,000 km (3,720 miles), the Tu-4 could perform combat missions only within the confines of Europe, North Africa, the Middle East and the Far East. Thus, increasing the heavy bomber's range became one of the directions of the Tupolev OKB's work in the late 1940s and early 1950s.

The first step on the path to creating a strategic bomber capable of reaching the territory of the main potential adversary – the USA – without resorting to in-flight refuelling resulted in the emergence of the 'aircraft 80'. This was a thorough modification of the Tu-4 aimed at rectifying the drawbacks of the progenitor's layout, improving its lift/drag ratio and enhancing the armament.

The new bomber featured a radio operator's work station in the front cabin, which simplified the interaction between the crew members (on the Tu-4 it was located in the cabin amidships). The bomb-aimer and the navigator were seated in the front part of the aircraft, which afforded them a considerably better view from their work stations. The problem of view distortion that had caused much vexation to Tu-4 pilots was rectified by introducing a stepped windscreen.

The targeted improvement of the lift/drag ratio was achieved through the following measures. Firstly, the engine nacelles were redesigned, the cross-section of all four

nacelles being reduced by 1.9 m² (20.4 sq ft) as compared to the Tu-4's engine nacelles. As a result, the power required for 'propelling' the nacelles of the 'aircraft 80' in maximum speed flight at sea level was reduced by 130 hp per engine.

Secondly, the defensive armament was 'cleaned up'. The forward dorsal barbette was made fully retractable in cruise flight, and two other barbettes (a dorsal and a ventral one) were recessed into the fuselage at an insignificant detriment to the field of fire. The lateral sighting blisters were made elliptical (instead of the hemispherical blisters used on the Tu-4) and were also semi-recessed into the fuselage, the sides of the pressure cabin amidships receiving a concave shape.

Finally, the antenna of the Kobal't radar was placed in a streamlined chin radome under the navigator's station instead of the Tu-4's retractable 'thimble' radome, creating a lot of drag when extended. True, this severely limited the radar scanner's travel; however, special research into the properties of different radomes showed that the resulting elongated pattern of the radar beam coverage was quite acceptable from the point of view of operational requirements. Subsequently such radomes became a standard feature on a whole range of combat and passenger aircraft created by the Tupolev OKB. The

lift/drag ratio of the 'aircraft 80' rose to 18 as compared to 17 in the case of the Tu-4.

The new bomber was powered by four upgraded ASh-73TKFN engines driving new AV-16U four-bladed propellers (although initially the aircraft had been designed to take ASh-2TK engines). This version of the ASh-73TK featured fuel injection instead of carburettors (hence the FN for *forseerovannyy, s neposredstvennym vpryskom* – uprated, with direct fuel injection); this resulted in a lower specific fuel consumption in take-off mode and the engine output rose to 2,360 hp at nominal power and 2,720 hp for take-off.

This package of measures aimed at improving the machine's aerodynamics, coupled with increasing the fuel tankage and reducing the SFC, made it possible to extend the range of the 'aircraft 80' to 8,200 km (5,095 miles), which was an improvement of 30-35% as compared to the Tu-4.

Apart from the alterations listed above, the following modifications were introduced on the 'aircraft 80' in comparison with the Tu-4:
- wing dihedral was reduced from 4° 30' to 1° 43';
- the wing leading edge was extended along the whole span;
- to retain the existing wing airfoil section while extending the leading edge, the thickness of the outer wing panels was increased

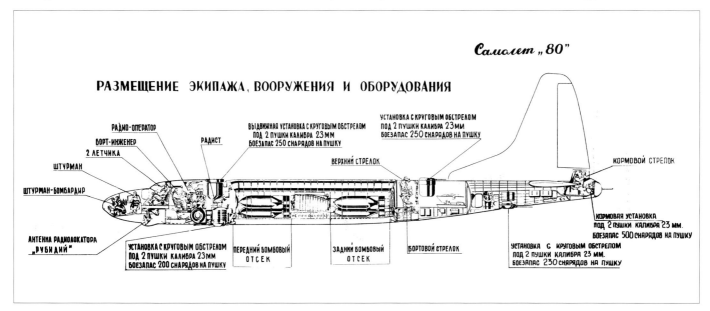

A cutaway drawing from the advanced development project documents showing the internal layout of the 'aircraft 80' bomber.

Above, below and head of opposite page: The 'aircraft 80' seen during manufacturer's flight tests. The new nose profile and recessed lateral sighting blisters are clearly visible, as is the bomber's pronounced nose-up attitude on the ground.
Opposite page, below: These photos give an excellent detail view of the 'aircraft 80' bomber's streamlined engine nacelles with AV-16U propellers during tests at LII in December 1949.

by building up the appropriate part of the upper skinning;

- flaps of increased area and span were installed;

- the wingtips received new fairings;

- bendable trim tabs (called *nozhee* – 'knives') were fitted to the trailing edges of all control surfaces for the purpose of adjusting the aerodynamic balance;

- the forward pressure cabin was extended by 3 m (9 ft 10 in) and reshaped;

- the forward fuselage was made more pointed and its diameter was reduced;

- new wing and stabiliser root fairings were introduced;

- the fin area was increased and the fin structure altered;

- the span of the horizontal tail was increased;

- the area of the elevator and rudder trim tabs was increased by increasing their span;

- the tips of the tail surfaces were recontoured.

The offensive armament system also underwent modifications. The bomb bays and their doors were lengthened – the forward bay by 38 cm (1 ft 3 in) and the aft bay by 40 cm (1 ft 4 in), making it possible to carry bombs of greater calibre. Greater length of the front cabin and of the bomb bays resulted in the overall length being increased by nearly 4 m (13 ft 1 in). Provision was made for carrying the bulky 9,000-kg (19,842-lb) FAB-9000 high-explosive bomb externally under the wing centre section.

To increase the effectiveness of the defensive armament, the 20-mm Berezin B-20 cannon were replaced by the 23-mm Nudel'man/ Sooranov NS-23 cannon.

Changes were introduced into the deicing system, too. Inflatable Goodrich-type de-icer boots on the wing leading edges gave place to more effective hot air de-icers, which were also more convenient in operation. The hot air came from special kerosene stoves. Subsequently such de-icers became a standard item on the aircraft designed by the Tupolev OKB.

A directive calling for the initiation of work on modifying the Tu-4 into the 'aircraft 80' was issued in June 1948, albeit the design work on the new bomber had already begun in March and April of the same year. The government task stipulated the construction of just one prototype, to be handed over for State acceptance trials in July 1949.

The advanced development project was completed at the end of November 1948 and work on detail drawings was initiated at the beginning of 1949. The full-size mock-up of the aircraft was presented to the commission together with the ADP documents. There were many critical observations concerning both the project and the mock-up, and agreement on all the outstanding questions was not reached until the end of 1949. Construction of the Tu-80 prototype (the bomber was also known under this designation) was initiated on 15th November 1948 and completed in July 1949. In August the finished aircraft was

moved to Izmaïlovo airfield for final assembly and adjustment work.

On 1st December 1949 the new bomber took to the air for the first time and stayed airborne for 23 minutes with test pilot F. F. Opadchiy at the controls. After that the aircraft was ferried to the LII airfield where the manufacturer's tests were commenced (they were conducted by test pilot A. A. Yefimov). In all, 30 flights were performed and a total of 29 hours 5 minutes was logged. The operation of the AV-16U feathering reversible-pitch propellers was checked in the course of the testing, as was the fuel tanks' inert gas pressurisation system. Generally the Tu-80 flew well; criticism coming from the test commission was concerned mainly with equipment and bombing armament.

However, the performance of the new bomber was not fully on a par with exigencies of the time. Besides, the OKB had started design work on a more advanced aircraft, the '85'. Therefore in September 1949, even before the manufacturer's tests had begun, it was decided not to submit the 'aircraft 80' for State acceptance trials and use the completed prototype for various experiments at LII.

In 1951 the 'aircraft 80' underwent stability and handling checks; simultaneously, measurements were made of elastic deformations of the wings, fuselage and the horizontal tail. For this purpose the aircraft was fitted with all sorts of instruments and sensors capable of recording deformations in the course of the flight experiment. This task was

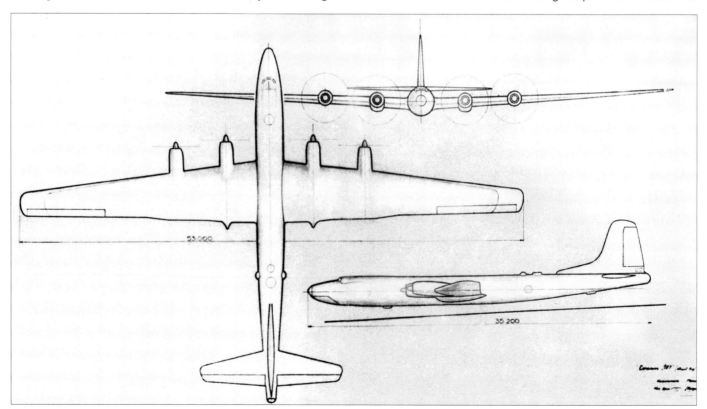

A provisional three-view drawing of the 'project 487' ultra-long-range bomber from the advanced development project files. Note the stippled lines in the upper view showing an alternative version with shorter-span wings.

undertaken by photographing different parts of the aircraft with S-13 gun cameras. The size of the deformation was determined by precise measurements of the pictures of the aircraft parts in flight and on the ground, with due allowance for scale, the measurements being made at different cross-sections of the structure.

The 'aircraft 80' had an inherent design fault of no small magnitude. In comparison with the Tu-4 its centre of gravity position was further forward while the arms of the control surfaces (ailerons, elevator and rudder) remained approximately the same. To compensate for this the area of the control surfaces was increased, but this proved to be inadequate. Therefore the 'aircraft 80' was flown with 900 kg (1,984 lb) of ballast located in the aft fuselage to keep the cg within acceptable limits.

The bomber ended its days as a target at a shooting range. Before the 'aircraft 80' was ferried to the shooting range, however, somebody at LII had removed the balancing weight from the aircraft, and the ferrying pilots narrowly escaped a crash during that last flight.

'Aircraft 85' (Tu-85) long-range heavy bomber

When the testing of the 'aircraft 80' prototype was completed, the Tupolev OKB took the decision to make use of the experimental materials thus obtained in the work on new heavy aircraft and, in particular, the 'aircraft 85' bomber.

Not only Soviet designers but also their American counterparts followed the path of updating an initial type for the purpose of increasing its range. After the end of the war the Boeing company modernised the B-29 bomber and started testing the B-50 derivative. The aircraft had greater dimensions and a higher top speed; it was powered by Pratt & Whitney R-4360 Wasp Major engines delivering 3,500 hp apiece and featured an aerial refuelling system. In March 1949 a non-stop flight around the world was made for the first time by a modified B-50A aircraft with four in-flight refuellings. At the same time the company evolved a project for a new strategic bomber, the B-54, which pushed the B-29 concept in the direction of a further increase in take-off weight (104 tonnes/229,278 lb) and range (15,000 km/9,321 miles), the design speed reaching 700 km/h (435 mph).

The project was not adopted because another bomber, the six-engined Convair B-36 Peacemaker, had entered series production by then. The B-36 was not inferior to the B-54 in performance and possessed a warload of 30 tonnes (66,138 lb); in consequence, it was capable of delivering all large-size and heavyweight munitions, including nuclear ones.

Above: A wind tunnel model of the 'aircraft 85' bomber illustrating the long fuselage and the high aspect ratio wings.

Analysis of the development of the USA's strategic aviation and creation of indigenous nuclear weapons by the Soviet Union (the first Soviet atomic bomb was exploded in 1949) prompted the designers of the OKB-156, led by Tupolev, to engage actively in creating a new strategic bomber that would be capable of delivering nuclear weapons to the North American continent.

Thus, work on the 'aircraft 80' logically transformed itself into work on the '85' project. A directive of the Council of Ministers of USSR calling for the construction of the '85' long-range four-engined bomber with a range of 11,000 to 13,000 km (6,835 to 8,078 miles) was issued on 16th September 1949. However, as was often the case, design work on the machine had started earlier (in August). Hence the performance requirements stipu-

lated by the directive were more or less realistic and were within the OKB's capabilities. The first prototype of the new bomber was to be submitted for State acceptance trials in December 1950, completion of the trials being envisaged for 1st August 1951.

The problem was that neither the aerodynamic characteristics of the wings of the Tu-4 and Tu-80 progenitor aircraft, nor the powerplant comprising ASh-73TK or ASh-73TKFN engines, no matter how modified, could ensure the possibility of obtaining the required range. Therefore, making use of the general layout of the Tu-80 and of some successful technical features evolved by that time, the Tupolev OKB created what was effectively a completely new aircraft.

When designing the '85' bomber (later it was also known as Tu-85), much attention

Another view of the same wind tunnel model.

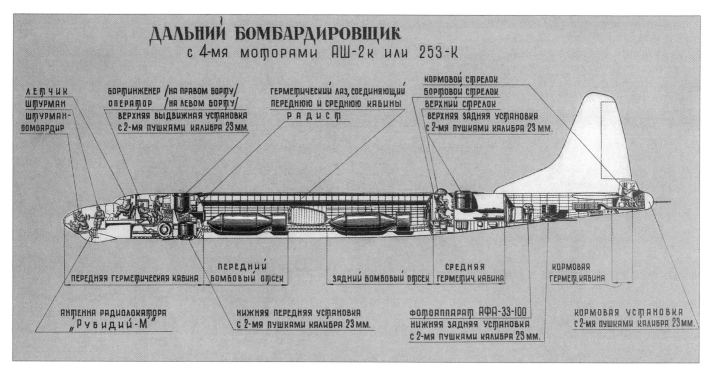

ДАЛЬНИЙ БОМБАРДИРОВЩИК
с 4-мя моторами АШ-2К или 253-К

ЛЕТЧИК
ШТУРМАН
ШТУРМАН-
БОМБАРДИР

БОРТИНЖЕНЕР /НА ПРАВОМ БОРТУ/
ОПЕРАТОР /НА ЛЕВОМ БОРТУ/
ВЕРХНЯЯ ВЫДВИЖНАЯ УСТАНОВКА
с 2-мя пушками калибра 23мм.

ГЕРМЕТИЧЕСКИЙ ЛАЗ, СОЕДИНЯЮЩИЙ
ПЕРЕДНЮЮ И СРЕДНЮЮ КАБИНЫ
РАДИСТ

КОРМОВОЙ СТРЕЛОК
БОРТОВОЙ СТРЕЛОК
ВЕРХНИЙ СТРЕЛОК
ВЕРХНЯЯ ЗАДНЯЯ УСТАНОВКА
с 2-мя пушками калибра 23мм.

ПЕРЕДНЯЯ ГЕРМЕТИЧЕСКАЯ КАБИНА
ПЕРЕДНИЙ
БОМБОВЫЙ ОТСЕК
ЗАДНИЙ БОМБОВЫЙ ОТСЕК
СРЕДНЯЯ
ГЕРМЕТИЧ. КАБИНА
КОРМОВАЯ
ГЕРМЕТ. КАБИНА

АНТЕННА РАДИОЛОКАТОРА
„РУБИДИЙ-М"
НИЖНЯЯ ПЕРЕДНЯЯ УСТАНОВКА
с 2-мя пушками калибра 23мм.
ФОТОАППАРАТ АФА-33-100
НИЖНЯЯ ЗАДНЯЯ УСТАНОВКА
с 2-мя пушками калибра 23мм.
КОРМОВАЯ УСТАНОВКА
с 2-мя пушками калибра 23мм.

Above: A drawing showing the fuselage layout of the 'aircraft 85' (referred to in this instance as a 'long-range bomber with four ASh-2K or [M-] 253K engines'). The bomb bays were large enough to accommodate even the biggest FAB-9000 HE bombs internally.

was devoted to a new wing structure and a new powerplant. The work on the wing design was conducted jointly with TsAGI. The new wings of high aspect ratio (11.75) employed TsAGI S-3 and S-5 laminar flow airfoil sections. As a result, the wings' lift/drag ratio reached 28.6 versus 26.5 in the case of the Tu-4; the overall L/D ratio was 19.5. Moreover, all the values of this ratio could be retained within the whole range of speeds up to the speeds equivalent to Mach 0.6. The design performance of the 'aircraft 85' obtained as a

result of perfecting the aerodynamic features of the wings placed this aircraft at the forefront of straight-wing bomber design.

OKB-156 engineers evolved a new design of outer wing flaps with a straight flap track which ensured high values of increase of the lift coefficient at small angles of deflection. This considerably enhanced the bomber's take-off performance. The flap design enabled the '85' bomber to obtain during take-off a lift increase equivalent to that obtained by the Tu-4 during landing.

The fuselage, crew accommodation and location of armament and equipment envisaged by the '85' bomber project were identical to those of the 'aircraft 80', the only exception being the increased length of the forward and aft bomb bays enabling the aircraft to carry FAB-9000 bombs internally.

The new project envisaged the possibility of aerial refuelling from an '85' sister ship in a tanker version, using the Shelest/Vasyanin 'wingtip-to-wingtip' system. This IFR system was under development at LII at the time, using modified Tu-4s as test aircraft.

Working jointly with TsAGI, TsIAM and the engine design bureaux, OKB-156 conducted comprehensive studies for the purpose of choosing an engine type and evolving the powerplant layout for the new bomber.

In the early 1950s, gas turbine engines, even in their turboprop guise, were considerably inferior to piston engines in terms of fuel efficiency. This consideration was especially important for long-range aircraft and, in particular, for heavy strategic bombers.

The 'aircraft 85' needed engines with a take-off rating of 4,300-4,500 hp and a specific fuel consumption (SFC) of 160-180 g/hp·hr (0.352-0.396 lb/hp·hr). Only then could the promised high performance characteristics be obtained in practice.

A large number of powerplant configurations were studied. As a result, a system was chosen that represented a combination of a piston engine, a constant-pressure turbine with a jet nozzle and pulse turbines using the kinetic energy of exhaust gases (power recovery turbines). This layout made it possible to

A model of the 'aircraft 85' in TsAGI's T-102 wind tunnel during tests in Laboratory 2.

obtain a specific fuel consumption of 155-170 g/hp·hr (0.342-0.375 lb/hp·hr), taking into account the use of exhaust jet thrust. Piston engines had an SFC of 240-270 g/hp·hr (0.530-0.595 lb/hp·hr) at best.

Such a power combination was dubbed a 'turbopiston engine' (ie, turbo-compound engine). Research conducted by TsAGI in 1948-1952 resulted in the emergence in the USSR of two engine types making practical use of this layout. These were the M-253K liquid-cooled engine (later renamed VD-4K) developed by Vladimir A. Dobrynin's OKB-36 and the ASh-2K air-cooled engine – a product of OKB-19 led by Arkadiy D. Shvetsov.

It was in September 1949 that the Dobrynin OKB was tasked with designing the new M-253K (VD-4K) engine delivering 4,300 hp for take-off. According to the requirements, specific fuel consumption in cruise flight was to be 185-195 g/hp·hr (0.408-0.430 lb/hp·hr) or, taking into account the use of residual jet thrust of the exhaust gases, 165 g/hp·hr (0.364 lb/hp·hr). The weight of the engine was to be within 1,500 kg (3,307 lb).

To create an engine featuring such a power output and fuel efficiency it was necessary to make the fullest possible use of all available resources. Therefore the designers opted for a combination layout comprising two units, one comprising the engine itself with three pulse flow turbines and the other comprising turbosuperchargers with adjustable jet nozzles. All the turbines and the jet nozzle used the energy of the engine's exhaust gases for the purpose of maximising thrust power output and fuel efficiency. The pulse turbines used the part of the gas flow energy which, when using the constant flow turbines, was dissipated in the exhaust gas piping and exhaust manifold. The VD-4K engine was also boosted through supercharging and rpm augmentation by injection of a water/methanol mixture. The new powerplant was provided with a specially developed electronic system for unit control which ensured the powerplant's stable and reliable operation within a wide range of modes.

Various measures were used to ensure high fuel efficiency of the VD-4K. Optimum values were chosen for all its parameters (ignition limiting angle, crankshaft rpm, compression ratio etc.). Engine parts were machined very carefully. The high degree of engineering perfection and the principle of using the energy of exhaust gases made it possible to create one of the most powerful Soviet piston engines, develop it to the stage of State acceptance trials and subsequently test-fly two prototypes of the 'aircraft 85' bomber powered by these engines.

Thus, while retaining the basic layout of the engine (a 24-cylinder radial made up of six cylinder banks), the Dobrynin OKB succeed-

Above: Another model of the 'aircraft 85' (designated 'object 119') in the TsAGI T-101 wind tunnel during a test on 14th December 1949.

ed in achieving an output as high as 4,300 hp by making the fullest possible use of collateral processes.

The first prototype VD-4K was completed by January 1950, and in February 1951 the prototype engine passed its 100-hour State acceptance trials. All its parameters met the required specification.

Another engine competing with the VD-4K at the design stage of the 'aircraft 85' project was the ASh-2K developed by the Shvetsov OKB. It featured the same turbo-compound layout but differed from the VD-4K in being air-cooled. Shvetsov's engine was just as complicated a system as the VD-4K, but it had a more traditional layout with 28 cylinders arranged in four radial rows. Its maximum take-off power output was as high as 4,700 hp. The cylinders of each successive row were somewhat offset in relation to the preceding one to ensure adequate cooling.

This was the most powerful piston engine built in the USSR. But it was plagued by bad luck: at the initial stage of testing of the 'aircraft 85' one of the prototype ASh-2K engines suffered a failure, and all subsequent testing of the bomber was conducted with VD-4K engines only.

The 'aircraft 85' was provided with a powerplant of high output and fuel efficiency, and it was up to the designers to make good use of the opportunities thus offered.

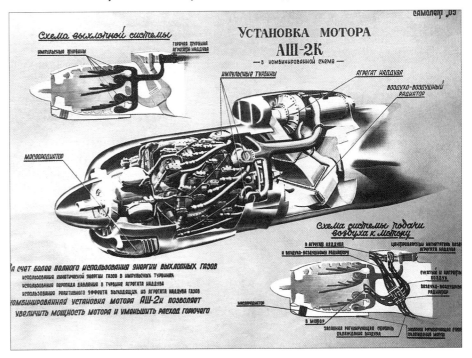

A cutaway drawing of the ASh-2K's engine nacelle, with additional diagrams showing the exhaust system design (including PRTs and the supercharger) and the intake manifold design (including the intercooler).

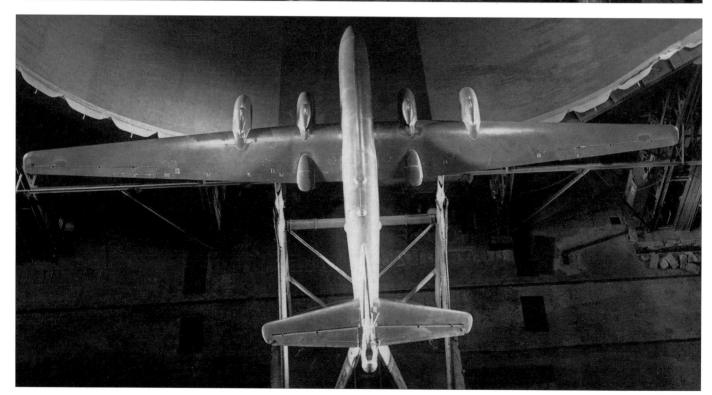

This page: A scaled-strength model of the 'aircraft 85' in the T-101 wind tunnel.

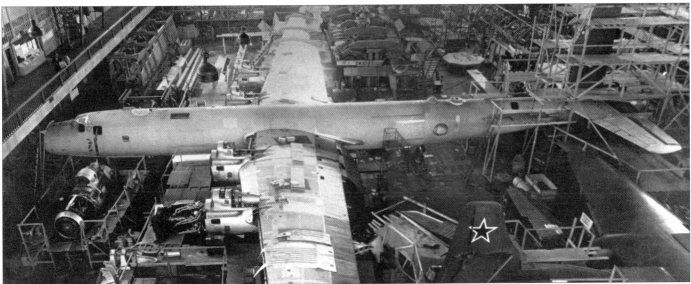

This page: The first prototype of the 'aircraft 85' nearing completion at the Tupolev OKB's experimental shop. Just visible beside the '85/1' is one of the prototypes of the Tu-14 *Bosun* twinjet tactical bomber. The lower photo shows the inboard flaps of the '85'.

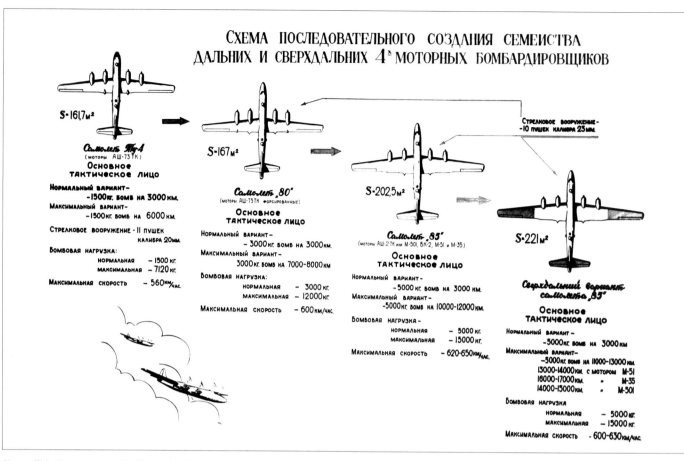

СХЕМА ПОСЛЕДОВАТЕЛЬНОГО СОЗДАНИЯ СЕМЕЙСТВА
ДАЛЬНИХ И СВЕРХДАЛЬНИХ 4х МОТОРНЫХ БОМБАРДИРОВЩИКОВ

S-161,7м²

Самолет Ту-4
(моторы АШ-73ТК)
Основное
тактическое лицо

Нормальный вариант-
-1500кг. бомб на 3000 км.

Максимальный вариант-
-1500кг. бомб на 6000 км.

Стрелковое вооружение - 11 пушек
калибра 20мм.

Бомбовая нагрузка:
нормальная — 1500 кг.
максимальная — 7120 кг.

Максимальная скорость — 560 км/час.

S-167м²

Самолет "80"
(моторы АШ-73ТК форсированные)
Основное
тактическое лицо

Нормальный вариант-
— 3000кг. бомб на 3000км.

Максимальный вариант-
3000кг. бомб на 7000-8000км

Бомбовая нагрузка:
нормальная — 3000 кг.
максимальная — 12000кг.

Максимальная скорость — 600 км/час.

S-202,5м²

Самолет "85"
(моторы АШ-2ТК или М-501, ВК-2, М-51 и М-35)
Основное
тактическое лицо

Нормальный вариант-
-5000 кг. бомб на 3000 км.

Максимальный вариант-
-5000кг. бомб на 10000-12000км.

Бомбовая нагрузка:
нормальная — 5000 кг.
максимальная — 15000 кг.

Максимальная скорость — 620-650км/час.

Стрелковое вооружение
-10 пушек калибра 23мм.

S-221м²

Сверхдальний вариант
самолета "85"

Основное
тактическое лицо

Нормальный вариант —
-5000кг. бомб на 3000 км

Максимальный вариант-
-5000кг. бомб на 11000-13000км.
13000-14000км. с мотором М-51
16000-17000км. " М-35
14000-15000км. " М-501

Бомбовая нагрузка:
нормальная — 5000 кг.
максимальная — 15000 кг.

Максимальная скорость - 600-630км/час.

Above: This diagram shows the line of development from the Tu-4 through the 'aircraft 80' to the 'aircraft 85' and the ultra-long-range version of the latter, with a comparison of warload and maximum speed.

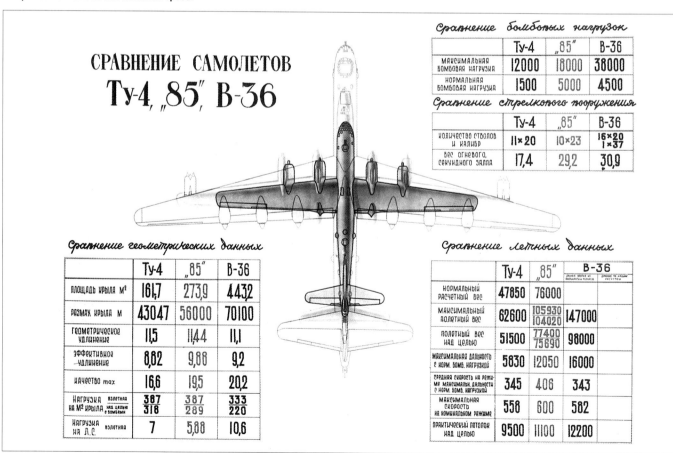

СРАВНЕНИЕ САМОЛЕТОВ
Ту-4, "85", В-36

Сравнение бомбовых нагрузок

	Ту-4	"85"	В-36
МАКСИМАЛЬНАЯ БОМБОВАЯ НАГРУЗКА	12000	18000	38000
НОРМАЛЬНАЯ БОМБОВАЯ НАГРУЗКА	1500	5000	4500

Сравнение стрелкового вооружения

	Ту-4	"85"	В-36
КОЛИЧЕСТВО СТВОЛОВ И КАЛИБР	11×20	10×23	16×20 1×37
ВЕС ОГНЕВОГО СЕКУНДНОГО ЗАЛПА	17,4	29,2	30,9

Сравнение геометрических данных

	Ту-4	"85"	В-36
ПЛОЩАДЬ КРЫЛА М²	161,7	273,9	4432
РАЗМАХ КРЫЛА М	43047	56000	70100
ГЕОМЕТРИЧЕСКОЕ УДЛИНЕНИЕ	11,5	11,44	11,1
ЭФФЕКТИВНОЕ УДЛИНЕНИЕ	8,82	9,88	9,2
КАЧЕСТВО max	16,6	19,5	20,2
НАГРУЗКА НА М² КРЫЛА взлетная / над целью с бомбами	387/318	387/289	333/220
НАГРУЗКА НА Л.С. взлетная	7	5,88	10,6

Сравнение летных данных

	Ту-4	"85"	В-36
НОРМАЛЬНЫЙ РАСЧЕТНЫЙ ВЕС	47850	76000	
МАКСИМАЛЬНЫЙ ПОЛЕТНЫЙ ВЕС	62600	105930/104020	147000
ПОЛЕТНЫЙ ВЕС НАД ЦЕЛЬЮ	51500	77400/75690	98000
МАКСИМАЛЬНАЯ ДАЛЬНОСТЬ С НОРМ. БОМБ. НАГРУЗКОЙ	5830	12050	16000
СРЕДНЯЯ СКОРОСТЬ НА РЕЖИМЕ МАКСИМАЛЬН. ДАЛЬНОСТИ С НОРМ. БОМБ. НАГРУЗКОЙ	345	406	343
МАКСИМАЛЬНАЯ СКОРОСТЬ НА НОМИНАЛЬНОМ РЕЖИМЕ	558	600	582
ПРАКТИЧЕСКИЙ ПОТОЛОК НАД ЦЕЛЬЮ	9500	11100	12200

Another chart providing a graphic comparison of the Tu-4, the 'aircraft 85' and the Convair B-36. The tables show, clockwise, the bomb loads, defensive armament, flight performance (normal/maximum AUW, speed and range) and external dimensions plus wing loading and power loading.

Above and below: The second prototype ('85/2') seen during trials.

Above and below: The first prototype ('85/1') on an unpaved airfield during initial flight tests. The large dorsal supercharger fairings of the VD-4 engines, incorporating the engine/intercooler air intakes at the front and exhaust pipes at the rear, are clearly visible.

Above and below: Two more views of the first prototype at the initial flight test stage. The stripes applied to the port side of the fin are photo calibration markings.

Above and below: A desktop model of the 'aircraft 85' as originally conceived with Shvetsov ASh-2K engines and five-blade propellers.

The advanced development project was completed by the end of 1949. At the end of January of the following year the Air Force, at last, submitted its specification for the 'aircraft 85'. In March the customer endorsed the full-size mock-up of the bomber.

Preparation of detail drawings was started as early as the first quarter of 1949; simultaneously, a decision was taken calling for the construction of two prototypes designated '85/1' and '85/2'. The latter was also known as the '85D' (*dooblyor*, literally 'understudy'; this term meaning 'second prototype' was used in the Soviet Union until the early 1960s). Manufacture of the first prototype was started. The two machines differed in certain structural elements and equipment items. Construction of the '85/1' bomber was completed on 15th September 1950.

The first taxying test was performed at the OKB's flight test facility in Zhukovskiy on 14th November 1950 (the '85' was the first Tupolev aircraft to be tested at this new facility). The second taxying was performed a full month later, on 10th December. Reliable information as to the reasons for so lengthy a delay is not available. One can only surmise that one of

the ASh-2K engines failed on the first occasion and this engine type, making up the powerplant of the Tu-85, had to be urgently replaced by the VD-4K. Some indirect evidence points to that: certain documents persistently mention that the testing of the 'aircraft 85' was initiated with ASh-2K engines. The engine nacelles were designed to accept both types of engines, so quite possibly it proved possible to re-engine the prototype with VD-4Ks within a month. The State acceptance trials of the latter engine commenced in January 1951, proceeding in parallel with the manufacturer's flight tests of the Tu-85.

Manufacturer's flight tests of the '85/1' were conducted by project test pilot A. D. Perelyot, lead engineer M. A. Ghenov, navigator S. S. Kirichenko, flight engineer A. F. Chernov, radio operator Ivannikov and various others.

On 9th January 1951 a crew captained by A. D. Perelyot took the new machine into the air for the first time. The flight lasted 31 minutes and was performed with the undercarriage down. During the second flight (on 12th January), the undercarriage was retracted for the first time; the crew checked the function-

ing of the powerplant and the aircraft's stability at 3,000 m (9,843 ft). The flight lasted for 1 hour and 51 minutes. On the following day one of the engines (the inboard starboard) cut out during a ground run and had to be replaced. Subsequent testing proceeded normally. In all, 59 flights were conducted by the first machine, the bomber logging 142 hours and 16 minutes. Manufacturer's flight tests of the '85/1' continued until 20th October 1951.

Despite the change of powerplant, the engines were the main source of complaints during the test programme. In the course of ten months all four engines were replaced in connection with failures (only the port outboard engine functioned normally); the first complete engine change took place as early as April and May due to the expiry of the very short designated service life.

The new Rubidiy M-85 radar was also a constant pain in the neck for the design personnel. Nevertheless, the machine seemed to hold promise and work on it continued.

Between 7th and 11th September, preparations were made for a long-distance flight with a view to determining the bomber's maximum range. On 12th and 13th September the '85/1' performed a flight at an altitude of 8,000 m (26,247 ft), covering a distance of 12,018 km (7,468 miles) in the course of 20 hours 38 minutes; the bomber's take-off weight was 107,225 kg (236,390 lb). The Tu-85 became the first Soviet aircraft with an all-up weight exceeding 100 tonnes (220,460 lb).

The report on the manufacturer's flight tests stated that the engine/propeller packages had functioned normally. Improvements to the Rubidiy M-85 radar were necessary, and to the electronic devices for automated engine control.

On 8th July 1951, while still undergoing manufacturer's flight tests, the '85/1' aircraft took part in the annual Tushino Air Display where it made a fly-past in the flagship role, escorted by MiG-15*bis* fighters.

In the course of flight-testing of the '85/1', the following flight performance figures were obtained:

- the maximum speed at 10,000 m (32,808 ft) was 638 km/h (396 mph);
- the maximum range at a take-off weight of 107,292 kg (236,538 lb) was 12,018 km (7,468 miles);
- the service ceiling at a take-off weight of 76 tonnes (167,550 lb) was 11,700 m (38,386 ft); it took the aircraft 61 minutes to reach this altitude;
- the bomber required 35 minutes to climb to 10,000 m (32,808 ft) at a take-off weight of 76.0 tonnes (167,550 lb);
- the take-off run at a 107,225-kg (236,390-lb) TOW was 1,640 m (5,381 ft); the take-off run took 46.5 seconds and the lift-off occurred at a speed of 207 km/h (129 mph),

the required take-off distance being 4,120 m (13,517 ft);

- the landing run at a landing weight of 76 tonnes (167,550 lb) was 1,500 m (4,921 ft), landing run time being 48.5 seconds.

Concurrent with the testing of the first machine the second prototype, the '85/2' (or '85D'), was being prepared for tests. Its construction began on 15th July 1950 and the aircraft was completed in June 1950. On 26th June it was rolled out of the final assembly shop for adjustments and installation of equipment.

The *dooblyor* was basically identical to the first prototype, with the exception of some details. The most noteworthy improvements were as follows: a sliding clear-view window was introduced in the navigator's station on the port side between fuselage frames 1 and 1a, and all single-pane glazing panels of the flight deck were replaced by double panes; the length of the bomb bay was increased by 50 mm (1.97 in); additional hatches were made in the lower fuselage skin between frames 26 and 33 (the central ones accommodated racks for TsOSAB coloured flare bombs and those on the sides were for a bomb loading hoist).

The glazing of the tail gunner's station was enlarged and the shape of the glazing frame was altered to improve the gunner's field of view and field of fire. A radome for the PRS-1 Argon gun ranging radar was installed above the gunner's station (the radar itself was not ready by the time testing of the '85/2' commenced and was not installed).

Wing area was reduced by 4.502 m² (48.46 sq ft). The basic airframe components were reinforced; this made it possible to revise the structure, eliminating additional bracing members in the wings which, in consequence, became lighter. Both the inboard and the outboard flaps were redesigned and the inboard engine nacelle fairings were recontoured. Rudder area was reduced by 0.48 m² (5.17 sq ft) due to the lower part of the rudder being cut down to provide space for the radome of the Argon gun-ranging radar.

The engines' liquid cooling system was altered to automatically maintain the correct coolant temperature. An additional underfloor fuel tank was installed in the fuselage; the existing oxygen system using gaseous oxygen was replaced by a liquid oxygen system featuring four KPZh-30 oxygen bottles, which resulted in a weight saving. The original Rubidiy M-85 radar was replaced by the improved Rubidiy-MM. Two PO-4500 AC converters (main and back-up) were installed as replacement for the three MA-750 converters; this arrangement was subsequently used in the aircraft designed by the OKB over the next 15 years.

Above: The upper portion of one of the Tu-85's engine nacelles prior to installation of the supercharger, showing the engine inlet duct (marked 1) and the intercooler ducts (marked 4).

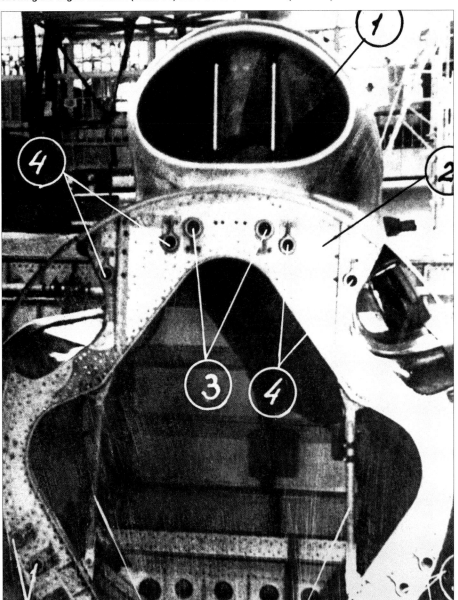

Front view of the nacelle prior to the installation of the ASh-2K engine, showing the design of the air intake with twin splitter plates and the firewall (marked 2). The lateral recesses are for the exhaust manifold.

Above: The tail unit and tail gunner's station of the '85/1'.

One of the main gear units seen from behind, with a support installed to avoid unnecessary tyre loading.

The ammunition supply of the rear fuselage dorsal and ventral cannon barbettes was increased. An electrical system for reversing the pitch of the AV-48 propellers was introduced. Finally, the elevator trim tabs were cable-actuated instead of being electrically controlled.

The *dooblyor* incorporating all of these changes was submitted for manufacturer's tests. Vyacheslav. P. Maroonov was appointed project test pilot, with N. S. Rybko as co-pilot, M. M. Yegorov as leading engineer, Yu. V. Liubimov as a gunner, G. F. Tatarinov as the flight engineer etc.

On 28th June 1951 the '85/2' performed its first flight which was of one hour's duration. The second flight, which took place on 29th June, was much longer, lasting four hours. The testing proceeded uneventfully. Powerplant operation was more reliable; there were fewer equipment failures. In all, 25 flights totalling 55 hours 14 minutes were performed on the second prototype in the course of manufacturer's flight tests; on one of the flights the '85/2' carried an FAB-9000 bomb weighing 9 tonnes (19,841 lb).

Testing of both machines went on relatively smoothly, giving rise to the impression that a long-range bomber capable of dealing nuclear strikes against the North American continent had, in effect, emerged. Preparations for series production were initiated. The new machine was to be produced by the same plants that were building the Tu-4: No. 22 in Kazan', No. 23 in Moscow and No. 18 in Kuibyshev.

However, July 1950 saw the outbreak of the Korean War in which the Soviet Union also came to be involved, albeit unofficially. The USSR sent fighter regiments equipped with MiG-15 and MiG-15*bis Fagot-A/B* jets to North Korea. From November 1950 onwards the MiGs were waging combat against the USAF. The most unpleasant surprise for the Americans was the fact that the piston-engined B-29s bombing targets in North Korea proved to be very vulnerable to attacks by the Soviet MiG-15s armed with heavy cannon.

From mid-1951 B-29 losses began to increase, reaching a peak on 30th October when, according to Soviet records, 12 Superfortresses were destroyed by MiGs in a single day. From that moment on the B-29s were switched to strictly nocturnal operations.

As a response to these events, all further work on piston-engined bombers in the USA was terminated and emphasis was placed instead on the programme which eventually resulted in the emergence of the Boeing B-52 Stratofortress.

In the USSR, too, studies were initiated on new strategic bombers powered by turboprop and turbojet engines and intended to achieve a range of 12,000-15,000 km (7,456-

9,323 miles) and a speed of approximately 900-1,000 km/h (559-621 mph). The Tupolev OKB initiated work on the 'aircraft 95' (the future Tu-95) powered by four NK-12 turboprops. The reborn OKB led by Vladimir M. Myasishchev started design work on the VM-25 (the future M-4) powered by four AM-3 turbojets.

The Government directive on the '95' heavy bomber was issued in July 1951, and on 15th November a similar directive was issued, terminating the flight testing of the '85/1' and '85/2' aircraft and stopping preparations for series production. The era of heavy piston-engined bombers came to a close; the epoch of jet-powered strategic aviation set in.

Nevertheless, the development of the 'aircraft 85' was not a waste of effort. Many technical features, units and equipment packages were transferred from this machine to the '95' bomber. The fuselage layout, crew accommodation, armament and equipment of the Tu-85 were derived from the appropriate elements of the 'aircraft 85'.

Having paved the way for the Tu-95 bomber, the 'aircraft 85' remained in the history of Soviet aviation as the last piston-engined heavy bomber.

Structural description of the 'aircraft 85' bomber

The 'aircraft 85' was an all-metal monoplane with unswept wings and a conventional tail unit. The aircraft's crew comprised 11 or 12 persons.

Fuselage: The fuselage structure was basically similar to that of the B-29, Tu-4 and 'aircraft 80', but differed in having greater dimensions.

To ensure normal operation at high altitudes the aircraft was provided with three pressure cabins. The forward pressure cabin accommodated the bomb-aimer, the navigator, two pilots, the flight engineer, the radar operator and the radio operator. The centre fuselage cabin accommodated the dorsal gunner and two gunners at lateral stations. The aft pressure cabin provided accommodation for the tail gunner. The front and centre pressure cabins were connected by a pressurised crawlway similar to the one used on the B-29, Tu-4 and 'aircraft 80'.

Wings: With a span of 56.0 m (183 ft 9 in) and an aspect ratio of 11.4, the wings consisted of a centre section and outer wing panels, each of which was built in two portions. The wing centre section was built integrally with the fuselage and carried the inboard (Nos. 2 and 3) engine nacelles, main undercarriage units and landing flaps. The centre section bays housed fuel tanks.

The inner detachable wing portions carried the Nos. 1 and 4 engine nacelles and the slotted flaps.

The bays of the inner detachable wing portions also housed fuel tanks.

The outer detachable wing portions, in a manner similar to the inner wing portions, represented a self-sufficient structural assembly. They also housed fuel tanks.

The wing skinning between the spars was considerably thicker and stronger, making possible a significant reduction in the weight of some wing spar components.

Tail unit: The tail unit featured a single fin and rudder and a cantilever horizontal tail. The rudder and elevator were aerodynamically balanced and fitted with trim tabs. The trim tabs and the wing flaps were electromechanically actuated.

Landing gear: Retractable tricycle landing gear with twin wheels on each unit and oleo-pneumatic shock absorbers. The nosewheels were non-braking, while the mainwheels were fitted with brakes. There was also a retractable tail bumper. Landing gear operation was effected by electromechanical actuators; there was a provision for emergency mechanical extension by means of manual winches.

Powerplant: Four 4,300-hp Dobrynin VD-4K 28-cylinder four-row radial engines rated at 4,300 hp for take-off and driving AV-48 four-blade feathering reversible-pitch propellers.

Control system: Conventional mechanical flight control system with no hydraulic boosters. Control inputs were transmitted directly to the control surfaces through a system of control cables and bellcranks. The aircraft's control system included an AP-5M autopilot.

Fuel system: The entire amount of fuel was accommodated in 48 bag-type fuel tanks; they were divided into groups installed in sealed bays of the wing centre section and outer wing panels. On the second prototype this tankage was supplemented by one more tank installed under the wing centre section torsion box. The total fuel capacity was 63,600 litres (13,991 Imp gal) for the '85/1' and 65,900 litres (14,497 Imp gal) for the '85/2'.

Electrical system: The aircraft had a single-wire electrical system; DC power was supplied by eight 12-kilowatt GSR-12000 gene- rators (two on each engine) connected in parallel to common collecting buses.

Back-up DC power was supplied by a 12-A-30 storage battery (on the '85/2' only) and a 5-kilowatt GS-5000 generator driven by an M-10 two-stroke engine housed in the unpressurised aft fuselage. AC converters catered for equipment using AC power.

Hydraulic system Pressure in the hydraulic system was created by an electrically driven hydraulic pump. The use of hydraulic energy was very limited – it was

employed for actuating the wheel brakes in normal and emergency operation modes and for raising the forward cannon barbette.

Armament: To provide protection from enemy fighters the 'aircraft 85' featured four remote-controlled barbettes and a remote-controlled tail barbette in the extreme aft fuselage; together they gave a 360° field of fire. Each barbette was equipped with two 23-mm Nudel'man/Rikhter NR-23 cannon. The total ammunition supply was 3,150 rounds for the '85/1' and 4,500 rounds for the '85/2'. There were plans to install the PRS-1 Argon gun ranging radar at the tail gunner's station.

The normal bomb load was 5,000 kg (11,023 lb) and the maximum bomb load reached 18,000 kg (39,683 lb). Bombs were accommodated in two bomb bays located fore and aft of the wings. The maximum bomb load was 9,000 kg (19,842 lb).

Avionics and equipment:

a) navigation equipment: RV-2 and RV-10 radio altimeters, ARK-5 ADF, the airborne part of the Meridian radio navigation system and the SP-50 Materik ILS;

b) communications equipment: 1RSB-70, RSB-D and RSIU-3 radios, SPU-14 intercom;

c) IFF equipment: Magniy-M interrogator and Bariy-M transponder;

d) radar equipment: Rubidiy M-85 (or Rubidiy-MM' on the '85/2') panoramic radar coupled to the OPB-5SR optical bombsight through the Tseziy (Cesium) interface;

e) photo equipment: one AFA-84/40 camera and one of three cameras: AFA33/50, AFA33/75 or AFA33/100 which could be replaced by an NAFA3S/50 camera for night photography.

Air conditioning and pressurisation system: Air for pressurised cabins was bled from the engine superchargers. Cabin air pressure corresponding to an altitude of 2,000 m (6,562 ft) was maintained up to 7,250 m (23,786 ft); at higher altitudes the system maintained a pressure differential of 0.4 kg/cm² (5.7 psi).

De-icing system: Electric de-icing of wing and tail surface leading edges, the front portions of engine nacelles near the air intakes and of the flight deck glazing. The propellers featured alcohol de-icing.

'Aircraft 85' long-range heavy bomber with TV-2F or TV-10 engines (project)

Before the commencement of work on the '95' aircraft the OKB studied various ways of converting the Tu-85 bomber to accept Kuznetsov TV-2F or TV-10 turboprop engines. In that instance the design range reached 16,000-17,000 km (9,942-10,563 miles), the maximum speed being 700-740 km/h (435-460 mph). However, the results of the studies proved disappointing and the idea was dropped.

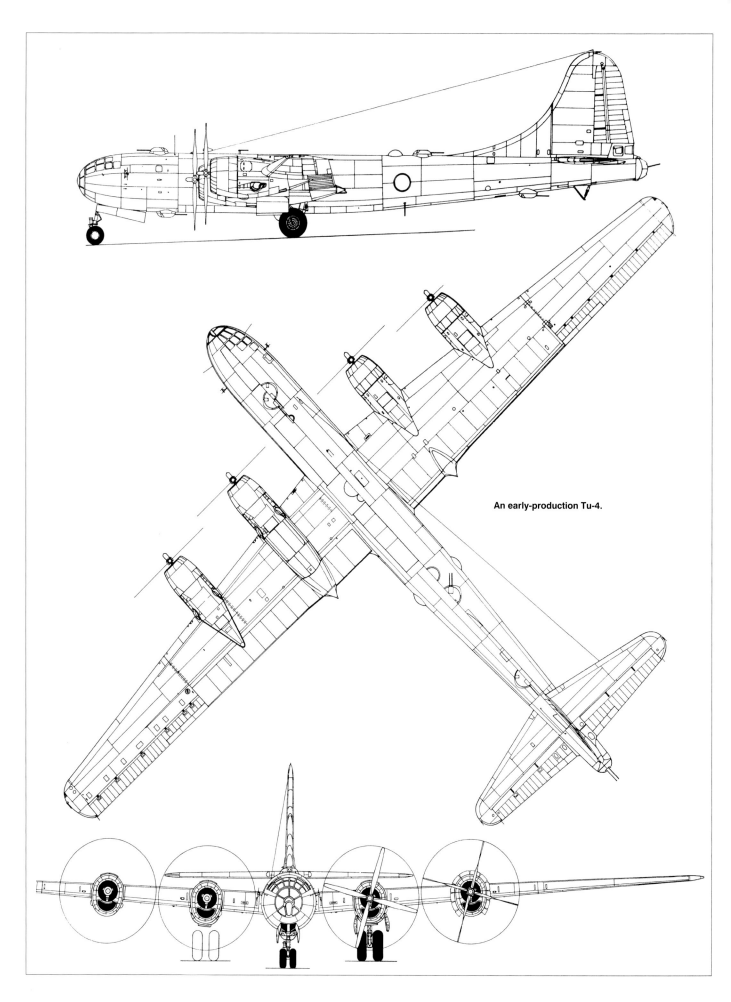

An early-production Tu-4.

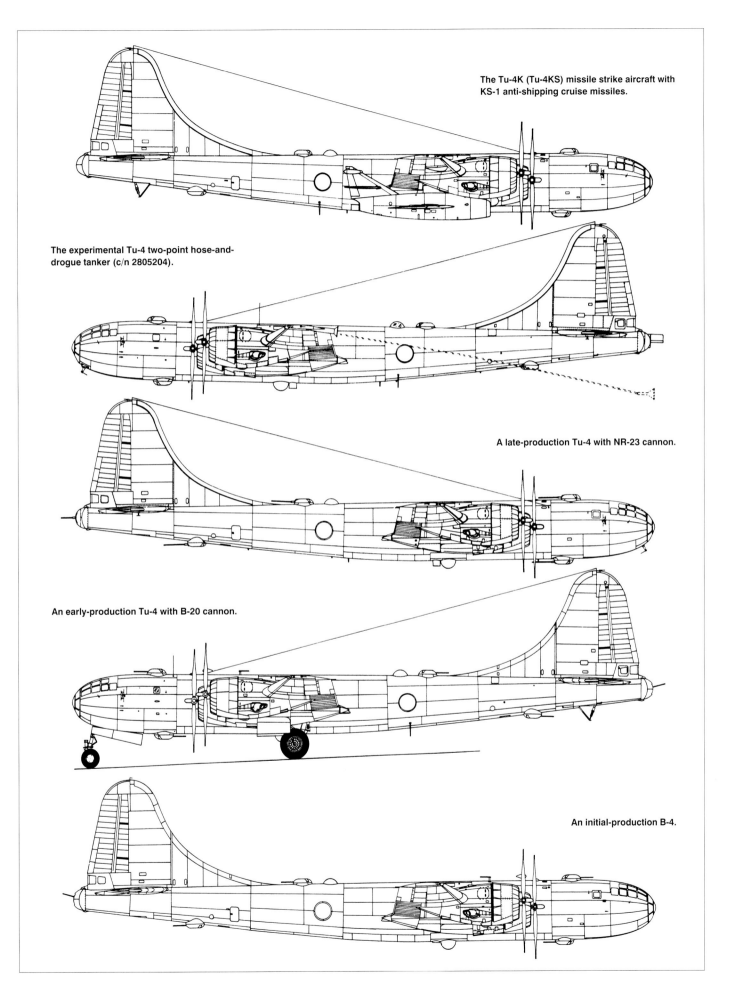

The Tu-4K (Tu-4KS) missile strike aircraft with KS-1 anti-shipping cruise missiles.

The experimental Tu-4 two-point hose-and-drogue tanker (c/n 2805204).

A late-production Tu-4 with NR-23 cannon.

An early-production Tu-4 with B-20 cannon.

An initial-production B-4.

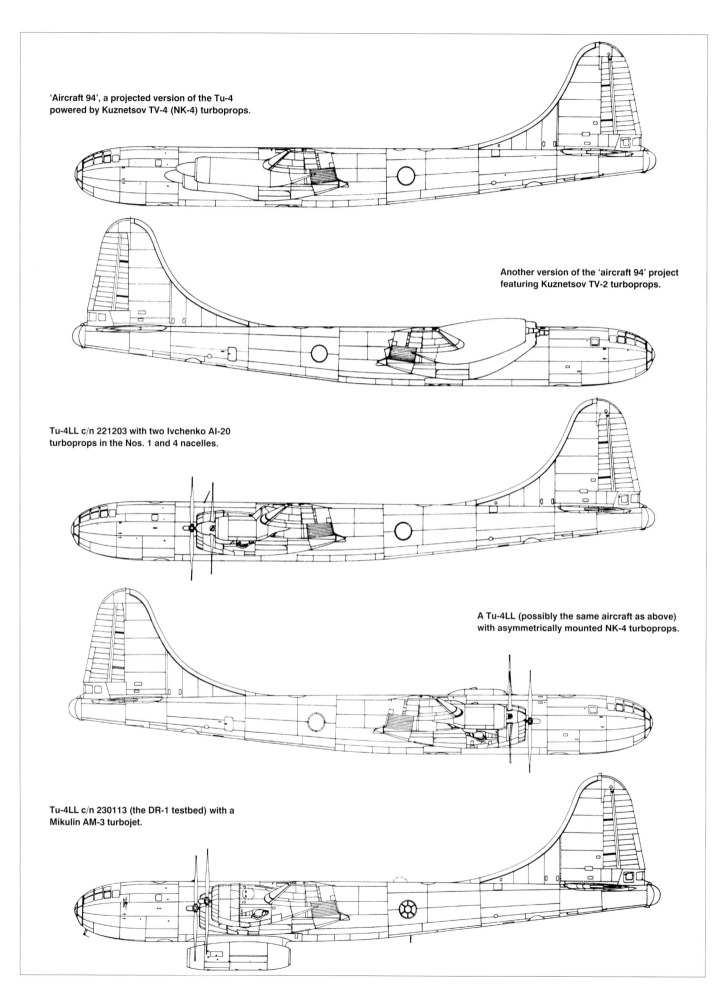

'Aircraft 94', a projected version of the Tu-4
powered by Kuznetsov TV-4 (NK-4) turboprops.

Another version of the 'aircraft 94' project
featuring Kuznetsov TV-2 turboprops.

Tu-4LL c/n 221203 with two Ivchenko AI-20
turboprops in the Nos. 1 and 4 nacelles.

A Tu-4LL (possibly the same aircraft as above)
with asymmetrically mounted NK-4 turboprops.

Tu-4LL c/n 230113 (the DR-1 testbed) with a
Mikulin AM-3 turbojet.

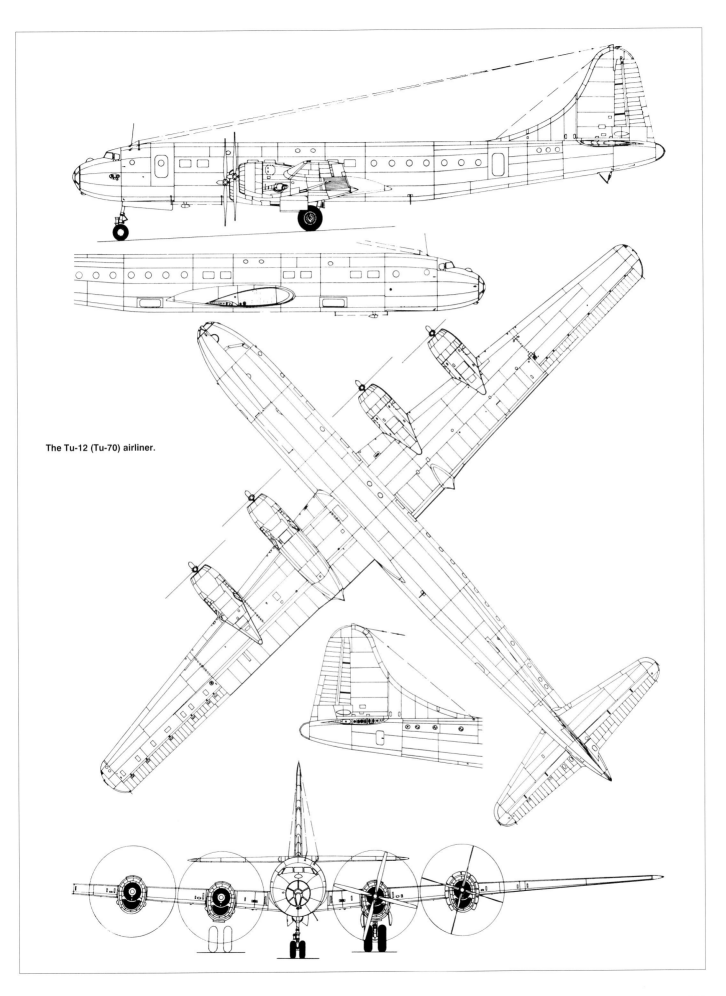

The Tu-12 (Tu-70) airliner.

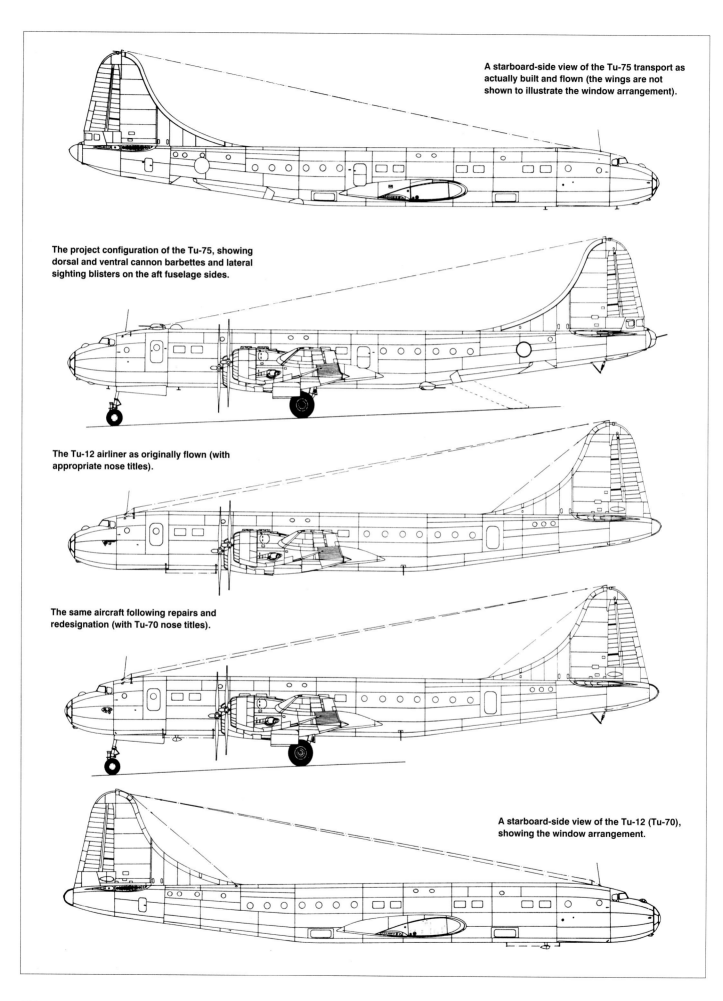

A starboard-side view of the Tu-75 transport as actually built and flown (the wings are not shown to illustrate the window arrangement).

The project configuration of the Tu-75, showing dorsal and ventral cannon barbettes and lateral sighting blisters on the aft fuselage sides.

The Tu-12 airliner as originally flown (with appropriate nose titles).

The same aircraft following repairs and redesignation (with Tu-70 nose titles).

A starboard-side view of the Tu-12 (Tu-70), showing the window arrangement.

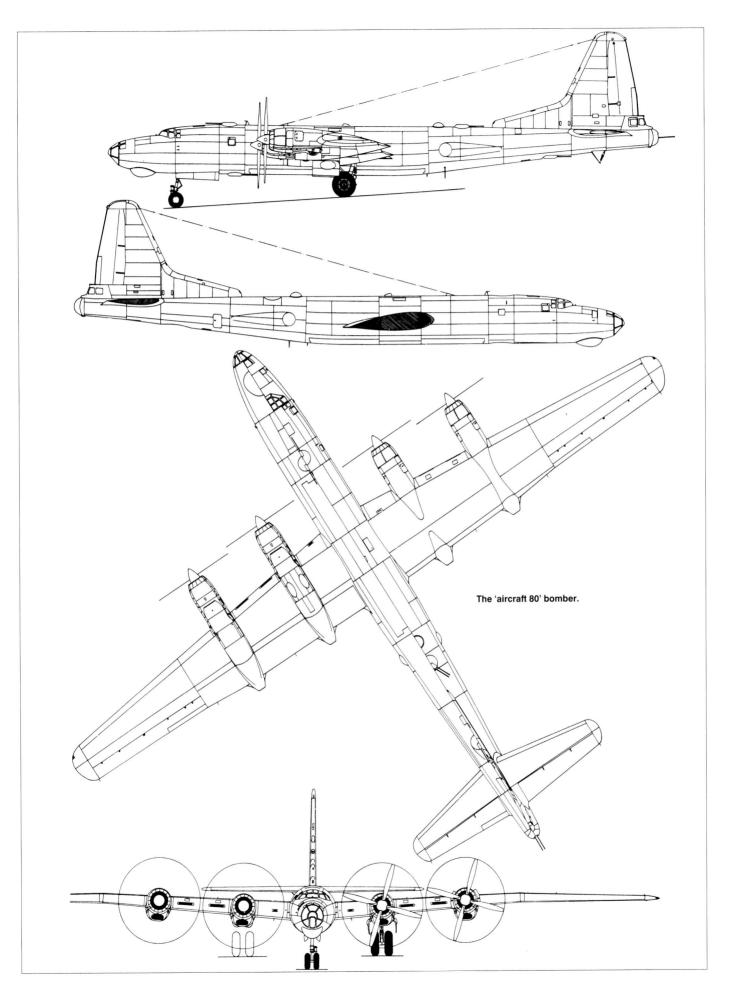

The 'aircraft 80' bomber.

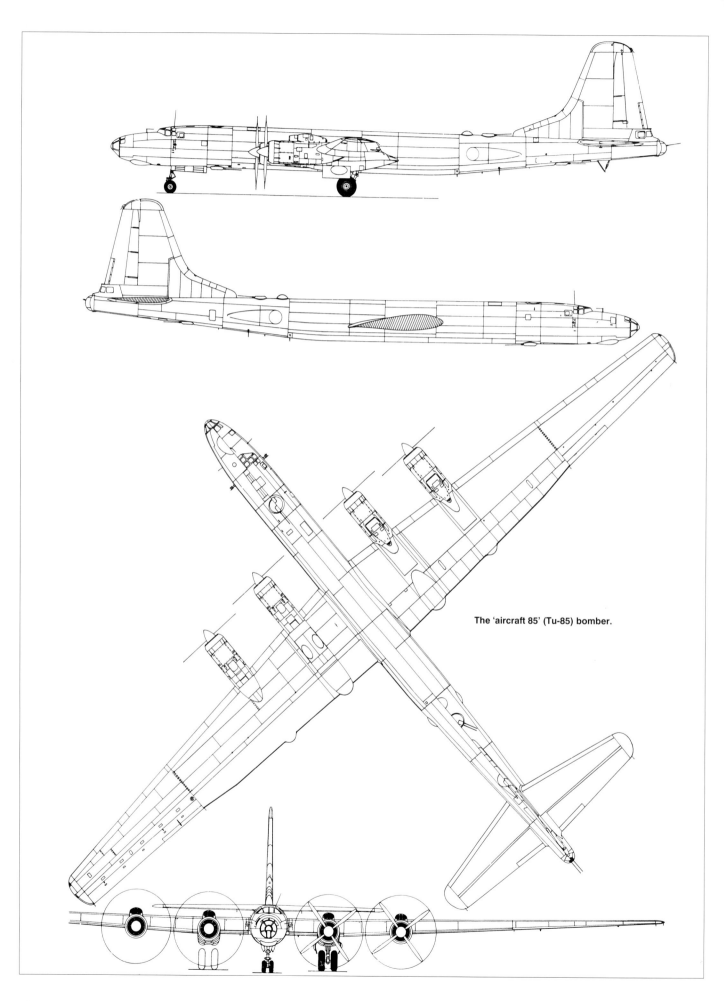

The 'aircraft 85' (Tu-85) bomber.

Above: A desktop model of the ultimate project version of the 'aircraft 64' bomber, showing the 'bug-eye' canopies.

A desktop model of the Tu-75 military transport. Note the lateral sighting blisters.

This page:

Left: This picture, showing technicians using a tall ladder to reach the aerials at the top of the Tu-4's fin, once graced the back cover of a very old issue of the *Aviatsiya i kosmonavtika* (Aviation and Spaceflight) magazine. However, this was not a colour photo. Quite simply, the magazine's artists took a black and white photo and painted it up (this was fairly common practice in the early days when colour film was scarce and expensive). In so doing they retouched away the c/n and tactical code for security reasons. In reality the aircraft in the foreground was coded '22 Red' (c/n 2805002); the code is still faintly discernible at the top of the fin. The other Tu-4 is '21 Red' (c/n 2805901).

Below: Another example of artistic skill caused by need. This pseudo-colour photo of the Tu-70 comes from a Tupolev OKB demonstration album intended for the Soviet government.

Opposite page:

Above: '01 Red' (c/n 2805103), the sole Tu-4 still in existence in Russia, is preserved at the Central Russian Air Force Museum in Monino near Moscow. This is one of the aircraft which was to participate in a bombing mission against Budapest in November 1956 (fortunately called off at the last moment). In the late 1980s the bomber had its c/n obliterated by excessively security-minded museum staff.

Below: Possibly the most non-standard Tu-4 ever! Chinese People's Liberation Army Air Force Tu-4 '4114 Red' (c/n 2806501) was at first re-engined with AI-20 turboprops and then converted to an AWACS testbed with a locally designed rotodome and other 'bumps and bulges'. It is seen here on display at the PLAAF Museum at Datangshan AB north of Beijing. No designation is yet known for the Chinese turboprop conversions of the *Bull*; a Western magazine referred to this variant as the Shaanxi AP-1 but this is doubtful, as the designation does not fit into the normal Chinese system of designating aviation hardware.

Red Star Volume 1
SUKHOI S-37 & MIKOYAN MFI

Yefim Gordon

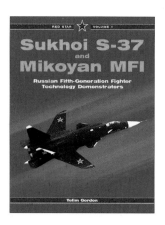

Conceived as an answer to the American ATF programme, the Mikoyan MFI (better known as the 1.42 or 1.44) and the Sukhoi S-37 Berkoot were developed as technology demonstrators. Both design bureaux used an approach that was quite different from Western fifth-generation fighter philosophy. This gives a detailed account of how these enigmatic aircraft were designed, built and flown. It includes structural descriptions of both types.

Sbk, 280 x 215 mm, 96pp, plus 8pp colour foldout, 12 b/w and 174 colour photos, drawings and colour artworks
1 85780 120 2 **£18.95/US $27.95**

Red Star Volume 2
FLANKERS: The New Generation

Yefim Gordon

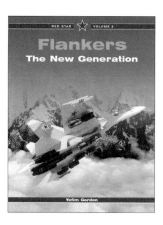

The multi-role Su-30 and Su-35 and thrust-vectoring Su-37 are described in detail, along with the 'big head' Su-23FN/Su-34 tactical bomber, the Su-27K (Su-33) shipborne fighter and its two-seat combat trainer derivative, the Su-27KUB. The book also describes the customised versions developed for foreign customers – the Su-30KI (Su-27KI), the Su-30MKI for India, the Su-30MKK for China and the latest Su-35UB.

Softback, 280 x 215 mm, 128 pages 252 colour photographs, plus 14 pages of colour artworks
1 85780 121 0 **£18.95/US $27.95**

Red Star Volume 3
POLIKARPOV'S I-16 FIGHTER

Yefim Gordon and Keith Dexter

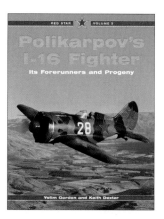

Often dismissed because it did not fare well against its more modern adversaries in the Second World War, Nikolay Polikarpov's I-16 was nevertheless an outstanding fighter – among other things, because it was the world's first monoplane fighter with a retractable undercarriage. Its capabilities were demonstrated effectively during the Spanish Civil War. Covers every variant, from development, unbuilt projects and the later designs that evolved from it.

Sbk, 280 x 215 mm, 128 pages, 185 b/w photographs, 17 pages of colour artworks, plus line drawings
1 85780 131 8 **£18.99/US $27.95**

We hope you enjoyed this book . . .

Midland Publishing titles are edited and designed by an experienced and enthusiastic team of specialists.

Further titles are in preparation but we always welcome ideas from authors or readers for books they would like to see published.

In addition, our associate, Midland Counties Publications, offers an exceptionally wide range of aviation, spaceflight, astronomy, military, naval and transport books and videos for sale by mail-order around the world.

For a copy of the appropriate catalogue, or to order further copies of this book, and any of many other Midland Publishing titles, please write, telephone, fax or e-mail to:

Midland Counties Publications
4 Watling Drive, Hinckley,
Leics, LE10 3EY, England

Tel: (+44) 01455 254 450
Fax: (+44) 01455 233 737
E-mail: midlandbooks@compuserve.com
www.midlandcountiessuperstore.com

US distribution by Specialty Press – see page 2.

Red Star Volume 4
EARLY SOVIET JET FIGHTERS

Yefim Gordon

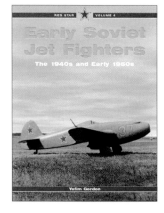

This charts the development and service history of the first-generation Soviet jet fighters designed by such renowned 'fighter makers' as Mikoyan, Yakovlev and Sukhoi, as well as design bureaux no longer in existence – the Lavochkin and Alekseyev OKBs, during the 1940s and early 1950s. Each type is detailed and compared to other contemporary jet fighters. As ever the extensive photo coverage includes much which is previously unseen.

Sbk, 280 x 215 mm, 144 pages 240 b/w and 9 colour photos, 8 pages of colour artworks
1 85780 139 3 **£19.99/US $29.95**

Red Star Volume 5
YAKOVLEV'S PISTON-ENGINED FIGHTERS

Yefim Gordon & Dmitriy Khazanov

This authoritative monograph describes this entire family from the simple but rugged and agile Yak-1 through the Yak-7 (born as a trainer but eventually developed into a fighter) and the prolific and versatile Yak-9 to the most capable of the line, the Yak-3 with which even the aces of the Luftwaffe were reluctant to tangle. Yak piston fighters also served outside Russia and several examples can be seen in flying condition in the west.

Sbk, 280 x 215 mm, 144 pages, 313 b/w and 2 col photos, 7pp of colour artworks, 8pp of line drawings
1 85780 140 7 **£19.99/US $29.95**

Red Star Volume 6
POLIKARPOV'S BIPLANE FIGHTERS

Yefim Gordon and Keith Dexter

The development of Polikarpov's fighting biplanes including the 2I-N1, the I-3, and I-5, which paved the way for the I-15 which earned fame as the Chato during the Spanish Civil War and saw action against the Japanese; the I-15*bis* and the famous I-153 Chaika retractable gear gull-wing biplane. Details of combat use are given, plus structural descriptions, details of the ill-starred I-190, and of privately owned I-15*bis* and I-153s restored to fly.

Softback, 280 x 215 mm, 128 pages c250 b/w and colour photos; three-view drawings, 60+ colour side views
1 85780 141 5 **£18.99/US $27.95**

Red Star Volume 8
RUSSIA'S EKRANOPLANS
Caspian Sea Monster & other WIGE Craft

Sergey Komissarov

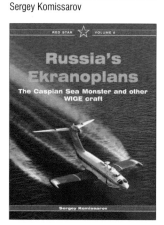

Russia has led development of wing-in-ground effect (WIGE) craft – in Russian *ekranoplans*; operating on the borderline between the sky and the sea, with the speed of an aircraft and better economics and the ability to operate anywhere on the world's waterways. They attracted the military's attention and thus have been veiled in secrecy until recently.

This describes the various WIGE craft in considerable fresh detail and is the most complete on the subject to date.

Sbk, 280 x 215 mm, 128pp, c150 b/w and colour photos, plus line drawings
1 85780 146 6 November 2002
£18.99/US $27.95